Acknowledgments

Theories of Adolescence has developed out of the author's unpublished dissertation "Theories of Adolescence: An Analysis of Selected American and European Positions," University of Illinois, 1957. Although the third edition has only limited resemblance to this earlier work, the author remains grateful to his doctoral committee: Norman Gronlund, Leon Helmer, Stewart Jones, Hobart Mowrer, and especially his adviser, Glenn Blair, who was instrumental in stimulating and guiding the early part of this endeavor.

The third edition owes a special thanks to my colleagues Joseph Martire, Jane Morrell, David Silk, and Eli Velder for critically reading much of the new material. Sincere appreciation is expressed to my secretary, Kay Cornell, for her reliable and competent assistance in putting the final manuscript together.

Most of all I am indebted to the students in my courses "Adolescent Development" and "Adolescents and the Secondary Schools" who have questioned and challenged ideas and continuously stimulated my thinking.

Finally, the writer is grateful to his wife, Gertrude, for proofreading and for patiently tolerating a mostly preoccupied husband during the months the new chapters were being written. The book is dedicated to my adolescent children: Gretchen and Michael.

R. E. M.

Contents

4

Erik Erikson's Theory of Identity Development 54

5

A *Geisteswissenschaftliche* Theory of Adolescence 85

6

Cultural Anthropology and Adolescence 96

7

Field Theory and Adolescence 116

8

Social Psychology and Adolescence 139

9

Arnold Gesell's Theory of Adolescent Development 145

10

Central European Stage Theories of Adolescent Development 158

11

Jean Piaget's Cognitive Theory of Adolescent Development 178

Theories of Adolescence
Third Edition

1

Introduction

The Purpose of Studying Theories of Adolescence

The process of human growth and development has long been the subject of much discussion and theorizing. However, since the turn of the twentieth century, special attention has been directed toward the period of development commonly referred to as "adolescence." The prodigious amount of recent literature dealing with adolescence shows the deep and sustained interest manifested by psychologists, educators, physicians, lawyers, psychiatrists, sociologists, and parents.

Numerous theories have been advanced to explain the phenomenon of adolescence. These theories have resulted in many conflicting viewpoints. In previous centuries, the opposing camps in developmental psychology built their arguments mainly on personal experiences and philosophical considerations. In recent years, they have relied more and more on systematic studies, controlled observation, and experimental research. These scientific methods of investigation have eliminated some of the earlier misconceptions of adolescent development, but they have not settled many of the controversial issues.

Problems have arisen owing to ambiguous terminology and to disagreement on basic assumptions as to what actually constitutes adolescence. In many instances, theoretical differences concerning adolescence stem from more basic disagreements on the methods and aims of psychological inquiry and the nature of psychological knowledge. Since an advocate of a particular position tends to cite research that supports his theory, there is a need for analyzing and, to some extent, integrating the different theoretical positions on adolescent development. It is not the aim of this book to derive a new theory or to combine several existing theories into an eclectic one. The main purpose is to give a systematic and comprehensive picture of different theoretical positions and to show whenever appropriate the relationship among them.

Adolescence and Pubescence: Their Definitions and Relationship

The word "adolescence" is derived from the Latin verb *adolescere* meaning "to grow up" or "to grow into maturity." For the purpose of this study, the following general definitions appear to be most suitable: Sociologically, adolescence is the transition period from dependent childhood to self-sufficient adulthood. Psychologically, it is a "marginal situation" in which new adjustments have to be made, namely those that distinguish child behavior from adult behavior in a given society. Chronologically, it is the time span from approximately twelve or thirteen to the early twenties, with wide individual and cultural variations. It tends to occur earlier in girls than in boys and to end earlier in more primitive societies (Benedict, 1950; Remplein, 1956). The terms "adolescence," "adolescent age," and "adolescent period" will be used interchangeably in this book. Laymen frequently use "teen-agers," but this term when properly used includes only the ages thirteen to nineteen. Furthermore, "teen-ager" connotes a somewhat condescending attitude, as does the term "juvenile," which some people invariably associate with delinquency. A more appropriate word for the period between childhood and adulthood is "youth," but this term has different meanings for different writers. Whereas Gesell (1956)* uses it as the title of his study of the years from ten to sixteen, others have used it to describe the late adolescent period. Keniston (1970) goes even one step further and defines "youth" as

*Throughout the text, references to Gesell's books, several of which are co-authored, will cite Gesell only.

a distinct new stage between adolescence and adulthood that has emerged only recently from the changing conditions in postindustrial society.

The words "puberty" and "pubescence" are derived from and related to the Latin words *pubertas,* "the age of manhood," and *pubescere,* "to grow hairy," "to reach puberty." Ausubel (1954) uses the term "pubescence" as the more restricted concept that refers only to the biological and physiological changes associated with sexual maturation. Adolescence is the broader, more inclusive concept that refers also to changes in behavior and social status. Stone and Church (1973) make a similar distinction between the cultural and behavioral on the one hand and the physical manifestations on the other. However, they further differentiate between "puberty," the point at which sexual maturity has been reached, and "pubescence," the period of approximately two years preceding puberty.

Pubescence is the time span of physiological development during which the reproductive functions mature; it is phylogenetic and includes the appearance of the secondary sex characteristics as well as the physiological maturation of the primary sex organs. Pubescence, then, corresponds to the period of early adolescence and ends with the appearance of all secondary sex characteristics and reproductive maturity.* These changes take place in a time span of approximately two years. At perhaps no other period in human life, except birth, does a transition of such importance take place. And though physiological change takes place at all age levels, the *rate* of change during this period is immeasurably greater than in the years that precede and follow it (Ausubel, 1954).

The relationship between pubescence and adolescence becomes more complicated if material from cultural anthropology concerning initiation rituals and initiation periods is considered. In some instances, the transition from childhood to adulthood is smooth and without social recognition; in other instances, *puberty rites* bring about a transition not from childhood to adolescence, but

---

*The exact age at which reproductive maturity occurs varies greatly and seems to be related to socioeconomic as well as geographic factors. It appears earlier in the temperate zone, in higher socioeconomic classes, and as a result of good nutrition; it appears later in both the tropical and arctic regions (Ausubel, 1954; Greulich, 1944).

from childhood to adulthood. Pubescence seems to be the only aspect of the process of maturation that some primitive societies recognize; after puberty the young man and woman obtain adult status and have adult privileges. The prolonged period of adolescence (in some cases nearly a decade) in more technically advanced societies is not a physiological, but a social invention.

It has been claimed that these initiation rituals may occur after, during, or even before the period of biological pubescence. While the duration of pubescence is determined by biological factors, the length of social adolescence is influenced by social institutions and the social group. They may coincide, but it is not necessary that they do so. The causal relationship between the physiological, especially endocrinological, changes during pubescence and the behavioral and social phenomena of adolescence has been denied, and it has been claimed that the behavior of adolescence is culturally determined. However, some of the questions involved are still at issue. Ausubel emphasizes that social initiation into adulthood either corresponds to or follows physiological maturation, but that attainment of biological sexual maturity "always precedes and never follows" the social inauguration of adolescence (Ausubel, 1954: 68). Sherif, after reviewing anthropological studies on the subject, concludes that the problems that adolescents face "vary from culture to culture, rendering the transition to adulthood more or less complicated, more or less conflicting, more or less prolonged" (Sherif and Cantril, 1947: 220). However, he does assert that the "basic psychological principles which operate in all of these social settings should be the same" (Sherif and Cantril, 1947: 220).

For a long time a specific causal relationship between puberal changes and the social psychological adjustment of adolescence had been assumed. This assumption is unwarranted, since the effects of physiological changes do seem to be greatly modified by social expectations and institutions. Psychological correlates, particularly noticeable in the area of sexual adjustment and social recognition, find behavioral expression and tie pubescence and adolescence together. Needless to say, the author does not imply that the kind of prolonged transition period found in Western societies is universal. Youth in Samoa has frequently been cited as a smooth, harmonious, and pleasurable adolescent transition period. However, even in Samoa there is evidence of change in status and conflict in sexual adjustment. The girl may be invited to a love affair by a *soa,* a messenger who may betray his friend in his own favor. The *moetotolo,* or "sleep crawler," hoping that the girl is expecting a lover may attempt a modified form of rape, since he has been unsuccessful in previous love affairs. Furthermore, prestige is enhanced for the families of both bride and bridegroom if the girl proves to be a virgin (Mead, 1950).

In Western culture, pubescence as a developmental period corresponds to pre- or early adolescence. The onset of pubescence can be ascertained by specific body changes that occur in the following sequence (Greulich, 1944). This sequence, according to Ausubel (1954), remains fairly constant, even with retarded or precocious individuals.

Girls	*Boys*
Skeletal growth	Skeletal growth
Breast development	Enlargement of testes
Straight pigmented pubic hair	Straight pigmented pubic hair
Maximum annual growth increment	Early voice changes
Kinky pigmented pubic hair	Ejaculation
Menstruation	Kinky pigmented pubic hair
Appearance of axillary hair	Maximum annual growth increment
	Appearance of downy facial hair
	Appearance of axillary hair
	Late voice change
	Coarse pigmented facial hair
	Chest hair

Any of these phenomena could be selected, and a variety of them have been used to determine the onset of pubescence. It is obvious that pubescence is not a single event but a constellation of events, none of them occurring instantaneously. Consequently, there is a great deal of overlapping in the developmental sequence. The main idea in the definition of puberty is attainment of reproductive maturity. Therefore, the most widely used single criterion for determining puberty in girls is the first menstruation (Shock, 1944;

Zeller, 1952). However, since it is generally believed that there is a period of one or more years of sterility between the first menstruation and the ability to conceive and reproduce (Mills and Ogle, 1936), even menstruation is not a valid criterion for the determination of reproductive maturity. Furthermore, there is no corresponding event in boys. Ejaculation has been considered (Ausubel, 1954), but since it is less dramatic and is frequently not remembered, it is less accessible for research investigation. Furthermore, there is no evidence that menstruation and ejaculation are corresponding biological events. Other criteria useful in determining the onset of pubescence are the appearance of straight pigmented pubic hair and the maximum annual growth increment (Shock, 1944). Neither of these is directly related to reproductive maturity.

The change in the excretion of gonadotropic hormones, determined through urinalysis, gives valid information concerning the endocrinological changes that accompany pubescence. Gonadotropic hormones are considered partly responsible (also partly responsible are the hormones produced by the adrenal cortex) for the development of primary and secondary sex characteristics and wholly responsible for the production of mature ova and spermatozoa. Studies have shown that few, if any, gonadotropic hormones are found in the urine of nonpubescent boys (Greulich, 1944; Shock 1944). The adequate production of gonadotropic hormones appears to be of great importance in determining the onset, normality, or deviations of pubescent development.

The upper age limit of adolescence is even less clearly marked than the onset of pubescence, since there are no objective physiological phenomena that can be used to define the termination. Observable social phenomena such as financial independence, successful employment, and marriage are useful. But, in the first place, they do not necessarily indicate psychological independence and maturity. Secondly, no agreement has been reached as to their relative importance. Finally, the psychological and even the sociological meaning of such phenomena differ according to the sociocultural environment; how to determine when adulthood, maturity, self-determination, and independence have been reached depends on the definition that these terms have in a given social setting.

In primitive society, the period of adolescence may be very brief and may be terminated by initiation rituals after which the individual obtains adult status. In contrast to this example of a short period of adolescence, the psychologist G. Stanley Hall wrote in 1904 that adolescence in the United States lasts until the twenty-fourth or twenty-fifth year. To speak of the termination of adolescence in terms of age is only possible if the sociocultural environment is taken into consideration.

In most cultures two different criteria have been applied to determine the end of adolescence. They are: (1) *functional definitions*—such as ability to support oneself—and (2) *status definitions*—such as having reached the age necessary to vote or having been given status through initiation or puberty rituals—(Committee on Adolescence, 1968). Status definitions are easily determined and more obvious, but often less meaningful, since they depend on arbitrary convention and often neglect individual differences in psychological development. Functional definitions are more related to the responsibilities that are required of adults to function effectively in a given society and relate to self, mate, offspring, and society.

In the United States the legal recognition of the end of adolescence is changing in line with the accelerating growth patterns and earlier maturation of adolescents today as compared to seventy or eighty years ago. Considerable evidence has accumulated (Muuss, 1970b) indicating that adolescents reach puberty earlier, experience the adolescent growth spurt earlier, and reach adult height earlier. The Twenty-sixth Amendment gives the eighteen-year-old the right to vote, and most states are following the federal law by redefining the definition of the end of adolescence and the beginning of adulthood. The legal age for buying liquor, to sue and be sued, and to enter into contracts is being lowered from twenty-one to eighteen in many states. Other legal rights not available to children—such as acquiring a license to drive a car, the option to drop out of school, permission to marry and enter full-time employment—may be granted at an earlier age with considerable variation from state to state. In a legal sense, the age of eighteen is increasingly recognized as the termination of adolescence, since at this age the law increasingly removes the last legal protective aspect of "immaturity" and gives a person his full rights, legal independence, and adult responsibilities.

Adolescence is widely recognized as a period of social, personal, sexual, religious, political, and vocational adjustments as well as a period of striving for increasing emotional and financial independence from parents. Therefore, from a psychological standpoint, the status definition for termination of adolescence is not related to a specific chronological age; it is instead the degree to which these adjustments have been made and the degree to which emotional and financial independence has been reached. A person who marries after graduation from high school and becomes successfully employed and financially self-sufficient is more likely to be regarded as having attained maturity—and is more likely to be recognized by society as an adult—than his friend who goes to college and is supported by his parents. Furthermore, a person can be old in a chronological sense and still show the behavioral and social characteristics of the adolescent. However, if appropriate age norms must be given, at least for the United States, they are suggested by the new school reorganization: preadolescence, nine to eleven, covers elementary schoolchildren; early adolescence, twelve to fourteen, coincides with middle school and frequently with pubescence; middle adolescence, fifteen to eighteen, covers the senior high school years; and late adolescence, nineteen to twenty-one, applies primarily to the college-bound segment of youth.

2

The Philosophical and Historical Roots of Theories of Adolescence*

Long before psychology became a science, there were philosophical, theological, educational, and psychological theories that contributed to an understanding of human nature and human development. G. Stanley Hall, as a result of his famous two-volume work *Adolescence* (1916), is considered the father of a scientific "psychology of adolescence." Prior to Hall it was frequently the philosopher-educator who was especially concerned with a theory of human development with its implications for teaching. This was the case with Plato, Aristotle, Comenius, Rousseau, Herbart, Froebel, and Pestalozzi.

One difficulty in identifying prescientific theories of adolescent development is that prior to Hall adolescence was not considered a separate part or stage of human development and received no special emphasis. The word "adolescence" first appeared in the fifteenth century, indicating that historically adolescence was subordinated to theoretical considerations about the general nature of human development. Contemporary theories of adolescence frequently have their historical roots in general theories of development. Some important ideas about human development come from philosophers who are primarily concerned with the question: What is the nature of man? For example, what Locke and Darwin had to say about the nature of man is so profound that it is utilized and

*Chapter 2 is a revision and extension of an article by the author, "Theories of Adolescent Development, Their Philosophical and Historical Roots," *Adolescence*, Vol. I, pp. 22–44, 1966.

reflected in the writings of Rousseau and Hall respectively and thus constitutes a philosophical basis for a theory of development.

In classifying theories of development, Ausubel (1958) distinguishes between preformationistic and predeterministic approaches to human development on the one side and tabula rasa approaches on the other side. The preformationistic theory is reflected in the theological proposition of man's instantaneous creation, in the homunculus theory, and in the doctrine of man's basic sinfulness as well as in the more recent theories emphasizing instincts and innate drives. Predeterministic theories postulate universally fixed stages of development, but allow for environmental influences, as is obvious in Rousseau's romanticism, Hall's theory of recapitulation, Freud's stages of psychosexual development, and Gesell's emphasis on maturation. In contrast to this are the tabula rasa approaches that minimize the biological and genetic factors and place the emphasis on environmental determinants of human development. As the name implies, this includes Locke's tabula rasa theory, the humanistic approaches, and the related modern theories of behaviorism, social learning theory, and cultural determinism.

Early Greek Concern with Human Nature

A historical approach to a theory of adolescence must begin with the early Greek ideas about human development. Their influence remained prevalent through the Middle Ages and is still noticeable today. The philosophical idea of dualism, for instance, is essentially Greek. Plato (427–347 B.C.) made a clear distinction between two aspects of human nature: soul and body. He expounded that body and soul are different substances and that although there is some interaction between them the soul is an entity in itself, capable of leaving the body without losing its identity. It can perceive more clearly and reach higher realities when freed from the body; *soma sema* ("the body is the grave of the soul") he declared. The body and sensuality are the fetters that hinder the soul in reaching those higher realities. Body is matter and has all the defects of matter. The idea of dualism between mind and body reappeared later in

Christian theology and became of primary importance in the philosophical thinking of the seventeenth century, especially under Des-
cartes, Leibnitz, and Spinoza.

Of greater interest from a developmental point of view is the idea
of the layer structure of the soul which Plato developed in the
dialogue *Phaedo*. According to Plato, the soul has three distinguishable parts, layers, or levels. Thus, probably for the first time
in the history of psychology, a threefold division of soul, or mind
is advanced. The lowest layer of the soul is described as man's
desires and appetites. Today we might describe this level in terms
of drives, instincts, and needs, and its resemblance to Freud's
concept "id" can hardly be denied. According to Plato, this part
of the soul is located in the lower part of the body and is primarily
concerned with the satisfaction of the physical needs. ". . . it fills
us full of love, and lusts, and fears, and fancies of all kinds, and
endless foolery, and . . . takes away the power of thinking at all"
(Plato, 1921: 450). The second layer of the soul, the spirit, includes
courage, conviction, temperance, endurance, and hardihood; aggressiveness and fierceness also originate here. Man has both the
first and the second layer in common with the animal world. These
two layers belong to the body and die with it. The third layer is
divine, supernatural, and immortal; it constitutes the essence of the
universe. This is the real soul, which Plato described as reason and
which has its temporary seat in the body. Plato's theory concerning
the layer structure of the soul closely resembles several contemporary central European personality theories, which are developed on
the assumption of a layerlike stratification of personality, especially
the theories of Lersch and Remplein to be discussed in Chapter 10.
They perceive development as a process by which the lower layers
mature earlier and are superseded by higher layers as the child
grows older. Plato had already postulated such a developmental
theory. Reason is latent during the first stage when perception is
most important. Among contemporary theorists Piaget maintains
that percepts develop into concepts. The second stage of development is characterized by conviction and understanding and brings
the second layer of the soul, spirit, into the foreground of psychological development. The third stage, which we might identify with
adolescence and maturity, but which, according to Plato, is not

reached by all people, relates to the development of the third part of the soul, reason and intelligence.

Interspersed in most of Plato's dialogues—but particularly in *Laws* and *The Republic*—are descriptive accounts of children and youth as well as advice concerning the control of their behavior. While this material does not constitute a theory of development as we understand it today, it does give insight into Plato's conception of the nature of development.

During the first three years of his life the infant should be free from fear and pain and sorrow. This point of view would be endorsed by many psychologists today. Interestingly enough, in the dialogue *Laws* Cleinias suggests that in addition to freeing the infant from pain we ought to provide him with pleasure. This is in agreement with Plato's basic goal, which is the possession of happiness. However, the Athenian Stranger objects that this would spoil the child, since during the early years "more than at any other time the character is engrained by habit" (Plato, 1953: 359). Character is formed at such an early age because the experiences and impressions leave a lasting influence. However, Plato did admit that "the characters of young men are subject to many changes in the course of their lives." The argument about the consistency of personality versus its modifiability has continued, and proponents for both of Plato's statements can be found today.

From three to six the child needs sports and social contact with age-mates in order to get rid of his self-will. Plato would punish but not disgrace the child. Social development is taken into consideration at this age, and children ought to come together in a kind of kindergarten arrangement under the supervision of a nurse. However, children should find for themselves the "natural modes of amusement" appropriate to their age.

Plato suggested a division of the sexes at six. "Let boys live with boys and girls . . . with girls." The boy now has to learn horsemanship, the use of bow and arrows, the spear, and the sling. Boys will not be allowed to drink wine until they are eighteen because of their easy excitability, "fire must not be poured upon fire." A related adolescent desire is argument for amusement's sake. In their enthusiasm they will leave no stone unturned, and in their delight over the first taste of wisdom they will annoy everyone with their arguments. Plato believed that the character is formed through habit at a very early age.

Plato developed his educational philosophy in *The Republic*. He perceived education as the development of the soul under the influence of the environment, "and this has two divisions, gymnastic for the body, and music for the soul." Reasoning in the young child is undeveloped, but since the young child is impressionable, Plato suggested establishing "a censorship of the writers of fiction," since "anything that he receives into his mind is likely to become indelible and unalterable: and therefore . . . the talks which the young first hear should be models of virtuous thoughts" (Plato, 1921: 642). Rational and critical thought develop mainly during adolescence. The training that began with music and gymnastics during childhood was continued through adolescence with mathematical and scientific studies. The latter brought out critical thought and dissatisfaction with direct sense knowledge; during this training students would develop methods of finding the truth and of distinguishing truth from opinion. In *Laws* Plato spoke of education as "that training which is given by suitable habits to the first instincts of virtue in children;—when pleasure, and friendship, and pain, and hatred are rightly implanted in souls not yet capable of understanding the nature of them, and who find them, after they have attained reason, to be in harmony with her" (Plato, 1953: 218). The meaning of education in this view is to provide experiences for children prior to the development of reason that are nevertheless in agreement with reason when it does develop during adolescence. Plato already recognized the importance of individual differences; children are born with different abilities and should be guided into those kinds of activities that are in line with their aptitudes.

Plato postulated that the attainment of knowledge might be explained by his doctrine of innate ideas. Though undeveloped, vague, and nebulous, innate ideas are nevertheless present at birth. Learning is a process of remembering these ideas, which once— probably before the soul entered the body—were clear. Sensations help in reawakening these partially lost ideas. The mind-body dualism is of relevance here, since the body contributes sensation while the mind contains the ideas. In this way, Plato's theory of innate ideas opens the discussion about the influence of heredity and environment.

Aristotle (384–322 B.C.), in contrast to Plato, denied the separation of body and soul and returned to the older Greek idea of the unity of the physical and mental worlds. Body and soul, according to him, are related in structure and function. The relationship between body and soul is the same as that between matter and form; body is matter and soul is form. Soul-life, for which Aristotle used the word "entelechy," is the principle by which the body lives. Aristotle accepted Plato's idea concerning the levels of the soul-life; however, he viewed soul structure from a biological, almost evolutionary, point of view. The lowest soul-life form is that of the plant, the life functions of which are supply of nourishment and reproduction. The next higher form of soul-life is also found in animals, its additional functions being sensation, perception, and locomotion. The third soul-life function is distinctly human and sets men apart from the animal world. It includes the ability to think and reason. Consequently, there are three layers of soul-life, the food-supplying or plant soul, the perceiving or animal soul, and the thinking or human soul. Aristotle further divided the thinking or human soul into two different parts, the practical soul by which we "deliberate about those things which depend upon us and our purpose to do or not to do" (Aristotle, 1925: 1196) and the theoretical soul, which deals with higher and abstract knowledge such as distinguishing between what is true and what is false.

Aristotle advanced a theory of development concerning the layer structure of the soul that appears to have some resemblance to Darwin's more scientific biological theory of evolution, even though it does not include the idea of evolution of one species to another. Furthermore, Aristotle made an impassable division between the different levels of soul-life. Plato, in describing the stages of development, held that the first (plant) soul level developed before the second (animal) soul level and this, in turn, was a prerequisite for the rational soul level. Aristotle followed this idea of the level structure of the soul and applied it to the development of the child, as becomes obvious from the following quotation:

As the body is prior in order of generation to the soul, so the irrational is prior to the rational. The proof is that anger and wishing and desire are implanted in children from their very birth, but reason and understanding are developed as they grow older. Wherefore, the care of the body ought to precede that of the soul, and the training of the appetitive part should follow; none the less our care of it must be for the sake of the reason, and our care of the body for the sake of the soul [Aristotle, 1941c: 1300–1301].

Aristotle divided the developmental period of the human being into three distinguishable stages of seven years each. The first seven years he named infancy; the period from seven to the beginning of puberty, boyhood; and from puberty to twenty-one, young manhood. This division of the period of development into three stages was generally accepted during the Middle Ages and recurs in some modern psychological theories of development, such as those advanced by Kroh, Remplein, and Zeller in Germany. Until recently twenty-one was the age at which the last limitations and protections of the "minor status" were removed.

Infants and animals are alike in that both are under the control of their appetites and emotions. "Children and brutes pursue pleasures" (Aristotle, 1941a: 1053). Aristotle emphasized that moral character is the result of choice, "for by choosing what is good or bad we are men of a certain character . . ." Even though young children are able to act voluntarily, they do not have choice; "for both children and the lower animals share in voluntary action, but not in choice, and acts done on the spur of the moment we describe as voluntary, but not as chosen" (Aristotle, 1941a: 967–968). This seems to imply that children first go through an animallike stage of development; what distinguishes them from animals is that children have the potential for higher development than animals, "though psychologically speaking a child hardly differs for the time being from an animal" (Aristotle, 1941b: 635). It is the characteristic of adolescence to develop the ability to choose. Only if the youth voluntarily and deliberately chooses, will he develop the right kind of habits and thus in the long run build the right kind of character. By making choices the adolescent actively participates in his own character formation. Voluntary and deliberate choice thus becomes an important aspect in Aristotle's theory of development, since it is necessary for the attainment of maturity. This idea is expressed by several modern writers. For example, both Margaret Mead and Edgar Friedenberg have stated that today with prolonged education and prolonged dependency we have reduced choices for adolescents to the extent that we interfere with their attainment of maturity.

Although Aristotle did not offer us a systematically stated theory of adolescence, in *Rhetorica* he provided us with a rather detailed description of the "youthful type of character," part of which resembles descriptive statements that could have been written by G. Stanley Hall or Arnold Gesell. "Young men have strong passions, and tend to gratify them indiscriminately. Of the bodily desires, it is the sexual by which they are most swayed and in which they show absence of self-control" (Aristotle, 1941d: 1403). Sexuality in adolescence is of concern in any contemporary text whether theoretically, empirically, or clinically oriented. Among the more recent theoretical positions, Otto Rank in particular describes promiscuity as an adolescent defense mechanism against sexual urges. Aristotle in his description of the adolescent commented on their instability: "They are changeable and fickle in their desires, which are violent while they last, but quickly over: their impulses are keen but not deep-rooted" (Aristotle, 1941d: 1403). Lewin and Barker among the contemporary writers deal with the instability of the psychological field of the adolescent since he stands in a psychological no-man's-land. This makes many sociopsychological situations unclear, indefinite, and ambiguous, and the resulting behavior is "changeable and fickle." "For owing to their love and honour they cannot bear being slighted, and are indignant if they imagine themselves being unfairly treated" (Aristotle, 1941d: 1403–1404). Adolescent complaints about being "unfairly treated" in home, school, and society in general are so common today that they need no further elaboration. The list of quotes from *Rhetorica* in which Aristotle described the characteristics of adolescence could be continued at length, and other analogies to contemporary theory, observation, and empirical data would not be too difficult to find. Aristotle discussed, among other issues, adolescents' desire for success, their optimism, trust, concern with the future rather than the past, their courage, conformity, idealism, friendship, aggressiveness, and gullibility.

The education of the adolescent in the fourth century B.C. was based on the study of mathematics and included astronomy, geometry, and the theory of music; these subjects taught abstraction but did not require the life experiences and the wisdom that were considered necessary in order to become a philosopher or a physicist.

Under the early impact of Christian theology, Aristotelian thought seemed to get lost; however, it was later combined with Christian ideas by Saint Thomas Aquinas. The Aristotelian Thomistic philosophy became dominant in the twelfth and thirteenth centuries, and its influence was felt during the Middle Ages— particularly in the form of scholasticism. Aristotle is also considered as influential in laying the foundation for a more scientific approach to science and psychology.

Medieval Christian View of Human Development

The theological view of human nature and development cannot as readily be identified in terms of one man, a specific historical period, or even a particular church. We find the idea of original sin expressed by Tertullian in the second century when he speaks of the depravity of human nature. It was emphasized by John Calvin in the sixteenth century and is prevalent in Catholic scholasticism, Protestant Calvinism, and American Puritanism.

The theological view of human nature and development as found in the medieval-early Reformation period encompassed several ideas relevant to our topic:

1. Man's unique position in the universe, being created in the image of God.
2. Man's evil due to Adam's original sin.
3. Man's dualistic nature, a spiritual, immortal soul and a material, mortal body. Salvation and the life after death places the immortal soul on a higher level of importance.
4. Knowledge as revealed to man from without. It comes from God and is revealed to us through the Bible.
5. The homunculus idea of instantaneous creation. The last point is not so much biblical as medieval.

Most of these ideas can be found in biblical sources, but they were also influenced by Greek philosophy, especially Plato's dualism. We will see later that theories that followed in the seventeenth, eighteenth, and nineteenth centuries, especially those advanced by Locke, Rousseau, and Darwin, can partly be understood as antitheses to these earlier theological ideas.

The idea that God created man in his own image and thus gave him a unique position in the universe is expressed in Genesis 1:27–28: "And God created man to his own image: to the image of God he created him: male and female he created them." Furthermore, he gives them the power to rule over all living creatures. Prior to Darwin man was seen as being divinely created and basically different from the animal world.

The second important idea concerning the nature of man is the theological doctrine of human depravity. The human being is seen as having innate tendencies toward ungodliness and sinfulness. Man is fundamentally bad, and his badness becomes stronger during the developmental years if it is not counteracted by stern discipline. The idea of original sin as based on Genesis 3:6–7 relates the sinfulness of each individual to Adam's first sin. And "as sin came into the world through one man and death through sin, and so death spread to all men because all men sinned. . . . Yet death reigned from Adam to Moses, even over those whose sins were not like the transgression of Adam . . ." (Romans 5:12–14).

This pessimistic view of human nature, prevalent in Catholic theology before the Reformation, received a new impetus with Calvin's theology and thus set the intellectual climate for Puritanism. The educational objective in this theory was to bring forth the innate ideas that are God given—knowledge of his laws and commands. Such a stern disciplinary approach to education was prevalent under the influence of Catholic scholasticism and Calvinism in Europe and Puritanism in New England. There was little room for individual differences, since the quality of the mind was the same for all individuals and the child who failed to learn was seen as willfully resisting the efforts of the teacher. The role of the teacher was defined by his authority and a belief that learning could be facilitated by physical punishment. The role of the child was defined by obedience. Calvin in particular expressed a strong faith in the value of education.

The theological point of view that man is the result of instantaneous creation results in preformationist thinking (Ausubel, 1958). During the Dark Ages, it was believed that the child came into the world as a miniature adult. The difference between a child and an adult was considered to be only a quantitative one, not a qualitative one. Therefore, girls wore long dresses and corsets of adult style, only smaller in size, as is obvious from many medieval paintings. The qualitative difference in body build, body function, and mental abilities was disregarded. Growth was understood to be only a quantitative increase of all physical and mental aspects of human nature, not a qualitative one. This is a regression of thought when contrasted with the logical theories of Plato and Aristotle. The theory of preformationism held that children had the same interests as adults and therefore should be treated correspondingly, which meant that adult requirements were put upon them and were enforced by stern discipline. According to this view, the child did not "develop," since he was preformed. Figure 1 illustrates the homunculus concept; it represents a view of the preformed "little man" in the sperm as conceived by seventeenth-century scientists. This idea of "homunculism" was utilized in prescientific theory of embryology.

> It was seriously believed that a miniature but fully-formed little man (i.e., an homunculus) was embodied in the sperm, and when implanted in the uterus simply grew in bulk, without any differentiation of tissues or organs, until full-term fetal size was attained at the end of nine months [Ausubel, 1958: 23–24].

This idea of homunculism was soon to be challenged by the beginning of modern science and advancements in the field of medicine. It was learned that the young child has qualitative and quantitative characteristics of his own and is not a miniature adult. One might speculate that the reason for the limited concern of pre-Hallian writers with the basic physiological changes that take place during pubescence—many of these changes are obvious to the keen observer, and their detection does not require medical knowledge or technology—is due to the theoretical position that the child is a miniature adult. If one were to accept this point of view, then it follows that there should be no difference in the physiological functions of the child and the adult. In the philosophical realm it was Rousseau who stated that "nature would have children be children before being man. If we wish to prevent this order, we shall produce precocious fruits which will have neither maturity

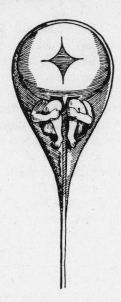

FIGURE 1. Drawing of a small man (that is, a homunculus) in a human spermatozoon.

Adapted from Hartsoeker, 1694.

nor flavor, and will speedily deteriorate; we shall have young doctors and old children" (Rousseau, 1911: 54). Thus a new conception of human nature contributed to a more scientific concept of growth and development.

John Amos Comenius' Development-Centered Theory of Education

The Renaissance may be seen as a revolt against authoritarianism in church, school, and society. The Aristotelian logic, the presupposition of universal ideas, and scholasticism in general were challenged by Erasmus and Vives. Vives felt that one had "to begin with the individual facts of experience and out of them to come to ideas by the natural logic of the mind" (Boyd, 1965: 179). Learning was no longer seen as a deductive process, but as an inductive process beginning with experiences, and he suggested that an understanding of the learning process came from psychology. Learning, it was believed, was determined by the mind of the learner, and, therefore, education became concerned with individuality in pupils.

Comenius (1592–1670) accepted these new ideas of the Renaissance, combined them with Aristotle's classification of development, and advanced a theory of education that was based on psychological assumptions. In his *Great Didactic* first published in 1657 Comenius suggested a school organization based on a theory of development. Rather than dividing the developmental period into three stages of seven years, as Aristotle did, Comenius proposed four developmental stages of six years each and a different kind of school for each of these four stages.

The suggested school organization was based on assumptions concerning the nature of human development and a specific theory of learning, that of faculty psychology. Interestingly enough, present-day school organization in parts of the United States closely resembles this pattern. Comenius argued that the temporal sequence of the curriculum content should be borrowed from nature; in other words, it should be suitable to the psychological development of the child. "Let our maxim be to follow the lead of nature in all things, to observe how the faculties develop one after the other, and to base our methods on this principle of succession" (Comenius, 1923: 257).

The child in the first six years of his life learns at home in the mother-school at his mother's knee. He should exercise the external senses and learn to discriminate among the various objects around him. The nature of the development of the faculty of sense perception is such that it precedes all other faculties, and, consequently, sensory experiences and sensory knowledge should be provided first. The significance of early sensorimotor experiences is emphasized in Piaget's contemporary theory of development.

The child from six to twelve attends the vernacular-school and receives a general well-rounded elementary education, which is provided for all children, rich or poor, boy or girl. Included in the curriculum are the correct use of the vernacular language, social habits, and religious training. The program at this level would emphasize training of the "internal senses, the imagination and memory in combination with their cognate organs." Comenius accepted the faculty psychology point of view in respect to memory. "The memory should be exercised in early youth, since practice develops it, and we should therefore take care to practice it as much as possible. Now, in youth, labour is not felt, and thus the memory developes without any trouble and becomes very retentive" (Comenius, 1923: 152).

For the next six years, from twelve to eighteen, which includes the adolescent period as we understand it today, education was to be provided in the Latin school. The psychological purpose of the school at this age was to train the faculty of reasoning. The student learned to "understand and pass judgment on the information collected by the senses." Included were judgments about relationships of the things perceived, imagined, and remembered. Understanding here implies utilization of the principle of causality. The curriculum of the school was divided into six years, which results in the following six classes: Grammar, Natural Philosophy, Mathematics, Ethics, Dialectics, and Rhetoric.

The following six years from eighteen to twenty-four consist of university education and travel, and during this period the faculty of the will is trained. Considering our present conception of will this appears to be a strange notion and becomes more meaningful only if we consider that the concept of will, as used by Comenius, includes the self-direction of one's life. Corresponding ideas can be found in the contemporary theories of Erikson and Nixon.

Comenius strongly advocated that the instructional procedure should fit the level of comprehension of the child in contrast to the scholastic education, which he attacked. For Comenius, development is not uniform, continuous, and gradual—as the homunculus theory of development implies—but each stage of development has its own characteristics, "teachable moments" as Havighurst would say today. Development was seen as a process in which the intellectual functions gain progressively more control over the other aspects of the soul.

> To attempt to cultivate the will before the intellect (or the intellect before the imagination, or the imagination before the faculty of sense perception) is mere waste of time. But this is what those do who teach boys logic, poetry, rhetoric, and ethics before they are thoroughly acquainted with the objects that surround them. It would be equally sensible to teach boys of two years old to dance, though they can scarcely walk [Comenius, 1923: 257].

The right time for the education of each of the faculties must be chosen correctly, and the sequence must be "borrowed from nature." In Comenius' continuous focus on what children can do, know, and are interested in at each stage of development, we seem to find the historical roots of a child-centered theory of education.

John Locke's Empiricism

The idea of homunculism with its emphasis on preformationism and Plato's theory of innate ideas—a basic scholastic principle—was most seriously challenged and opposed by John Locke (1632–1704). Locke was influenced by Thomas Hobbes' (1588–1679) idea that the human being, both body and mind, is part of the natural order; he further expanded Hobbes' theoretical position, known today as empiricism, that all of our knowledge is derived from sensation. Hobbes stated in *Leviathan* that "there is no conception in man's mind, which has not at first, totally, or by parts, been begotten upon the organs of sense" (Hobbes, 1651: 7). Locke further developed the theory that there are no innate ideas; ideas that we hold in our consciousness are either obtained through our senses directly or are derived from those ideas that have been obtained through sensations previously. The child's mind at the time of birth is, according to an analogy used by Locke, a tabula rasa, a blank tablet. He made the following famous statement concerning the nature of the human mind:

> Let us then suppose the mind to be, as we say, white paper, void of all characters, without any ideas:—How comes it to be furnished? . . . To this I answer, in one word, from EXPERIENCE. In that all our knowledge is founded; and from that it ultimately derives itself. Our observation employed either, about external sensible objects, or about the internal operations of our minds perceived and reflected on by ourselves, is that which supplies our understandings with all the materials of thinking. These two are the fountains of knowledge, from whence all the ideas we have, or can naturally have, do spring [Locke, 1753: 76].

This assumption has had far-reaching influence in social theory and has with amplification become the cornerstone of democracy. Since the mind of each person at birth is a tabula rasa, all ideas and knowledge that men have come from experience; since present differences and inequalities that can be found in people are due to environment and experiences, men are completely equal at birth. Thus the principle of democracy is in part derived from a philosophical-psychological theory concerning the child's mind at birth. Locke discussed his views concerning democracy in *Treatise of Civil Government* (1768). He blamed environmental conditions, such as poor education and poor social environment, for the human misery in the world and gave hope to those who lived under unfavorable conditions. Thus emerged a theory that is an expression of faith in the perfectibility of the human race.

Locke found rather enthusiastic followers in Helvetius and Condillac in France. They carried his empiricism to its extreme, since for them even the powers of faculties of the mind were the result of sensation. Furthermore, since poor living conditions existed for the French lower and middle classes prior to the Revolution, many people in France were especially susceptible to such ideas. Thus the words *liberté, égalité, fraternité* became the powerful symbols of a new concept of human nature. A new hope emerged: that by changing the environment, human nature could be changed. Mankind could determine its own destiny.

Locke's proposition that there are no innate ideas and that the human mind is a tabula rasa contrasts sharply with several theories of human development already discussed. The more outstanding examples are:

1. The doctrine of human depravity and original sin appeared to be in open contradiction to Locke's new concept of the human mind. If our mind is formed by experience only, then it follows that whether a child becomes "good" or "bad" is due to environmental experiences. Locke's psychology stresses nurture rather than nature.

2. The medieval class system of Europe was based on what we would consider today as hereditary assumptions. The nobility was noble by birth, regardless of personal merits and qualities. This notion was challenged by the empiricist assumption that "all men are born equal." If everyone is alike and begins life at the same point, then everyone should have the same rights and opportunities to obtain better social position. King and subject, rich and poor, begin life at the same zero point. Therefore, support for social

mobility is found in this theory. Locke's early form of environmentalism, even though it is not directly related to behaviorism, social learning theory, and cultural relativism, may be viewed as a historical forerunner to these schools of thought.

3. The doctrine of innate ideas was interpreted during the medieval period to imply that the child is a miniature adult and grows only quantitatively. Locke's tabula rasa concept implied that the child at birth is fundamentally different from the adult both qualitatively and quantitatively. If ideas are not innate, then the newborn child is radically different from the adult in respect to intellectual properties. Locke pointed out that the child's personality is basically different from that of the adult and thus laid the foundation for a new theory of child development; he also urged the scientific study of human nature. Development, he believed, occurred in a gradual process from mental passivity in the early years of childhood to increased mental activity in adolescence. The rational faculty emerges toward the end of this developmental process and therefore was seen as characteristic of the period of adolescence.

Locke himself, even though he advanced many important ideas about human nature, foreshadowed rather than developed a specific theory of human development. It was Rousseau who, influenced by Locke, proposed a new theory of human development.

Jean Jacques Rousseau's Romantic Naturalism

Rousseau (1712–1778) was greatly influenced by Locke's ideas, but he developed his own theoretical positions concerning human nature. While for Locke reason was the most important aspect of human nature, Rousseau considered human nature as primarily feeling. While Locke was concerned with constitutional government, Rousseau made a great plea for individualism and individual freedom and directed his criticism and attack against society and social institutions. Although he, too, was concerned with the social well-being of all, he distinguished between the "will of all" (majority will, determined by vote) and the "general will" (that which is really best for every member of the society). Rousseau was not truly democratic, for he was afraid that a majority vote could be as bad as any monarchy. Ideally the majority will and the general will would coincide. This, however, was only possible if men were educated and wise.

Rousseau brought about a revolutionary change in thought concerning the nature of human development with its corresponding educational implications, the main ideas of which he expressed in *Émile,* originally published in 1780. The traditional approach toward childhood education had been to see the child from the adult point of view, adult interests, and adult social life. Rousseau claimed that such an approach is not only false, it may even be harmful. He started with the needs and interests of the child and saw development as a natural preplanned process. If one were to free the child from the restrictions, unnatural limitations, and rigid discipline of the adult world, nature would assure a harmonious and healthy development. The child was innately good, but the restrictions of adult society and poor education had corrupted the child. To correct this, he advocated a natural development in a sound and healthy environment, which for him was one that posed few restrictions on the child, especially in the first twelve years. Rousseau was one of the strongest proponents of individualism in education, basing his proposition on a deep faith in the natural good of man.

Rousseau advocated a revision of the treatment children received at home and in school as well as changes in the methods of instruction; if development were left to the laws of nature, the outcome would be most desirable. Each of Rousseau's four stages of development had specific psychological characteristics. Consideration of these characteristics resulted in definite educational objectives, the attainment of which helped children grow toward maturity. The educational methods, the content to be taught, and the educational objectives at each age level were to be determined by the characteristics of the child at that developmental level. Learning was most effective if the child had freedom and could learn and grow according to his own impulses.

Rousseau (1780) most strongly opposed the homunculus idea and asserted that it was the plan of nature that children play, live, and behave like children before they become adults. "Childhood has its own way of seeing, thinking, and feeling, and nothing is more foolish than to try to substitute ours for them" (Rousseau, 1911: 54). Rousseau advised teachers and parents, "You ought to be wholly absorbed in the child—observing him, watching him without respite, and without seeming to do so, having a presentiment of his feelings in advance" (Rousseau, 1911: 169). Even though Rousseau himself had only limited and not always successful educational experiences—his five children lived in a foundling asylum—his theory had a tremendous impact on educational practice in the latter part of the eighteenth and most of the nineteenth centuries. Rousseau's ideas are obvious in the works of Pestalozzi, Froebel, Basedow, Spencer, Horace Mann, and Dewey and are reflected in a child-centered approach to education.

Rousseau, like Aristotle, saw the development of the child occurring in certain stages—however, he identified four stages rather than three—and believed that teaching and training should be in harmony with the developmental nature of each of these stages. According to Rousseau, these various stages are breaks in the developmental process, and each can be distinguished by its special characteristics and functions. He spoke of a metamorphosis that takes place when the child changes from one stage to another. Thus, Rousseau introduced a saltatory theory of human development according to which the nature of development is seen as change that is more sudden at certain age levels than at others. He, like G. Stanley Hall, spoke of puberty as a new birth. New functions may emerge rather suddenly and become dominant in the psychological organization. We might better understand this saltatory aspect of development in Rousseau's theory in the light of his own temperamental saltatory experiences.

The first stage, that of infancy, includes the first four to five years of life. The child is dominated by the feeling of pleasure and pain. This period is called the animal stage, because the child is like an animal in regard to its physical needs and undifferentiated feelings. This notion we encountered earlier in the writings of Aristotle. Education, such as training motor coordination, sense perception, and feeling, is primarily physical. He advocated to mothers that the method of nature be followed in everything and proposed the following rule: "Observe nature, and follow the route which she traces for you. She is ever exciting children to activity; she hardens the constitution by trials of every sort; she teaches them at an early hour what suffering and pain are."

The second stage, which Rousseau characterized as the savage stage, includes the years from five to twelve. Dominant during this stage is the faculty of sense. Sensory experiences are provided by play, sport, and games, and the curriculum is centered on the training of the senses. During this stage self-consciousness and memory develop, and human life in the proper sense begins here. The child still lacks reasoning ability and is not yet sufficiently aware of moral considerations. Education during this stage should be free from external, social, and moral control. Formal training in reading and writing are seen as harmful and therefore postponed until the beginning of the third developmental stage. In the first twelve years education

> . . . ought to be purely negative. It consists not at all in teaching virtues or truth, but in shielding the heart from vice, and the mind from error. If you could do nothing and allow nothing to be done, if you could bring your pupil sound and robust to the age of twelve years without his being able to distinguish his right hand from his left, from your very first lesson the eyes of his understanding would be open to reason [Rousseau, 1911: 59].

Rousseau's method of "negative education," based on the assumption that there is an innate developmental plan in the organization that cannot be improved upon by environmental factors, finds its corresponding modern psychological concept in "maturation." The defenders of the maturational concept of development frequently advocate, as did Rousseau, a permissive and unrestricted atmosphere for childrearing.

The third stage, from the age of twelve to fifteen, is characterized by an awakening of the rational functions, including reason and self-consciousness. Youth at this age possess an enormous amount of physical energy and strength. The excess of energy leads to curiosity, which the school curriculum should utilize by encouraging exploratory behavior and the desire to discover what is true about the world. The only book that should be read during this stage is *Robinson Crusoe*. Rousseau saw in Crusoe the great model and ideal for the preadolescent, since his style of life was characterized by exploration of the world and a primitive curiosity and corresponds to the needs and interests of this developmental stage. The curriculum should be geared to the study of nature, astronomy, science, art, and crafts. Rousseau in agreement with contemporary educational theory emphasizes the learning process rather than the product. "He is not to learn science, he is to find out for himself." This is the age of reason; curiosity and personal utility are the main motives for behavior; social conscience and emotionality are still undeveloped. It is interesting to observe that, in opposition to other developmental theories, the rational aspect of personality develops prior to the emotional. Rousseau's theory was a reaction to the historically earlier philosophy of rationalism. Modern theory of personality stratification sees in emotionality the deeper and therefore the historically and developmentally earlier layer of personality.

The fourth period, adolescence proper, from the age of fifteen to twenty, finally culminates in the maturation of the emotional functions and brings about a change from selfishness to self-esteem and social consideration. The adolescent is no longer self-sufficient but develops a strong interest in other people and a need for genuine affection. This stage is characterized—late by comparison to knowledge about youth today—by the emergence of the sex drive, which Rousseau considered a second birth. "We have two births, so to speak—one for existing and the other for living; one for the species and the other for the sex" (Rousseau, 1911: 193). Now conscience is acquired, and morals and virtues become possible. This is the period of preparation for marriage, which ideally coincides with the attainment of maturity.

Maturity could be considered as a fifth stage in the process, but it appears to be less clearly defined. The faculty that becomes dominant during this period is will. Comenius also placed the development of the will at the time of late adolescence. The will is the faculty of the soul by which we choose between two alternatives.

These stages of development, according to Rousseau, correspond to certain stages in the development of the human race. Thus it was assumed by this recapitulation theory that the human race had gone through the stages of animallike living, the stage of savagery, the stage of reason, and, finally, through a stage of social and emotional maturity. He used the historical development of the race in order to explain the development of the individual child. This hypothesis was taken up again and further developed by educators, such as Froebel and Ziller, as well as by G. Stanley Hall and the Child Study Movement of America.

Critics have pointed out that Rousseau overemphasized the individual nature of human growth and development and underemphasized the importance that education, society, and culture have in the developmental process and especially in the formation of the human personality. He saw the influence of society and culture as negative forces in personality development; he wanted to remove them to make possible the free natural development of what is good in the child.

Charles Darwin's Theory of Biological Evolution

A new trend of thought concerning the nature of development emerged with the publication of Darwin's *Origin of Species* (1859). Darwin's (1809–1882) idea of evolution—growth and development from the simpler to the more complex forms of organic life—has been one of the most revolutionary and influential ideas in man's thinking about himself and the nature of his development. Every living organism from the simplest organic structure to the most complex, man himself, is brought together under the order of natural explanation. The psychological implications resulting from this biological concept of development were accepted, elaborated, and applied to adolescent development by G. Stanley Hall, thus leading to a science of adolescent development.

Since Darwin's theory is well known, only its basic principles will be stated. Darwin collected substantial, though not complete, evidence for a theory that claimed that the evolution of biological life is continuous, from a single cell organism, through numerous higher developmental stages, to the complexity of human mind and body. This evolutionary theory assumed variability and adjustability in all organisms as well as the overproduction in the number of offspring of each species. Darwin showed that the overproduction of offspring threatened their capacity to survive. The result is a "struggle for existence." In this struggle of the selection of some and elimination of others, a "natural selection process" takes place by which the increase in population is checked. The stronger, healthier, faster, more immune, more intelligent, and physically better developed and adjusted organisms survive and reproduce, while the weak, sick, and less adaptable species perish. In time this leads to the "survival of the fittest." The qualities that account for the survival of the fittest are inherited by the offspring. Since the conditions for survival frequently differ in various kinds of environments, basic changes in the organism occur. Thus in the selection process, variations, new kinds, new races, and eventually new organisms come into existence. This process began with the simple one-cell organism, and from the lower forms of organic life more and more complex forms have developed. The last link in this biological evolution is the human being. Since climatic, geological, and general life conditions change, the evolutionary process is a perpetual one.

This theory of evolution is in complete contrast to the theological doctrine of the divine creation of each individual. Through Darwin's theory man was placed in the order of nature. Most theological and many philosophical positions previous to Darwin's —for example, that of Aristotle—had postulated an essential dichotomy between man and nature. This absolute distinction between human nature and the nature of the organic world was seriously challenged by Darwin. Man was now seen as part of the organic world, albeit a more advanced and more intelligent species.

G. Stanley Hall's Biogenetic Psychology of Adolescence

G. Stanley Hall (1844–1924) was the first psychologist to advance a psychology of adolescence in its own right and to use scientific methods in his study of adolescence. It can be said that he bridged the philosophical, speculative approach of the past and the scientific, empirical approach of the present.

Hall expanded Darwin's concept of biological "evolution" into a psychological theory of recapitulation. In this theory he stated that the experiential history of the human species had become part of the genetic structure of each individual. The law of recapitulation asserted that the individual organism, during its development, passes through stages that correspond to those that occurred during the history of mankind. That is, the individual relives the development of the human race from early animallike primitivism, through a period of savagery, to the more recent civilized ways of life that characterize maturity.

Hall assumed that development is brought about by physiological factors. He further assumed that these physiological factors are genetically determined, that internal maturational forces predominantly control and direct development, growth, and behavior; there was little room in this theory for the influence of environmental forces. It follows that development and its behavioral concomitants occur in an inevitable and unchangeable pattern that is universal, regardless of the sociocultural environment. Cultural anthropologists and sociologists were able to challenge this point and to show that Hall's position was extreme and untenable in the light of accumulated evidence. They further refuted the claim that the behavioral predispositions of physiological drives, as expressed in the recapitulation theory, are highly specific. Hall held that socially unacceptable types of behavior—those characteristic of earlier historical phases—must be tolerated by parents and educators, since they are necessary stages in social development. He advocated childrearing practices of leniency and permissiveness. However, he reassured parents and educators that unacceptable behavior would disappear in the following developmental stage without any corrective educational or disciplinary efforts. Remnants of this assumption can be found in Gesell's conception of maturation.

A corollary of Hall's theory of recapitulation is his concept of stages of human development; the characteristics of a certain age in the development of the individual correspond to some primitive historical stage in the development of the human race. Hall did not divide human development into three stages as advocated by Aristotle and many present-day "stage" psychologists. He followed a four-division pattern similar to that proposed by Comenius and Rousseau. Hall's developmental stages are infancy, childhood, youth, and adolescence.

The period of infancy includes the first four years of life. While the child is still crawling, he is reenacting the animal stage of the human race when the species was still using four legs. During this period, sensory development is dominant; the child acquires those sensorimotor skills that are necessary for self-preservation.

The period of childhood—the years from four to eight—corresponds to the cultural epoch when hunting and fishing were the main activities of man. This is the time when the child plays hide-and-seek, cowboys and Indians, uses toy weapons, and so on. The building of caves, shacks, and other hiding places parallels the cave-dwelling culture of early history.

Youth—from eight to twelve—includes the period that today is commonly referred to as "preadolescence." During this stage the child recapitulates the "humdrum life of savagery" of several thousand years ago. This is the period of life when the child has a favorable predisposition to practice and discipline, when routine training and drill are most appropriate.

> Never again will there be such susceptibility to drill and discipline, such plasticity to habituation, or such ready adjustment to new conditions. It is the age of external and mechanical training. Reading, writing, drawing, manual training, musical technic, foreign tongues and their pronunciation, the manipulation of numbers and of geometrical elements, and many kinds of skill have now their golden hour, and if it passes unimproved, all these can never be acquired later without a heavy handicap or disadvantage or loss [Hall, 1916: xii].

Adolescence is the period from puberty (about twelve or thirteen) until full adult status has been attained. According to Hall, it ends comparatively late, between the twenty-second and twenty-fifth years. Hall described adolescence as a period of *Sturm und Drang,* "storm and stress." In German literature, the period of *Sturm und Drang* includes, among others, the works of Schiller and the early writings of Goethe. It is a literary movement full of idealism, commitment to a goal, revolution against the old, expression of personal feelings, passion, and suffering. Hall saw an analogy between the objectives of this group of young writers at the turn of the eighteenth century and the psychological characteristics of adolescence. In terms of the recapitulation theory adolescence corresponds to a time when the human race was in a turbulent, transitional stage. Hall described adolescence as a new birth, "for the higher and more completely human traits are now born" (Hall, 1916: xiii).

The characteristics of adolescent *Sturm und Drang* are pictured in detail by Hall in the chapter "Feelings and Psychic Evolution." He perceived the emotional life of the adolescent as an oscillation between contradictory tendencies. Energy, exaltation, and supernatural activity are followed by indifference, lethargy, and loathing. Exuberant gaiety, laughter, and euphoria make place for dysphoria, depressive gloom, and melancholy. Egoism, vanity, and conceit are just as characteristic of this period of life as are abasement, humiliation, and bashfulness. One can observe both the remnants of an uninhibited childish selfishness and an increasing idealistic altruism. Goodness and virtue are never so pure, but never again does temptation so forcefully preoccupy thought. The adolescent wants solitude and seclusion, while he finds himself entangled in crushes and friendships. Never again does the peer group have such a strong influence over him. At one time he may exhibit exquisite sensitivity and tenderness; at another time, callousness and cruelty. Apathy and inertia vacillate with an enthusiastic curiosity, an urge to discover and explore. There is a yearning for idols and authority that does not exclude a revolutionary radicalism directed against any kind of authority. Hall (1916) implies these antithetical impulses of Promethean enthusiasm and deep sentimental *Weltschmerz* in his use of the concept of *Sturm und Drang*, which for him is so characteristic of the adolescent.

In late adolescence the individual recapitulates the stage of the beginning of modern civilization. This stage corresponds to the end of the developmental process: he reaches maturity. Hall's genetic psychology did not see the human being as the final and finished product of the developmental process; it allowed for indefinite further development.

3

The Psychoanalytic Theory of Adolescent Development

Although G. Stanley Hall's theory of adolescence probably had little direct influence on Sigmund Freud (1856–1939), it is noteworthy that Hall was the first person in the United States who gave Freud academic recognition by inviting him to give a series of lectures at the twentieth anniversary of Clark University in 1909. Furthermore, Hall helped to promote Freud's ideas in the United States, as indicated by the fact that he wrote the preface to the American edition of *A General Introduction to Psychoanalysis* (1953). In the lectures that Freud gave during the period 1915–1917, a comprehensive statement of his theory of libido development can be found.

The psychoanalytic theory of adolescent development has one fundamental idea in common with Hall's evolutionary theory of recapitulation: both consider adolescence as a period that is phylogenetic. Psychoanalysis does not incorporate a specific theory of recapitulation, but Freud did maintain that the individual goes through earlier experiences of mankind in his psychosexual development.

According to psychoanalytic theory, stages of psychosexual development are genetically determined and are relatively independent of environmental factors. An outstanding example is the psychoanalytic assumption that the Oedipus complex is a universal phenomenon.* Latency ends with the growth and maturation of

*Since there is evidence disproving this psychoanalytic claim, a critical comment needs to be inserted. Malinowski, studying the natives of the Trobriand Islands,

the genitals, a biological characteristic. Since pubescence refers to those body changes associated with the maturing of the reproductive functions, it is undoubtedly seen as a universal phenomenon. Along with the physiological changes of sexual maturation go the psychological components such as the sex instinct—libidinal energies seeking tension release—as well as other phenomena of adolescence. Therefore it must be inferred that adolescence, which includes behavioral, social, and emotional changes, is a universal phenomenon. According to Freud, there is a close relationship between physiological changes and body processes on the one hand and psychological changes and self-image on the other. During adolescence, behavioral changes such as aggressiveness and awkwardness are linked with the physiological changes. Furthermore, self-concept and body image relate to other people. Thus, there are somatically rooted social changes, such as breaking the oedipal ties, building up (at least for a short period) homosexual relationships, and later heterosexual attachments. Finally, physiological changes are related to emotional changes, especially an increase in negative emotions, such as moodiness, anxiety, loathing, tension, and other forms of adolescent behavior.

Freud's theory of psychosexual development stimulated consideration of personality development in general and adolescent development in particular. However, in the original version of his theory, with its discovery of infantile sexuality, Freud placed relatively little emphasis on pubescence and adolescence. Neo-Freudians seem to agree that the period of adolescence had been neglected in early psychoanalytic literature (A. Freud, 1948; Spiegel, 1951). Personality development obviously continues beyond the oedipal situation; personality formation does occur during the puberty crisis and as a result of its resolution. Anna Freud (1948) explains the neglect of adolescence in this way: psychoanalysis developed the revolutionary idea that the sexual life of the human being

---

found no rivalry or conflict between father and son. Therefore, he asserted that the universality of the Oedipus complex was disproved. He emphasized cultural determinants in human development in opposition to the universality of psychosexual stages of development. The natives of the Trobriand Islands live in a matrilineal society and develop a matrilineal complex, which is quite different in origin and symptomatology from the Oedipus complex. Malinowski believed that "the nuclear family complex is a functional formation dependent upon the structure and upon the culture of a society" (Malinowski, 1927: 143).

begins not at puberty, but in early infancy. Many hitherto over-looked aspects of normality and abnormality, such as the capacity for love, are determined in the pregenital phases of sexual development. Moreover, one of Freud's basic assumptions was that the first five years of childhood are the most formative ones for personality development. Freud's stage theory of development holds that the young child goes through five definite phases in the first five or six years of life and only two more in the remaining fifteen childhood and adolescent years.

Beginning with birth—in the passive oral stage—the child gets pleasurable autoerotic stimulation from such manipulations of the oral erogenous zone as sucking, drinking, and eating. In the second phase—the oral-sadistic stage—the child exhibits sadistic tendencies through biting during the cutting of teeth. At the end of the second year, the anal stage begins, changing the source of pleasure from the oral to the anal region. He "holds back" and "lets go" to get more pleasure and to exert power over his parents. The oral and anal stages—basically autoerotic—are sometimes called pre-ego periods, since the id impulses are not yet restrained by the ego.

The phallic phase—sometimes referred to as "little puberty"—begins with interest in manipulation of the sex organs. Infantile masturbation and "impulses for knowledge and investigation" appear in this phase (S. Freud, 1925: 55). His newly developed intellectual curiosity draws the child to the problem of sex. The discovery of the ego accompanies the beginning of narcissism. The development of the ego changes the child's total outlook toward the world. The reality principle becomes increasingly important, subordinating the pleasure principle to the reality-testing functions of the ego.

At puberty, the sexual impulses break through to produce the "subordination of all sexual component-instincts under the primacy of the genital zone" (S. Freud, 1953: 337). Whereas pleasure-seeking was the aim of all the infantile forms of sexuality, physiological puberal changes create another sexual aim: reproduction. This phase of psychosexual development is called the genital stage. Pubescent sexuality manifests itself in three different ways: (1) through external stimulation of the erogenous zones; (2) through internal tension and a physiological need to release sexual products, a condition not present in childhood sexuality; and (3)

through psychological "sexual excitation," which may be influenced by the former two. Psychological excitement now "consists of a peculiar feeling of tension of a most urgent character"
(S. Freud, 1925: 69). This leads to what Freud called "onanism of
necessity," which occurs in the years of the pubescent period.
Empirical support for this psychoanalytic claim can be found in the
Kinsey report, according to which "the highest frequencies of
masturbation . . . occur in the period between adolescence and age
15" (Kinsey, 1948: 238). "Adolescence" here means the *onset* of
adolescence, which Kinsey sets at about age thirteen.

Pubescent development not only awakens sexuality but also
enormously increases nervous excitement, anxiety, genital phobia,
and personality disturbances "because of the outstanding power of
the lust dynamism and the comparative hopelessness of learning
how he . . . can do anything about it" (Sullivan, 1953: 267). Biological changes bring about behavioral changes and adjustment difficulties, since one's lust collides with one's security. Sexual maturity
influences the total nervous system; it not only produces increased
excitability, but at the same time decreases resistance to the development of hysterical and neurotic symptoms. During adolescence,
therefore, a person is especially vulnerable to the development of
psychopathology. G. Stanley Hall discussed at great length the
marked increase of "disease of the mind" during adolescence. On
the other hand, Dennis (1946), in reviewing the literature on the
subject, maintains that there is a lack of evidence for the claim of
a direct relationship between puberty and increasing mental disease.

Increased sexual tension during adolescence revives many of the
incestuous objects of the earlier phallic period and directs the libido
toward them. Freud speaks of a second oedipal situation during
pubescence (S. Freud, 1925, 1953). However, during the latency
period the development of the superego has proceeded to the point
at which an internalized "incest barrier" will repress these feelings.
Freud (1925) commented that during adolescence a boy's first
serious love object is most likely to be a mature woman, and a
young girl's an older man—that is, mother and father figures.

But these are not the greatest dangers an adolescent faces in his
further development. Freud saw several developmental tasks to be

mastered. One is "not missing the opposite sex" (S. Freud, 1925: 87). There exists the danger that friendship ties that are too strong will bind boys and girls to their own sex, with the possibility of inversion of the sex object. Related to the oedipal situation is the adolescent's task of freeing himself from his dependency upon his parents. The boy's libidinal attachment to his mother has to be released, and he must also free himself from the dominance of the father. Unsuccessful attempts to resolve either situation will result in neurosis, since they will interfere with the selection of a hetero-sexual love object. Detachment from the incestuous object brings the "problem of generation" into the foreground and gives it its psychological explanation. The emotional detachment results, at least for a time, in rejection, resentment, and hostility toward parents and other authority, an adolescent phenomenon that has been described frequently in literature and that is a rather common concern of parents. The main task of the adolescent as seen by psychoanalytic theory may be summarized as being the "attain-ment of genital primacy and the definitive completion of the proc-ess of non-incestuous object finding" (Spiegel, 1951: 380).

Since the stages of psychosexual development occur in a prede-termined sequence, it must be assumed that they are predomi-nantly biological in nature. The biological nature of Freud's theory is further emphasized by his frequent use of the instinct concept. In his earlier theory, the two biological instincts are self-preserva-tion and reproduction. The self-preservation instinct includes such ego motives as hunger, fear, and self-assertion. The reproductive instinct is sexual and is closely related to the psychic energy called libido, which is a pleasure-seeking drive. The libido energy stems from the id which "contains everything that is inherited, that is present at birth, that is fixed in the constitution . . ." (A. Freud, 1949: 14).

Freud has frequently been criticized for his overemphasis of the biological, instinctual nature of man (Ausubel, 1954; Erikson, 1950; Sherif and Cantril, 1947). While he undoubtedly does over-emphasize instinctual and biological factors, Freud has not com-pletely neglected the operation of social forces. In his theory, environmental factors are secondary to innate tendencies, but he does not deny their importance. The morals, aspirations, and ambitions of each society become part of the individual through the development of his superego, which we may also call his conscience. Sexuality is the opposite of conscience, since it is present at birth, whereas conscience is acquired through social interaction. Thus, the developmental process, especially in latency and pubescence, is a dynamic struggle between the biological-instinctual id forces and the socially oriented superego.

Erikson (1950), Fromm (1932), Horney (1939), and Sullivan (1953) have modified the orthodox psychoanalytic position, with its emphasis on instincts and biological determinism, in the developmental process. They have pointed out that social factors can modify development and id impulses. Fromm (1936) recognizes that father and son are not sexual rivals in many societies. Sears maintains that there is no evidence for a "universal cross-sex preference" (Sears, 1943: 134). If the Oedipus complex is found only in certain cultures, the orthodox claim that it is universal is no longer warranted.

The psychoanalytic system is flexible enough to allow for some continuity, at least in normal development. "These phases are certainly only theoretical constructs . . . but necessary and valuable . . ." (S. Freud, 1953: 336). The stages are not rigidly defined and limited; they allow for overlapping in the successive maturation of the erogenous zones that are characteristic for each of the phases—oral, anal, phallic, and genital. At this point we should consider two ideas that Freud expressed at different times and that are important in his stage theory. His earlier position held that the stages follow consecutively and that each is the prerequisite for the next. "The libido function . . . goes through a series of successive phases unlike one another; . . . changes occur . . . like those in the development of the caterpillar into a butterfly" (S. Freud, 1953: 337). Thus anal gratification comes about only after preoccupation with the oral region. However, in his later approach, Freud developed the concept that one psychosexual stage is not finished and outgrown when the next one is reached: ". . . each earlier phase persists side by side with, and behind, later organizations" (S. Freud, 1933: 137). This second idea sees sexual development not as sequential, but rather as continuous expansion and integration. Autoeroticism, narcissism, and object-love may exist in an individual at the same time.

Anna Freud's Theory of Adolescent Defense Mechanism

Anna Freud (1895–   ) takes more pains than did her father in spelling out the dynamics of adolescent development. Furthermore, she assigns greater importance to puberty as a factor in character formation. In her discussion of childhood and pubescence, she puts greater emphasis on the relationship between the id (instinctual impulses), the ego (which is governed by the reality principle), and the superego (conscience). It is obvious to her that the physiological process of sexual maturation, beginning with the functioning of the sexual glands, influences directly the psychological realm. This interaction results in the instinctual reawakening of the libidinal forces, which, in turn, bring about psychological disequilibrium. The painfully established balance between ego and id during the latency period is disturbed by puberty, and internal conflict results. Thus, one aspect of puberty, the puberty conflict, is the endeavor to regain equilibrium.

During the latency period the child's superego develops through an assimilation of the moral values and principles held up to him by people with whom he identifies, such as his father. This process replaces his childhood fear of the external world with the internally produced anxiety of the superego or conscience. He develops a sense of right and wrong and ensuing guilt feelings when his behavior is inconsistent with his moral code. Thus, superego anxiety is a result of identification with and internalization of the moral value system of the parents or other important authority figures.

During childhood the inhibition of id impulses is most likely to be due to ego fear of punishment that results when the id-inspired behavior materializes. Behavior is also controlled by the parental power of physical and psychological reward. During pubescence, the ego, yielding to id impulses, comes into conflict with the now internalized moral standards of the superego. A child experiences external frustration, since the father or other authority figure interferes with the attainment of the goal-object. The pubescent, on the other hand, experiences internal frustration, since the attainment of the goal-object is interfered with by internal inhibitions arising from his conscience. The superego also has the power to give reward by way of the ego ideal. During prepubescence, the quantity of instinctual energy begins to increase and can be attached to any id impulse, not only to sexual impulses. This change from an external to internal mechanism of control brings the mental balance into a state of disequilibrium. Thus, we can observe an intensification of aggressive tendencies, naughtiness, preoccupation with dirt and disorder, brutality, and exhibitionistic tendencies. "If we scrutinize this struggle for supremacy between the ego and the id, we realize that almost all the disquieting phenomena of the prepubertal period correspond to different phases in the conflict . . ." (A. Freud, 1948: 160).

When the attainment of sexual maturity creates a disturbing increase in libidinal influence on the psychological sphere, there is a temporary revival of or regression to earlier developmental stages. Anna Freud claims a second Oedipus complex occurs at the onset of pubescence, producing castration fears in boys and penis envy in girls, as in the first oedipal stage. During pubescence, the oedipal impulses, if they become conscious at all, are usually fulfilled on a fantasy level only. The newly developed superego enters the conflict, produces anxiety, and thus calls forth all the methods of defense the ego has at its disposal: repression, denial, and displacement. These defenses reverse the libidinal impulses and "turn them against the self" (A. Freud, 1948: 160) causing fears, anxiety, and neurotic symptoms.

"Increased activity of phantasy, lapses into pregenital (i.e., perverse) sexual gratification, aggressive or criminal behavior signify partial successes of the id, while the occurrence of various forms of anxiety, the development of ascetic traits and accentuation of neurotic symptoms and inhibitions denote a more vigorous defence, i.e., the partial success of the ego" (A. Freud, 1948: 161).

The onset of actual puberty brings a qualitative change. The instinctual cathexis, previously undifferentiated and general, now becomes differentiated and specific as genitality, the final phase of psychosexual development, takes over. Anna Freud claims that the "turmoil of boorishness, aggressiveness, and perverse behavior has vanished like a nightmare" (A. Freud, 1948: 161). This relates to a similar observation of this event in Bühler's (1935) and Hetzer's (1948) concept of the "negative phase." In that concept, too, actual onset of pubescence, defined by Hetzer as corresponding to the first menstruation in girls, brings about a rather sudden change from negative behavior to a more positive period of gushing exuberance. It is interesting to note that even though Anna Freud operates within a different theoretical construct, she agrees with Hetzer on this point. Furthermore, we find a brief account of prepuberal negativism by Spiegel: "the girl is described as being full of rage and hatred as well as of dependent, clinging feelings toward the mother" (Spiegel, 1951: 382).

Anna Freud (1948) deals mainly with deviant or pathological development and pays little attention to normal sexual adjustment. But she describes clearly two possible dangers to normal development: (1) the id may override the ego "in which case no trace will be left of the previous character of the individual and the entrance into adult life will be marked by a riot of uninhibited gratification of instincts" (A. Freud, 1948: 163); (2) the ego may be victorious over the id and confine it to a limited area, constantly checked by numerous defense mechanisms.

Among the many defense mechanisms that the ego can use, Anna Freud considers two as typical of pubescence: asceticism and intellectualization. Both are available before pubescence, but they become especially important during this period. Asceticism in an adolescent is due to a generalized mistrust of all instinctual wishes. This mistrust goes far beyond sexuality and includes eating, sleeping, and dressing habits. The increase in intellectual interests and the change from concrete to abstract interests are accounted for in terms of a defense mechanism against the libido (Spiegel, 1951). This naturally brings about a crippling of the instinctual tendencies in adult life, and again the situation is "permanently injurious to the individual" (A. Freud, 1948: 164). She speculates that "ego-institutions which have resisted the onslaught of puberty without yielding generally remain throughout life inflexible, unassailable and insusceptible of the rectification which a changing reality demands" (A. Freud, 1948: 164).

She indicates that a harmonious balance between the id, ego, and superego is possible, but she does not develop it further. The establishment of this balance is more likely to be the actual result in most normal adolescents.

Anna Freud asserts that the factors involved in adolescent conflict are:

1. The strength of the id impulse, which is determined by physiological and endocrinological processes during pubescence.
2. The ego's ability to cope with or to yield to the instinctual forces. This in turn depends on the character training and superego development of the child during the latency period.
3. The effectiveness and nature of the defense mechanism at the disposal of the ego.

Otto Rank's Emphasis on the Adolescent Need for Independence

Otto Rank (1884–1939), a follower of the psychoanalytic school of thought, had been "completely under the influence of Freudian realism" (Rank, 1945: 209). However, he later developed his own theory and then challenged some of Freud's basic assumptions. Rank approached human development from a more positive point of view: he saw human nature not as repressed and neurotic, but as creative and productive. He criticized Freud's emphasis on the unconscious as a storehouse for past experiences and impulses. Rank reversed this assumption and returned to the conscious ego as the proper field of psychoanalysis.* Consequently, he was in opposition to Freud and basically in agreement with Lewin on the relationship of past and present. Rank pointed out that the past is of importance only to the degree that it acts in the present to influence behavior. Furthermore, Rank places less emphasis on instinctual forces and instinctual behavior. He claims that Freud actually neglected the role of the ego and gave value to it only as a repressive force. Rank wanted to restore the balance of power in the psychic realm.

The core concept in his theory is "will," a positive factor, a force that actively forms the self and modifies the environment. By "will" he meant a "positive guiding organization and integration of self which utilizes creatively, as well as inhibits and controls the instinctual drives" (Rank, 1945: 112). The ego is no longer caught between the instinctual id forces and the externally enforced su-

---

*It is interesting to note that this idea is a predecessor to contemporary ego psychology and to Rogers' nondirective approach in counseling and guidance.

perego; rather, it is the dominating force that utilizes and directs them both. Rank objected strongly to an interpretation that might identify his "will" concept with Freud's "wish" concept. While it is more closely related to Freud's "ego" concept, they are not synonymous, since Rank places more emphasis on choice and activity.

We must examine the place that adolescent development has in this psychoanalytic theory based on consciousness and "will." Sexuality is no longer the strongest determining factor in the developmental process. It has found its counterpart in "will," which can, at least to some degree, control sexuality. Consequently, the emphasis shifts from early childhood to adolescence, since it is predominantly in this period that a most crucial aspect of personality development occurs—the change from dependence to independence. *Does it happen at this time?*

During the latency period, the "will" grows stronger, more independent, and expands to the point where it turns against any authority not of its own choosing. The actual origin of the "will" goes further back into the oedipal situation. It is here that the individual will encounters a societal will, represented by parents and expressed in a moral code centuries old.

In early adolescence, the individual undergoes a basic change in attitude; he begins to oppose dependency, including both the rule of external environmental factors (parents, teachers, the law, and so on) and the rule of internal cravings, the newly awakening instinctual urges. Establishing volitional independence, which society values and requires, becomes an important but difficult developmental task for the adolescent.* This newly developed need for independence and the struggle for the attainment of independence lie at the root of many adolescent personal relationships and their complications.

The onset of the physiological sex drive during pubescence threatens the newly established independence. This threat does not originate through an external person or force, but by an internal need. Rank sees no necessity for external sexual restrictions and

---

*This developmental task corresponds closely to two of Havighurst's developmental tasks (to be discussed in Chapter 8): "emotional independence of parents and other adults" (Havighurst, 1951: 37), and "achieving assurance of economic independence" (Havighurst, 1951: 40).

inhibitions, since the struggle is one in which the individual's will strives for independence against domination by biological needs.

> Sexuality, however, as it awakens in the individual about the time of puberty is an incomparably stronger power than all the external authorities put together. . . . It is so strong and dominates the individual so extremely that he soon begins to defend himself against its domination, just because it is a domination, something that interferes dictatorially with his own will as individual, appearing as a new, alien and more powerful counter-will just as the ego is strengthened by puberty. . . . The reason the individual defends himself so strongly against it is because the biological sex drive would force him again under the rule of a strange will, of the sexual will . . . while the ego has just begun at this time to breathe a little freely out from under the pressure of strange authoritative wills [Rank, 1945: 258].

 (Because of this forceful striving for independence, the individual is unable to form strong emotional attachments that would bring him back into a personal love relationship of dependency) The adolescent can rely on two forms of defense mechanism in his endeavor to maintain independence: promiscuity or asceticism. By being promiscuous, he satisfies sexual urges without losing his newly acquired independence, since sexual gratification takes place without genuine love and ego involvement. By being ascetic, as expressed also by Anna Freud, he retains his independence, because he willfully rejects any kind of involvement. Periods of asceticism may take turns with periods of instinctual gratification. In both instances the adolescent avoids the real love relationship in which self-restraint, self-subordination, and dependency are necessary. Rank (1945) considers personality development to be a continuous expansion, differentiation, and integration of the external "self-other" relationship as well as of the intrapsychic self-other system.

Rank, too, says that an individual has to go through evolutionary stages to develop and strengthen his will and to achieve both the described external self-other and the intrapsychic self-other relationship.

The first stage is the freeing of the will from both the external and internal forces that dominate it. Rank comments that the average man probably never passes beyond this stage, but that he can live harmoniously because he accepts reality and adjusts his own mode of living to it; this type of person is duty-conscious.

The second stage is characterized by a division in personality. There is a disunity between the will and the counterwill. This moral struggle contains both neurotic and creative possibilities that were unknown in the first stage. As a type, this individual is guilt conscious. He either indulges in self-criticism, inferiority feelings, and neurotic symptoms, or he moves on to a third stage and becomes productive and creative. He is compelled to oppose the norms of the external world, since he has not yet accepted and internalized ideals that correspond with his self-concept.

The third stage of development is the integration of will, counterwill, and ideal formation. The individual is no longer in conflict with the demands of the external world as is the person in the second stage; he is in harmony with himself and his own ideals. Rank characterized this type as the genius; he is conscious of his potential and is self-assured. He has overcome the compulsion of the second stage through freedom.

It follows that the neurotic who may be in the second stage is in a higher form of psychological development than the normal person in the first stage who sacrifices creativity and individual ideals for the quiet of the conforming adjustment to the external world. There are two factors that might prevent an individual from passing from the second to the third stage of development: guilt that immobilizes his will, and a disintegration that influences both his external relationship with others and his self-concept and ego structure.

Educational Implications

Freud assumed that "frustration of normal sexual satisfaction may lead to the development of neurosis" (S. Freud, 1953: 319). Even at the risk of overgeneralizing, the psychoanalytic argument may be stated as follows: frustration causes neurosis; discipline involves frustration; therefore, if a parent does not want his child to be neurotic, he must not discipline him. This statement implies that educators should avoid frustrating adolescents unnecessarily, and questions the prudish Victorian attitude toward sexuality prevalent at Freud's time. But since "sexuality" for Freud is defined rather broadly—that is, to include everything that relates to and grows out of a person's love life—one might go one step further and assume that parents and educators should keep frustrations to a minimum, especially those frustrations that block the satisfaction of basic human needs. What is needed instead is an atmosphere of leniency, love, affection, approval, and attention in which the child can grow up feeling secure, wanted, and loved.

A similar idea was expressed in Rousseau's natural Romanticism and especially in his emphasis on "negative education." More recently psychoanalytic ideas have been influential in the creation of a variety of educational experiments, the best known of which is Neill's school, Summerhill in Leiston, England. Summerhill attempts to remove all restrictions and frustrations from the educational process, including many of the common restrictions on children's sexual curiosity and exploratory sex behavior. The school is designed to fit the child rather than to make the child fit the school, and Neill hopes that the result is to make Summerhill the happiest school in the world.

But even for the regular classroom teacher in a more conventional setting some of Freud's ideas can be applied for the benefit of the pupil and the educational process. Applying psychoanalytic thought to classroom management, discipline becomes less authoritarian and therefore less frustrating. Even when the kind of freedom provided in Summerhill may be inappropriate, there can be a genuine concern with the underlying causes and dynamics of disturbing, disruptive, antisocial, acting-out behavior. Even for a teacher with only rudimentary understanding of psychoanalytic principles, misbehavior can no longer be viewed as arbitrary, as simple meanness or a personal affront, but as a symptom of underlying conflicts and causes (Muuss, 1962). What an individual does or says is not meaningless but has a cause. Just as errors in conceptual development reflect lack of understanding, use of a false method, or incorrect reasoning, so errors in self-control or rudeness serve a psychological purpose. A basic assumption of psychoanalytic theory is that all behavior is meaningful. Dreams, neurotic behavior, even a slip of the tongue, and forgetting and losing things are motivated; and if there is no conscious motive, there must be an unconscious one.

Education has been slow in providing a place for the "affective domain" in its structure and curriculum. However, much of the recent efforts to legitimize emotions in the educational process have their roots in the writings of Freud and are made explicit in the writings of some of his followers, Anna Freud (1948), Lawrence Kubie (1960), and Richard Jones (1960):

> The child's fifth freedom is the right to know what he feels; but this does not carry with it any right to act out his feelings blindly. This will require a new mores for our schools, one which will enable young people from early years to understand and feel and put into words all the hidden things which go on inside of them . . . [Kubie, 1960: vii–viii].

Psychoanalytic theory assumes that talking about and acting out of dreams, fears, aggressive feelings, and feelings of hostility not only brings them out into the open but cleanses them and reduces their magnitude. In addition, openly sharing emotional problems in a classroom of peers leads to the realization that others have similar, if not the same, fears and feelings. "The freedom of one individual to express what another individual inhibits often results in freeing the latter" (Jones, 1960: 16). Adolescents in their concern about normality in regard to physical development, sexual needs, social sensitivities, and personal problems can benefit from the realization that their concern and most personal thoughts are not really too different from those of their peers.

The inhibition or frustration of sexual energies that most Western societies demand of their youth is the basis of Freud's concept of sublimation. Damming up libidinal energies "must swell the force of the perverse impulses, so that they become more powerful than they would have been had no hindrance to normal sexual satisfaction been present" (S. Freud, 1953: 319). It follows that early infantile sexual activities should not be repressed or pushed into the unconscious, unless normal sexual development be perverted. If libidinal energies are forced to regress to earlier stages of sexual development and denied any normal satisfaction, substitute satisfactions in the form of fetishism, homosexuality, sadism, masochism, narcissism, or other neurotic symptoms may manifest themselves. Yet psychoanalytic theory does not advocate uninhibited gratification of sexual impulses. Freud suggested redirecting sexual energy by means of sublimation. In Western culture most societies oppose unrestricted sexual gratification and assume that uninhibited sexuality would create new conflicts. Furthermore, since society's values are already represented in the adolescent's personality structure by means of the superego—which develops during the latency period—the sociosexual conflict is a psychological, internal one, a conflict of the conscience. Freud does not make a specific statement about adolescent sexual gratification. But since during this time the sexual drive and internal and external forces controlling the expression of sexuality are strong, sublimation can be a means of guiding these energies into productive educational activities thus contributing constructively to the learning process.

In practicing sublimation an individual finds substitute forms of satisfaction and tension release for unsatisfied libidinal energies. It is assumed that nonsexual aims and socially useful activities absorb some of the sexual energy. Hence many educationally desirable activities may be stimulated by denying sexual gratification. For a long time football players and athletes have been advised prior to major sports events to abstain from sexual activity. Through sublimation "sources of sexuality are discharged and utilized in other spheres, so that a considerable increase of psychic capacity results" (S. Freud, 1925: 95). The connection between sexual energy and productivity in the fields that appeal more to emotion such as music, art, poetry, and literature is one of the assumptions of psychoanalytic theory. Freud himself went much further. He developed a theory of culture and civilization in which all human creations—from the learning of language to the composition of symphonies and scientific inventions—are due to sublimation. "Sexual impulses have contributed invaluably to the highest cultural, artistic, and social achievements of the human mind" (S. Freud, 1953: 27). Since sexual urges appear to be strongest in the late adolescent period—if Kinsey's "outlets" are taken as an indication of the strength of sexual drive—and since internal and external restrictions are also strongest during this period, at least for middle-class American youth, sublimation appears to be one important educational objective in this period. If society can use sublimation to provide a harmonious balance between realistic denial of gratification and fulfillment of basic needs without repression and utilization of sexual energies and thus avoid the two extremes of maladjustment—neurosis and immoral behavior—the productivity and creativity of the individual could be vastly increased. Sublimation remains a theoretical model, and Freud stated quite frankly that very little is actually known about the physiological and neurological processes of sublimation.

Freud believed that applying psychoanalysis to education was most important. But he admitted quite openly that he had no "special understanding of it" (S. Freud, 1933). He did credit his daughter, Anna, with making this aspect of psychoanalysis her life work and thus expanding his theories. Her interest in child psychology and education is expressed in most of her publications, but it is especially clear in "The Relationship Between Psychoanalysis and Pedagogy."

4

Erik Erikson's Theory of Identity Development*

Erik H. Erikson's (1902–) theory reflects his psychoanalytic training, but it embraces social forces and the socialization process more than Freud's theory does. As a young artist, with little more than a German high school (gymnasium) education, Erikson attended art schools and traveled in Italy apparently in search of his own identity. He was offered a teaching position in a private school in Vienna that served the children of Sigmund and Anna Freud's patients. As a teacher he was invited to undergo analysis with Anna Freud, and slowly his interest changed from art and teaching to the theoretical study of psychoanalysis. He graduated from the Vienna Psychoanalytic Institute in 1933. Later that year he became associated with the Harvard Psychological Clinic, and after a rich professional life in a variety of famous institutions he returned to Harvard in 1960. Erikson has published extensively, his best known and most widely read book being *Childhood and Society,* which was published in 1950 and revised in 1963. Of particular significance to an understanding of adolescence is his *Identity: Youth and Crisis* (1968). However, the idea of identity appears not only in other book titles, such as *Identity and the Life Cycle* (1959), but is the underlying theme of much of Erikson's writing. Even when he examines historical figures, as in *Young Man Luther*

*Chapter 4 has been published as two articles, "Erik Erikson's Theory of Identity Development" and "James Marcia's Expansion of Erikson's Concept 'Identity vs. Role Diffusion,' " *Adolescence,* 1974, (in press).

(1958) and *Gandhi's Truth* (1969), he is concerned with the identity crisis of each of these men as well as the historical identity crisis in their respective countries, Germany and India. One cannot separate "the identity crisis in individual life and contemporary crises in historical development because the two help to define each other and are truly relative to each other" (Erikson, 1968: 23). More recently Erikson has written about his own identity crisis and the philosophical and psychoanalytic development of the concept in "Autobiographic Notes on the Identity Crisis" (1970).

Erikson in his chapter "Eight Stages of Man" (1950) modifies, elaborates, and expands the Freudian theory of psychosexual development. He does this in the light of anthropological findings and thus shifts the emphasis from the sexual nature of the stages of development to a new theory of psychosocial development. The core concept in Erikson's theory is the acquisition of an ego-identity, and the identity crisis is the most essential characteristic of adolescence. Although a person's identity is established in ways that differ from culture to culture, the accomplishment of this developmental task has a common element in all cultures. In order to acquire a strong and healthy ego-identity the child must receive consistent and meaningful recognition of his achievements and accomplishments.

Human development proceeds according to the *epigenetic principle,* which states "that anything that grows has a ground plan, and that out of this ground plan the parts arise, each part having its time of special ascendancy, until all parts have arisen to form a functional whole" (Erikson, 1968: 92). In the epigenetic chart (Figure 2) Erikson represents the basic ground plan of increasing psychosocial differentiation. The diagonal axis, beginning with "Trust vs. Mistrust," shows the sequence of Erikson's well-known eight stages of man. Movement along the diagonal axis through time shows the successive differentiation of the originally undifferentiated structure and thus reveals maturation of personality. The diagram demonstrates:

1. that each item of the vital personality is systematically related to all others, and that they all depend on the proper development in the proper sequence of each item;
2. that each item exists in some form before "its" decisive and critical time normally arises [Erikson, 1968: 93, 95].

FIGURE 2. Erikson's Epigenetic Diagram

	1	2	3	4	5	6	7	8
VIII								INTEGRITY vs. DESPAIR
VII							GENERA-TIVITY vs. STAGNATION	
VI						INTIMACY vs. ISOLATION		
V	Temporal Perspective vs. Time Confusion	Self-Certainty vs. Self-Consciousness	Role Experimentation vs. Role Fixation	Apprenticeship vs. Work Paralysis	IDENTITY vs. IDENTITY CONFUSION	Sexual Polarization vs. Bisexual Confusion	Leader- and Followership vs. Authority Confusion	Ideological Commitment vs. Confusion of Values
IV				INDUSTRY vs. INFERIORITY	Task Identification vs. Sense of Futility			
III			INITIATIVE vs. GUILT		Anticipation of Roles vs. Role Inhibition			
II		AUTONOMY vs. SHAME, DOUBT			Will to Be Oneself vs. Self-Doubt			
I	TRUST vs. MISTRUST				Mutual Recognition vs. Autistic Isolation			

Handwritten annotations: 0 - 18mo - 0   18 mo - 3½   3½ - 6

From *Identity: Youth and Crisis,* by Erik Erikson, © 1968 by W. W. Norton, New York. Reproduced by permission.

In each of the eight developmental stages that Erikson describes, a conflict that has two opposing possible outcomes arises. It is this social crisis or central developmental problem that gives each stage its name, rather than the body parts that give pleasure in the original Freudian theory. If the conflict is worked out in a constructive, satisfactory manner, the positive quality is built into the ego and further healthy development is enhanced. But if the conflict persists or is resolved unsatisfactorily, the developing ego suffers because the negative quality is incorporated into the personality structure. The negative quality will interfere with further development and may manifest itself in psychopathology.

Each crisis or conflict is never completely solved but is purest at the age level at which it is placed. However, as in psychoanalytic theory, these stages occur in a lawful sequential order. Ego "identity is never 'established' as an 'achievement' " as something static or unchangeable, but is a "forever to-be-revised sense of the reality of the Self within social reality" (Erikson, 1968: 24, 211). While the identity crisis is most pronounced in and especially characteristic of the period of adolescence, redefinition of one's ego-identity is not uncommon when the college freshman leaves home and again later with the first job, marriage, parenthood, divorce, unemployment, serious illness, widowhood, and retirement. The ability to cope with each of these identity issues that result from changes in one's role in life may well depend on the degree of success with which the adolescent identity crisis was mastered.

The vertical sequence in Figure 2, beginning with "Mutual Recognition vs. Autistic Isolation" and ascending until it coincides with "Identity vs. Identity Confusion" in the diagonal sequence, demonstrates how each of the four stages preceding adolescence contributes significantly to the development of an ego-identity during adolescence, or how it may contribute to identity diffusion. Thus "Mutual Recognition," "The Will to Be Oneself," "Anticipation of Roles," and "Task Identification" are secondary outcomes of earlier stages in psychosocial development that are essential prerequisites to the achievement of an identity in adolescence. On the other hand, failure in the earlier stages resulting in "Autistic Isolation," "Self-Doubt," "Role Inhibition," and a "Sense of Futility" leads to "a particular estrangement or identity confusion" in adolescence.

The horizontal sequence in Figure 2 beginning with "Temporal Perspective vs. Time Confusion" lists the

> derivatives of earlier relative achievements which now become part and parcel of the struggle for identity. It is necessary to emphasize [that] the early relative achievements [diagonal] when considered at a later stage [any horizontal below the diagonal] must be . . . renamed in terms of that later stage. Basic Trust, for example, is a good and a most fundamental thing to have, but its psychosocial quality becomes more differentiated as the ego comes into the possession of a more extensive apparatus, even as society challenges and guides such extension [Erikson, 1959: 140–141].

The symptoms of confusion that make up the negative alternative on the horizontal sequence represent the earlier failures to progress and resolve conflict and are therefore reflected later in identity confusion. The common experience of time confusion during adolescence, for example, arises out of the undifferentiated mistrust that occurred earlier; it may develop into an attitude of not trusting time or interpreting an unnecessary delay or wait as deceit.

The Relationship of Erikson's "Stages of Man" to the Adolescent Identity Crisis

During infancy—the first stage of life—the major developmental issue is between becoming a trusting or a mistrusting person. Trust includes being trustful of others, as well as a sense of one's own trustworthiness. The basic healthy experience for the development of trust is maternal love. Initially, the infant "lives through, and loves with, his mouth" (Erikson, 1968: 97). Feeding results in trust. However, the infant is receptive to maternal love in many other ways besides orally. The trusting child has learned that mother does come and take care of him regularly. He thus learns that he lives in a predictable, secure world, a world that he can trust because his basic needs are satisfied. Later, as his motor skills develop and as he is given freedom to explore his world, he also learns to trust himself and his own body, especially as he begins to control his body movements such as grasping, holding, and reaching, and later crawling, standing, and walking.

The mistrust of time and *time confusion* that Erikson sees as "more or less typical for all adolescents at one stage or another" (Erikson, 1968: 182) grow out of negative experiences at this early stage and are related to the regularity of the cycle in which the infant's needs are satisfied. Repeated delay or irregularity in basic body satisfactions results in mistrust of time. **?**

The conviction that emerges from this receptive state is: "I am what I am given," and Erikson refers to it as an incorporative stage. The positive outcome of this stage is trusting others and trusting oneself. Later in the life cycle the ability to experience faith is a result of this early stage. The trusting infant has achieved the first step in developing confidence, optimism, and finally a feeling of security. He recognizes people and smiles at them as they talk to him. *Mutual recognition* and mutual trustworthiness are the earliest and most undifferentiated experiences of what is later to become a sense of identity.

The negative outcome of this stage is mistrust of others and mistrust of oneself. Lack of trust in childhood recurs as identity confusion in adolescence. Absence of the experience of trust during infancy may impair the "capacity to feel identical" with others during adolescence (Erikson, 1968: 105). *Autistic isolation* in infancy is the earliest contribution to identity diffusion in adolescence.

The issue at the second stage of life is between becoming an *autonomous and creative individual* and a dependent, inhibited, and *shameful individual filled with self-doubt;* it falls approximately between the ages of eighteen months and three-and-a-half years. The child during this stage—although still dependent on others in many ways—begins to experience the autonomy of free choice. He is developing both the motor ability and the intellectual capacity to experience himself as an entity in his own right, as a person who is different from father and mother. This newly gained autonomy is used freely, although it is not always effective socially. The battle for autonomy may show in stubborn refusal, temper tantrums, and the "yes-no" syndrome. During this stage the child begins to learn self-control, which is particularly important in Western civilization in the control of body waste products. Toilet training means "holding on and letting go" when the child wishes, representing definitely autonomous activities over which nobody else has any direct control. The child can retain body wastes even though his mother may want him to let go. On the other hand, he can release them even though his mother wishes him to hold back. However, with proper training—that is, in a general sense as well as in regard to toilet training—he can develop a feeling of mastery for a job well done and a sense of autonomy of choice in that he can determine when and where to hold back and let go.

The conviction that emerges during this stage is: "I am what I will to be." The child's sense of autonomy is primarily "a reflection of the parents' dignity as autonomous beings" (Erikson, 1968: 113). The positive outcome is pride, control, self-assurance, autonomy, *self-certainty,* and the *will to be oneself.* The development of a rudimentary form of the will to be oneself during the autonomy stage is an essential prerequisite for the development of a mature ego-identity during adolescence. "There are clinical reasons to believe that the adolescent turning away from the whole childhood milieu in many ways repeats this first emancipation" (Erikson, 1968: 114). The contribution of the autonomy quality to the formation of an identity in adolescence is the conviction: I am an independent person who can choose freely and who can guide my own development and my own future.

The negative outcome is shame, *self-doubt,* dependency, *self-consciousness,* and meek compliance resulting from too many restrictions, unfair punishment, and the parents' frustration in marriage, work, and citizenship. The identity crisis of adolescence revives and grows out of an unresolved autonomy crisis. Since autonomy is an essential ingredient for the development of identity during adolescence, the battle for autonomy in decision making is a familiar issue in the adolescent's struggle for independence from his family. The adolescent may become so self-conscious and lacking in autonomy that he is afraid of being seen in an exposed or vulnerable situation. He may question the reliability of the whole experience of childhood and therefore be unable to find an identity. On the other hand, entering adolescence with too much autonomy may cause shameless defiance of parents, teachers, and other authorities.

The psychosocial conflict in the third stage of life is the growth of a *sense of initiative versus a sense of guilt.* The conflict at this level is between an aggressive intrusion into the world by way of activity, curiosity, and exploratory behavior or an immobilization by fear and guilt. The child from about three-and-a-half to six years of age is characterized by exuberance, a feeling of power, curiosity, a high level of activity, and surplus of energy. The child during this play age moves around more freely and more aggressively, develops an increasingly larger radius of operations, and begins to aim for goals further away. This is also the stage during which language develops rapidly. The child expresses his intellectual initiative by his many questions. Beginning between ages three and four there are endless numbers of "what" questions and, a year later, "why" questions, which are basically learning tools, since new words, concepts, and ideas are learned through questions. One can observe aggressive manipulation of toys. The child takes his toys apart to see what is inside, not because he is destructive but because he is curious; but if his curiosity is interpreted as destructiveness, he is made to feel guilty and as a result his initiative may wane. The child will also explore and manipulate his own body as well as those of his friends, and sexual exploration becomes frequent. His aggressive behavior and his exploration of other people is accompanied by rudimentary forms of cooperation with others in play activity.

The conviction that emerges from this intrusive mode is: "I am what I can imagine I will be." The intrusive mode is characterized by a variety of thoughts, wishes, behavior, and fantasies:

> (1) the intrusion into space by vigorous locomotion, (2) the intrusion into the unknown by consuming curiosity, (3) the intrusion into other people's ears and minds by the aggressive voice, (4) the intrusion upon or into other bodies by physical attack, (5) and, often most frighteningly, the thought of the phallus intruding the female body [Erikson, 1968: 116].

If the crisis of this stage is mastered successfully, a sense of initiative emerges that will later become the basis for curiosity, ambition, and *experimentation with different roles* as the child's play activities already reflect an *anticipation of different roles*. The sexual self-image and the differentiation between masculine (making) and feminine (catching) initiative are important prerequisites for the sexual identity crisis during adolescence. The initiative state contributes to the development of an identity in adolescence through the anticipation of what one might become and of one's future role in life by "freeing the child's initiative and sense of purpose for adult tasks which promise a fulfillment of one's range of capacities" (Erikson, 1968: 122).

A negative outcome becomes likely if parents resist and restrain the newly developing initiative too much by making the child feel guilty if his explorations lead to destruction—such as the destruction of the toy taken apart. If his sexual explorations encounter too stern taboos, the result may be an immobilization by guilt, inhibition by fear, *role inhibition, role fixation,* and too much dependence on adults; and thus in a broader sense these problems may contribute to a negative identity in adolescence.

The task at the fourth stage is the development of a *sense of industry versus the development of feelings of inferiority.* Freud's view of a period of sexual latency that follows the Oedipus conflict is utilized by Erikson. Unable to marry his mother, the boy must learn to become a potential provider so that he too may become a man, a husband, and a father. Therefore, this period between school entry and puberty becomes a period of learning and mastering the formal and basic skills of life. Children now acquire their fundamental knowledge, and, even more important, a desire to do well in their work. This period is described as *the apprenticeship* in life. In all cultural groups children during this stage receive some kind of formal training, although not necessarily the kind of schooling provided in Western societies. The child learns to win approval, recognition, and a feeling of success by producing things and doing his job well. An important aspect of industry is the "positive identification with those who know things and know how to do things" (Erikson, 1968: 125). The free play of the earlier period now becomes subordinated to rules and regulations. The child learns to follow and respect rules and develops the idea of cooperation in team efforts and fair play. Through team activities, games, and play he learns to anticipate the behavior, roles, and feelings of others and thus prepares himself for cooperative participation later in life.

The conviction that emerges is: "I am what I will learn" or "I am what I can learn to make work." If the task is mastered successfully, the child will need and want accomplishments later in life and strive for completion of his tasks and recognition from others. He will develop a sense of duty, a feeling for workmanship and work participation, and an attitude of striving for mastery that is based on a desire for industriousness and provides a feeling of success. The contribution of this stage to ego-identity is "the capacity to learn how to be, with skill, what one is in the process of becoming" (Erikson, 1968: 180)—that is, an *identification of the task* ahead and a willingness to learn and master it.

If the child fails at this stage to acquire a feeling of success and recognition, there will be a lack of desire for accomplishment and a feeling of uselessness. He may not develop the feeling of enjoyment and pride for work well done. He will be plagued by feelings of inadequacy and inferiority, and he may become convinced that he will never be "any good." As a result there is *work paralysis* and a *sense of futility* that contribute to ego diffusion in the next stage.

Adolescence has been characterized by Erikson (1950) as the period during which the individual must establish a *sense of personal identity* and avoid the dangers of *role diffusion and identity confusion*. This implies that the individual must assess what his liabilities and assets are and how he wants to use them. He must answer for himself the questions of where he came from, who he is, and what he will become. Identity, or a sense of sameness and continuity, must be searched for. Identity is not given to the individual by society, nor does it appear as a maturational phenomenon, like pubic hair; it must be acquired through sustained individual efforts. Unwillingness to work on one's own identity formation carries with it the danger of role diffusion, which may result in alienation and a lasting sense of isolation and confusion.

The search for an identity involves the production of a meaningful self-concept in which past, present, and future are linked together. Consequently, the task is more difficult in a historical period in which the past has lost the anchorage of family and community tradition, the present is characterized by social change, and the future has become less predictable. In a period of rapid social change the older generation is no longer able to provide adequate role models for the younger generation. Keniston (1965) has even suggested that in a rapidly changing society the search for an identity is taking the place of the socialization process, which implies that there actually are stable socially defined roles into which children can be socialized.

Since the older generation no longer provides effective role models to the adolescent in search of a personal identity—or if they do provide them, he may reject them as inappropriate for his situation

—the importance of the peer group in the process of finding out "Who am I?" cannot be overemphasized. To find an answer to this question depends on social feedback as to what others feel and how they react to the individual. Therefore, adolescents "are sometimes morbidly, often curiously, preoccupied with what they appear to be in the eyes of others as compared with what they feel they are and with the question of how to connect to earlier cultivated roles and skills with the ideal prototypes of the day" (Erikson, 1959: 89).

Since an identity can be found only through interaction with other people, the adolescent goes through a period of compulsive peer group conformity as a means of testing roles to see whether and how they fit him. The peer group, the clique, and the gang do help the individual in finding his own identity in a social context, since they provide the individual with both a role model and direct feedback about himself. The bull session and the seemingly endless telephone conversation, for example, serve this feedback function. As long as adolescents depend on role models and feedback about themselves, the in-group feeling that the peer group or the gang provides remains strong, and the ensuing clannishness and intolerance of "differences"—including petty aspects of language, gesture, hair style, and dress—is explained by Erikson as the "necessary defense" against the dangers of self-diffusion that exist as long as an identity has not yet been achieved. Particularly during the time when the body image changes drastically, when genital maturity stimulates imagination, and when intimacy with the opposite sex appears as a possibility with simultaneous positive and negative valences, the adolescent relies on his peers for comfort by stereotyping himself, his ideals, and his adversaries. Eventually, he has to free himself from this peer group orientation in order to become himself—that is, to attain a mature identity. Such an identity, once it has been found, gives the young adult "a sense of 'knowing where one is going,' and an inner assuredness of anticipated recognition from those who count" (Erikson, 1959: 118).

Pubescense, according to Erikson, is characterized by rapidity of body growth, genital maturity, and sexual awareness. Because the latter two aspects are qualitatively quite different from those experienced in earlier years, an element of discontinuity with previous development occurs during early adolescence. Youth is confronted with a "physiological revolution" within himself that threatens his body image and interferes with the formation of an identity. Erikson maintains that the study of identity has become more important than the study of sexuality was in Freud's time. Particularly for the adolescent, identity—the establishment and reestablishment of sameness with one's previous experiences and a conscious attempt to make the future a part of one's personal life plan—becomes subordinated to sexuality. The adolescent must establish ego-identity and accept his pubescent body changes and libidinal feelings as part of himself. The identity crisis depends at least in part on psychophysiological factors. If ego-identity is not satisfactorily established at this stage, there is the danger that role diffusion will endanger further ego development. "Where this is based on a strong previous doubt as to one's sexual identity, delinquent and outright psychotic incidents are not uncommon" (Erikson, 1950: 228).

Falling in love, which is a common occurrence at this age, is not so much of a sexual nature as it will be at a later age; but it is an attempt to project and test one's own diffused and still undifferentiated ego through the eyes of a beloved person in order to clarify and reflect one's own self-concept and one's ego-identity. "In this connection, the 'serious' love affairs through which the adolescent passes contribute to the development of the ego as one identification succeeds another, and the adolescent is aided in defining and revising his own definition of his ego" (Harsch and Schrickel, 1950: 216). Crushes and infatuations, which are not uncommon at the high school and even the college level, serve a genuine developmental purpose. "That is why many a youth would rather converse, and settle matters of mutual identification, than embrace" (Erikson, 1950: 228).

Of great concern for many adolescents is the still unsettled question of vocational identity. During the initial attempts to establish a vocational identity some role diffusion frequently exists. Adolescents at this stage hold glamorized and idealized conceptions of their vocational goals, and it is not uncommon that goal aspirations are higher than the individual's ability warrants. Frequently, vocational goal models are chosen that are attainable for only a very few: movie heroes, rock musicians, athletic champions, car racers, astronauts, and other glamorized "heroes." In the process the adolescent overidentifies with and idolizes his heroes to the extent that he yields his own identity and presumes he has theirs. At this point a youth rarely identifies with his own parents; on the contrary, he rebels against their dominance, their value system, and their intrusion into his private life, since he must separate his own identity from that of his family. Once more he must assert his autonomy in order to reach maturity.

The search for a personal identity also includes the formation of a personal ideology or a philosophy of life that can serve to orient the individual. Such a perspective aids in making choices and guiding behavior, and in this sense, a personal identity influences the individual for the rest of his life. In a society such as ours, in which many ideologies compete for followers and new ideologies emerge constantly, the formation of a personal ideology that has both consistency and conviction is made increasingly difficult. While it is easier to adopt an already existing ideology, it is often less satisfactory than developing one's own. The adopted ideology rarely becomes personal and can, therefore, lead to foreclosure in adolescent development.

The positive outcome of the identity crisis is dependent on the young person's willingness to accept his past and establish continuity with previous experiences. To complete his search for an identity the adolescent must find an answer to the question "Who am I?" He must establish some orientation toward the future and answer the questions: "Where am I going?" "Who am I to become?" He must develop a commitment to a system of values—religious beliefs, vocational goals, a philosophy of life—and accept his sexuality. Only through the achievement of these aspects of ego-identity, which can be called "adult maturity," can intimacy of sexual and affectional love, deep friendship, and personal self-abandon without fear of loss of ego-identity become possible.

If the adolescent fails in his search for an identity, he will experience self-doubt, role diffusion, and role confusion, and the individual may indulge in self-destructive one-sided preoccupation or activity. He will continue to be morbidly preoccupied with what others think of him, or, even worse, he may withdraw and no longer care about himself and others. Ego diffusion and personality confusion, when they become permanent, can be found in the delinquent and in psychotic personality disorganization. In its more severe form the clinical picture of identity diffusion leads to suicide or suicide attempts. "Many a late adolescent, if faced with continuing diffusion, would rather be nobody or somebody bad, or indeed, dead . . . than be not quite somebody" (Erikson, 1959: 132).

Once a personal identity has been established, the need for personal intimacy moves into the foreground of psychosocial development of the young adult. The conflict now is between *finding intimacy or isolation in interpersonal relationships*. At this stage peer group conformity has lost much of its importance. While it did aid in finding an identity, it does not directly provide for intimacy. Intimacy involves establishing psychological closeness to other people as a basis for enduring relationships. Sexual and affectional intimacy is only part of that process. A basic theoretical insight emerges from the sequence of Erikson's stages: The prerequisite for genuine and lasting intimacy is the achievement of an ego-identity, since intimacy implies the fusion of identities. It follows that ego-identity must be established before marriage should be considered. One has to find an answer to the question "Who am I?" before one can select a person with whom to live the rest of his life. "The giving of oneself to another, which is the mark of true intimacy, cannot occur until one has a self to give" (Constantinople, 1969: 359). If marriage is begun before one or both partners have established an identity, the chances for a happy, lasting marriage are low. This may help in explaining the very high divorce rate of teen-age marriages, which is three out of four, whereas the ratio in general is one out of four.

Douvan and Adelson (1966) in *The Adolescent Experience* have suggested that for women the psychosocial crisis of "intimacy" may be closely related or even be concurrent with the psychosocial crisis of "ego-identity." Erikson seems to agree with this when he claims "that something in the young woman's identity must keep itself open for the peculiarities of the man to be joined and of the children to be brought up" (Erikson, 1968: 283).

The conviction that emerges during this stage is: "We are what we love." The plural pronoun "we," rather than "I," is a significant reflection of the intimacy of the relationship. The positive outcome of this stage in the human life cycle is intimacy, including sexual intimacy, genuine friendship, stable love, and lasting marriage. The negative outcome is isolation and loneliness, and if intimacy is not based on permanent identity, divorce and separation may result.

The young adult who has basic uncertainties in his identity will shy away from interpersonal relationships or he may seek promiscuity without intimacy, sex without love, or relationships without stability. As a counterpoint to intimacy, detachment and distancing in interpersonal relationships may develop—that is, "the readiness to repudiate, isolate, and, if necessary, destroy those forces and people whose essence seems dangerous to one's own" (Erikson, 1968: 136).

The developmental issue of adulthood is the achievement of *generativity, and the negative possibility is stagnation.* This stage encompasses the productive years of the human life cycle, and generativity is the driving force in men's behavior. Erikson discusses in some detail why he prefers the term "generativity" to the more widely used synonyms "productivity and creativity." Generativity is a productive creativity in terms of vocational and professional contributions to society. Marriage, giving birth to children, and guiding the growth of children are creative, productive activities. If this stage is successfully completed, the mature man wants to be useful and productive, he wants to be needed; and the conviction that emerges is: "I am what I create, or I am what I produce." The giving of oneself to another person, an ideal, or one's work leads to an expansion of ego interests. If failure occurs at this stage, there is no further development and stagnation results. Stagnation implies that there is repetition in vocational activities as well as social stagnation, and boredom becomes dominant. The individual becomes egotistical, self-absorbed, and self-indulgent. He expects to be indulged. Stagnation at this stage implies that "individuals begin to indulge themselves as if they were their own one and only child" (Erikson, 1968: 138).

The last stage of life encompasses old age and retirement from the productive life. The developmental task of this stage is between the achievement of *ego integrity* versus *disgust and despair.* The conflict here is between combining, integrating, and appreciating one's life experiences and coming to terms with the finality of the human life cycle. The fruits of the successful resolution of the seven preceding stages culminate in integrity. The conviction that emerges is: "I am what survives of me." The positive outcome at this last stage in life is an acceptance of one's self and of one's life without bitterness and regret. There is independence and maturity, rather than a regression to childlike dependency. Ego integrity is based on self-discipline and the wisdom that can give old age its positive quality.

The negative outcome, on the other hand, is a feeling that one's life has been wasted and a basic discontentment with one's life, one's self, and others. There is fear of death and a regression to childhood dependence that characterizes the disintegration of old age resulting in disgust and despair.

James Marcia's Expansion of Erikson's Concept "Identity Versus Role Diffusion"

James Marcia wrote his dissertation "Determination and Construct Validity of Ego Identity Status" at Ohio State University in 1964. Subsequently, in his work at the State University of New York at Buffalo he has continued his interest in ego-identity status of adolescents and has devoted much effort to provide empirical support to Erikson's theory of identity development. What emerges from Marcia's work (1966, 1967, 1968, 1970) constitutes an interesting expansion and elaboration of Erikson's adolescent stage "identity formation versus role diffusion," in that Marcia identifies various patterns and common issues of youth coping with the adolescent identity crisis.

According to Marcia, the criteria for the attainment of a mature identity are based on two essential variables: crisis and commitment. "Crisis refers to times during adolescence when the individual seems to be actively involved in choosing among alternative occupations and beliefs. Commitment refers to the degree of personal investment the individual expresses in an occupation or belief" (Marcia, 1967: 119).

In applying Marcia's criteria of crisis and commitment to Erikson's developmental stage "identity versus role diffusion," four identity statuses that provide a typology or a taxonomy of adolescence emerge.

1. The *identity diffused or identity confused subject* has not yet experienced an identity crisis, nor has he made any commitment to a vocation or a set of beliefs.

2. The *foreclosure subject* has not experienced crisis, but he has made commitments; however, these commitments are not the result of his own searching and exploring, but they are handed to him, ready-made, by others, frequently his parents.

3. The *moratorium subject* is in an acute state of crisis; he is exploring and actively searching for alternatives, and he is struggling to find his identity; but he has not yet made any commitment or has only developed very temporary kinds of commitments.

4. The *identity achieved subject* has experienced crises but has resolved them on his own terms, and as a result of the resolution of his crises he has made personal commitments to an occupation, a religious belief, a personal value system, and he has resolved his attitude toward sexuality.

These four identity statuses may be perceived as a developmental sequence, but not in the sense that one is necessarily and inevitably the prerequisite for the other as is true of Erikson's "Eight Stages of Man." Only the moratorium appears to be an essential prerequisite for identity achievement, since identity cannot be achieved without the kind of searching and exploring that is so characteristic of the moratorium. Any one identity status could become terminal, but this danger is, of course, greater for the foreclosure than for the moratorium status.

An individual in the process of moving to the next higher status may well exhibit some of the characteristics of two or even three statuses at the same time. He may have developed a commitment to a vocation, for example, while still searching for a personal value system and holding on to a puritanical attitude toward sex indoctrinated by his parents or church. Marcia found that as students moved through the four years of undergraduate college experiences, the proportion of identity diffused subjects declined significantly while the proportion of identity achieved subjects increased steadily. This was not a function of college selectivity but of increased maturity. Constantinople reports a "consistent increase in successful resolution of identity, both from freshman year to senior year across subjects and from one year to the next within subjects" (Constantinople, 1969: 367).

In Marcia's research (1966, 1967, 1970) the individual's identity status is determined by means of an individual interview that was developed to find out a student's commitment to and the extent to which he has experienced crises in regard to a vocation, a personal value system, religious beliefs, and for females, their attitude toward their sexuality.

The remainder of this chapter will deal with a closer examination of the four identity statuses.

1. *Identity Diffusion*. The identity diffused individual has no apparent personal commitment to occupation, religion, or politics. He has not experienced an identity crisis in respect to these issues, or he has not made an active struggle in terms of reevaluating, searching, and considering alternatives. Identity diffusion is a kind of psychological chaos experienced by the early adolescent. Erikson (1968) maintains that identity diffusion is not a diagnostic entity, but it is the description of a developmental problem—which if it persists, but only if it persists, could become a diagnostic picture. Consequently, identity diffusion can encompass a variety of different behavior or personality patterns. This appears to be one of the reasons why research findings of the identity diffused subject are more inconsistent than for the other three identity statuses.

First, identity diffusion may exist due to the precrisis lack of commitment, which is not at all uncommon when entering the period of adolescence. Thus, some degree of identity diffusion may be characteristic of normal early adolescence. Second, there is also the playboy type of identity diffusion. He lives and lets live and attempts to get for himself whatever he can get away with. Apparently suffering from an unresolved ego crisis of the first stage, "trust versus mistrust," and not being able to trust people, he uses them. Third, identity diffusion exists when the individual avoids crises and confrontation by means of drugs, alcohol, or sex, or by otherwise denying that crises exist. Finally, prolonged stagnation in the identity diffusion stage may lead to personality disintegration, thus becoming a diagnostic entity and leading to schizophrenia or suicide.

The identity diffused subject is in a state of psychological fluidity, remaining uncommitted to any values; consequently he is open to all kinds of influences, and when opportunities arise, he will take advantage of them often without design or purpose. He may take a smorgasbord approach to ideological systems and be most influenced by and too receptive toward whatever politician or minister he heard last. The diffused college student can become quite vehement in his demands on the professor to tell him which of the various theories is best, which is right, or which one to believe. Erikson (1965) maintains in *The Challenge of Youth* that the high percentage of recidivity of criminality in young offenders can be explained by the fact that during the years of identity formation, especially identity diffusion, these youths were forced by society into intimate contact with criminals.

On Kuhn's (1954) Twenty Statement Test the identity diffused subject may reveal his confusion over the question "Who am I?" with answers such as: "I'm a nobody," "I don't know who I am," "I wish I weren't me," "I wish I knew who I am," "I'm confused," "I'm mixed up," "I'm not me," "I'm unsure of what I am," "I'm dead," "I wish I were dead," "I'm intelligent"/"I'm stupid," "I'm a child of God"/"I'm the devil." Identity in these responses is defined negatively by the lack of something, the reversal of an identity, the denial of an identity, death, and contradictory statements revealing confusion.

The classical example of identity diffusion in literature is Prince Hamlet. He, too, is confused about his sex role: "Man delights me not, no, nor woman either." He is also estranged from love and procreation, as when he says "I say we will have no more marriage." And finally he appears alienated from the ways of his country ". . . though I am native here and to the manner born . . ." (Erikson, 1965: 6). In Arthur Miller's *Death of a Salesman* Biff admits his identity diffusion quite clearly: "I just can't take hold, Mom, I can't take hold of some kind of life."

In Marcia's studies (1966, 1967) subjects were independently classified as to their identity status. In addition, personality tests were administered to all subjects. Identity diffused male subjects showed little resistance to self-esteem manipulation—that is, they quite readily changed their own opinions about themselves. They were vulnerable to evaluative feedback about themselves, since they did not yet have a stable identity. Gruen (1960), too, found that ego diffused subjects were more willing to accept incorrect personality sketches about themselves than subjects who had achieved an identity. Marcia's subjects scored low on a stressful concept attainment task; they had low self-esteem, and experienced more difficulty than other subjects in interpersonal relationships. Marcia's (1970) identity diffused female subjects, even though they were not less intelligent, were enrolled in the easiest college majors as compared to the other three identity statuses. They, too, obtained low self-esteem scores, but high anxiety and authoritarianism scores. Block (1961) found a direct relationship between role variability and the individual's identity status. That is, subjects lacking a clear identity behaved quite differently in interaction with people playing different roles, such as lover, boss, parent, peer, or acquaintance. Identity achieved subjects revealed more internal consistency in their interpersonal behavior. Bronson (1959), contrasting the person who has achieved an identity with one who has not, characterized the latter as follows:

1. He is less certain about the relationship between the past and the present as it pertains to himself and his self-concept; his current self-concept is not firmly rooted in his earlier identifications.
2. The identity diffused shows a high degree of internal tensions and anxiety.
3. He was found to be less certain about his own personality traits, and he experienced variability over short periods of time as to his own feelings about himself. He does not know who he is and cannot estimate his own personality traits effectively.

Bunt (1968) finds that "the ego diffused group of adolescents had a significantly greater self-concept minus other-concept discrepancy than did the adolescent group with strong ego identity." Apparently the identity diffused subject views himself differently from the way he feels others perceive him. Cross and Allen (1969) found the fathers of the identity diffused subjects to be more controlling than the fathers of any of the other three identity statuses. The controlling father—especially if he is ineffective from the adolescent's point of view—interferes with the search for an identity and independence, which is essential for reaching maturity. It has been demonstrated that there is a strong relationship between un-resolved trust-mistrust conflicts in early childhood and identity confusion during adolescence (Rasmussen, 1964). Marcia suspects that identity diffusion is very much on the increase in society today.

2. *Foreclosure*. The foreclosure subject is committed to goals and values, an occupation, and a personal ideology. Consequently, in everyday life he may appear very much like an identity achieved subject, with whom he actually has some characteristics in common. He has not, however, experienced psychological crisis or seriously considered other goals and values. The goals he works for and the values he holds were determined for him by others, his parents or his peers. The foreclosure subject frequently tends to become his parents' alter ego. When asked what he wants to be, he may answer "I want to be a dentist," and when asked why, he might respond "Because my father is a dentist." And even further probing does not change the essence of his first response. No personal reason is given; no personal searching seems to have occurred. It appears as if other alternatives were never seriously considered. When talking to a foreclosure subject, it becomes difficult to distinguish between his own goals and those that parents have planned and emphasized for him. College serves mainly to reconfirm his own childhood value system and provide him with an opportunity to attain his goals, rather than as a process by which to determine his goals. He may become solidified in his position and authoritarian in his attitude and, consequently, is somewhat less likely than the moratorium subject to reach the status of identity achievement. There appears to be a certain rigidity in his personality structure. If he is not sufficiently challenged in his preprogrammed assumptions and values, foreclosure may become a permanent part of his personality structure and he may remain dependent on others.

On Kuhn's (1954) Twenty Statement Test the foreclosure subject seems to define his identity in terms of relationships to other people or the extensions of other people. The following responses from the present author's files of three college students in response to the question "Who am I?" may serve as an illustration: (1) daughter, sister, aunt, sister-in-law, niece; (2) girl, daughter, my father's little girl; (3) my mother's daughter, my father's daughter, my sister's sister, my brother's sister, my boyfriend's girl friend, my girl friend's friend, my next door neighbor's neighbor, my aunt's niece, my cousin's cousin.

Responses from Marcia's (1968) interview records can serve to illustrate the commitment of the foreclosure subject to parental values. One adolescent comments on his political affiliation with a Republican ideology quite similar to that of his parents: "You still pull that way, Republican, if your parents are that way. You feel like it is where you should be." Another student who holds the same religious beliefs as his parents states: "Maybe it's just a habit with me, I don't know. I have thought a lot and you meet all kinds of people here, but I really haven't changed any of my beliefs. . . . I plan to bring up my children in the church, just the way dad did with me." Keniston seems to be referring to the foreclosure phenomenon when he writes that "total lack of conflict during adolescence is an ominous sign that the individual's psychological maturity may not be progressing" (Keniston, 1971: 364).

The foreclosure males and females in Marcia's research (1967, 1970) scored by far the highest on authoritarianism. Foreclosure subjects show respect for authority; they conform to others and go along with conventional approaches. Foreclosure males score low in the concept attainment task; they perform relatively poorly under stress. They maintain a high level of aspiration and hold on to a high level of aspiration in spite of failure experiences. Apparently, they possess less ability to evaluate themselves critically and have no flexible adjustment mechanisms. The foreclosure male and female scored lowest of the four groups on the anxiety scale. The foreclosure females but not the males have the highest self-esteem scores. Marcia speculates that foreclosure may have a different meaning and may be a more adaptive status for women than for men. Waterman and Waterman (1970) studied the relationship between the satisfaction with college and the individual's identity status. They found that students who had never experienced a crisis in respect to their vocational choice, but who were committed to a vocational goal, held the most favorable attitude toward their education, their college experience, and the college administration. Cross and Allen (1969), focusing on the parental antecedent of the identity status of college males, reported an intermediate degree of control from the fathers of foreclosure subjects, who provided more control than the fathers of moratorium and identity achieved subjects. The father is seen by his foreclosure son as neither too harsh nor too lenient; apparently, the father is quite effective in guiding his offspring into the preconceived role that he, the father, has determined.

Foreclosure as an identity status is most frequently referred to as being determined by the subject's own parents, as was emphasized in the previous discussion. However, the concept may also apply to a situation in which the individual's identity is predominantly determined by his peer group—or any other influential group for that matter. For a time, the young adolescent may lose himself, and he may lose his budding identity to the crowd. Apparently, foreclosure occurs when the individual's identity submerges into the role given to him by others and when he defines himself primarily by his group membership and acts, dresses, selects food and entertainment, uses language and slang predominantly in the light of peer group standards and expectations. (Intolerance and even cruelty toward those that are different is not uncommon.) The youth group movements of the totalitarian system (for example, Hitler Youth) provide such a group identity, as do the gang structure, the hippie culture, and other youth subcultural groups. Many a junior high school student conforms to peer group standards in order to be accepted by the group and gain a peer group identity. He overidentifies with the peer group, with its heroes and idols, to the extent that he may lose for some time his own personal values and decision-making capacity. According to Keniston, if the "conformity to peer group norms merely replaces conformity to parental norms ... adolescent development is foreclosed before real self-regulation and independence are achieved" (Keniston, 1971: 377).

The youth group of the totalitarian system can serve as an illustration of political foreclosure, since the youth movement provides the adolescent with a ready-made political system of beliefs and even a personal identity that the democratic system does not provide. The appeal that the totalitarian system makes to the adolescent might be based on these considerations, since the totalitarian system supplies convincing and suitable identities for this age group. Democratic identity has less appeal and is harder to attain because it involves freedom of choice; it does not supply a ready-made identity but insists on self-made identity. Adolescent imagery, which tends frequently to classify into black and white, has an affinity to the totalitarian system that supplies this kind of dichotomy. The democratic system, in contrast, allows for many different shades of ideological beliefs and therefore provides more ambiguity. It requires that a person have ego-identity to withstand ambiguity, but it gives less help in establishing this identity.

3. *Moratorium*. The word "moratorium," in a general sense, is a period of delay granted to somebody who is not yet ready to meet an obligation or make a commitment (Erikson, 1968: 157). The adolescent moratorium is defined as a developmental period during which commitments have not yet been made or are rather exploratory and tentative. However, there are many crises and many unresolved questions. There is an active struggle to find an answer, explore, search, experiment, try out different roles, and play the field. It is in this sense that the moratorium is considered the adolescent issue *par excellence*. According to Marcia, about 30 percent of today's college students are in this stage.

Erikson, as well as Margaret Mead (1961), has postulated that the adolescent period is a psychological moratorium, or an "as if period" during which the individual can try on different roles "as if" he were committed to these roles; however, since it is an "as if period," he is not really committed and is not held fully accountable. He can still change his values and commitments, and he frequently does so as he becomes more mature. Therefore, the "as if period" is society's delay granted its offspring to try on different roles—as when buying clothes—to see which fits best. In this sense the moratorium subject tries different political ideologies (such as a radical philosophy); he may try new religious beliefs (such as Oriental mysticism); he may even try different vocational endeavors (such as in volunteer social work or the Peace Corps); he may try new relationships with the opposite sex (such as coed apartment living).

If the adolescent, while experiencing his moratorium, has sufficient opportunity to search, experiment, play the field, and try on different roles, there is a good chance that he will find himself, develop an identity, and emerge with commitments to politics, religion, and a vocational career. His final commitments are frequently less extreme than some of his tentative and exploratory commitments during the moratorium. Moratorium really is an essential prerequisite for identity achievement. However, at the time the adolescent is in this stage, the world does not look very stable or predictable and does not appear to be a very desirable place; rather he views it as badly in need of improvement. The moratorium subject challenges what he sees. He wants to change government, politics, education—in short, "the system." While he frequently is a very good diagnostician in pointing to the ills, imperfections, and limitations of "the system," he is not equally effective in producing viable, realistic alternatives that require identity and a lasting kind of commitment.

In responding to Kuhn's (1954) test question "Who am I?" moratorium subjects typically reveal their lack of commitment and their search for an identity with such responses: "I am searching, I am confused, I am thinking, I am wondering, I am calculating"; "I am a discontented person, I am a person striving for meaning"; "I am a curious person, I am unsure of what I am, I am many people at different times, I seek new experiences to find out what I really am, I am looking for something for myself."

Marcia's studies (1966, 1967, 1970) show that both male and female moratorium subjects have the lowest authoritarianism score. He also found (Podd, Marcia, and Rubin, 1970) that moratorium subjects in crises were rebellious and less cooperative with people in authority. Moratorium males respond with greater variability on a concept attainment task than any of the other subjects —that is, their performance is rather unpredictable. They are less vulnerable to self-esteem manipulation, but they obtained high scores on an anxiety test. This may mean that they are highly anxious beeause they experience crises, but it could also mean that they are more willing to admit anxiety. Waterman and Waterman (1970), investigating the relationship between commitment to a vocation and college satisfaction, found that the students who were not sure whether or not they had selected the right major and were not at all sure about their vocational choice evaluated their college experience, their education, and the college administration least favorably. Cross and Allen (1969) found that the moratorium and the identity achieved subjects reported the least amount of control at home. Moratorium subjects seem to remember their fathers as being least coercive and restrictive. It appears as if the moratorium father has encouraged his son's search for independence and for an identity.

Mead and also Friedenberg have expressed concern that in our emphasis on success as symbolized by boy scout badges, good grades, promotions, honors, and diplomas we exert too much pressure and deprive the adolescent of his opportunity for a moratorium. It has been found that the need for a moratorium is reflected in the motives for volunteering for the Peace Corps and may be one of the reasons for the existence of the hippie cultures.

4. *Identity Achieved.* After a person has experienced a psychological moratorium and has resolved his adolescent identity crises and as a result begins to develop lasting personal commitments, an identity has been achieved, which contributes to an increment in ego strength. Identity achievement means that adolescent development has been successfully completed and maturity has been attained. Successful adolescent development is defined by Keniston as ". . . integration of impulses into life . . . the humanization of conscience, . . . the stabilization of a sense of self . . ." (Keniston, 1971: 363).

An identity has been achieved after the individual has seriously and carefully evaluated various alternatives and has considered different choices, but has come to his conclusion and decision on his own terms. Actually, he may take a position that is really fairly close to his parents' values, but his values are now his own, since he has considered other alternatives, accepted or rejected them, and then made the final choice on his own terms. This process contrasts with the foreclosure subject, who stays very close to his parents' values and expectations, without making a genuine personal choice in the matter and without really having seriously questioned his parents' values. The achievement of an identity gives the individual an awareness of and an acceptance of his personal continuity with the past and a projection into the future. "A new synthesis between the past and the present has been found." Keniston speaks of the "synthesis within the self of new values and purposes." Once an identity has been achieved, there is self-acceptance, a stable self-definition, a willingness to make commitment in terms of a vocation, a religion, a political ideology and in terms of intimacy, engagement, and marriage. To achieve a mature identity the individual must overcome "his irrational rebelliousness as well as his irrational urge to conform" (Keniston, 1971: 364). In other words, he must overcome the moratorium issues as well as the foreclosure issues of adolescent development.

An individual who has attained an identity, according to Erikson (1968), feels in harmony with himself, accepts his capacities, limitations, and opportunities. He realizes "where he fits (or knowingly prefers not to fit) into" social situations in terms of his own personal development.

Four college students' responses to the "Who am I?" test from the author's file may again serve to illustrate this sense of identity: "the future Mrs. Jones, a future English teacher; a future resident of Colorado, a happy-go-lucky person"; "a woman, a potential wife, a potential mother, a student, a teacher"; "I am me, outgoing, well liked, intelligent"; "a contained person, a free-willed individual, a leader, self-sufficient, young adult." These responses convey a feeling that adolescence has been or is about to be terminated, there is a sense of direction and a positive orientation toward the future, which is characteristic of the identity achieved individual.

Marcia's (1966, 1967, 1970) research subjects who had achieved their identity scored highest on the concept attainment task; they set goals for themselves that were more realistic than those of subjects who had not yet achieved an identity. Identity achieved subjects are less likely to accept false personality sketches about themselves. They are less inclined to subscribe to authoritarian values, and they are less vulnerable to the stress situation of being evaluated. They show a sense of self, self-acceptance, and interpersonal role expectations (Podd, Marcia, and Rubin, 1970). The personal profile of the identity achieved female is not quite as positive; this group scored lowest of all four groups on self-esteem. Prior to Women's Liberation it may have been more threatening to women to have to decide for themselves who or what they were, either because of a greater emphasis on dependence in their childhood socialization or because they still perceived their identity in relationship to a husband. Block (1961) found that identity achieved subjects seem to behave consistently but flexibly when interacting with other people, regardless of the role of the other person: lover, boss, parent, peer, and so on. Bunt (1968) maintains that for identity achieved subjects there is less of a discrepancy between their own self-perception and the perception of others viewing them. Rasmussen (1964) reported that subjects who have achieved an ego-identity are more effective in interpersonal interaction and in general show better psychosocial adjustment. Gruen's (1960) identity achieved subjects did not accept false information or glib statements about themselves as true. Just like the father of moratorium subjects, the fathers of identity achieved subjects are seen as more relaxed and less controlling, apparently encouraging their sons' striving for psychological autonomy (Cross and Allen, 1969). The similarity of the attitudes of the fathers of both moratorium and identity achieved subjects is consistent, since most moratorium subjects in due time will achieve identity.

Educational Implications

One of the basic issues regarding education during adolescence that emerges from Erikson's theory is: To what extent and how do educational institutions contribute to and enhance youths' efforts in self-finding? Contemporary romanticists and critics of the school system—Dennison, Friedenberg, Goodman, Holt, Silverman, and others—have maintained that schools require adolescents to submit and suppress their creativity, individuality, and identity to the demands of the skill- and knowledge-oriented curriculum in order to succeed. Thus, schools seem to be encouraging foreclosure, since they demand conformity to the way things are and submission to authority, rather than aiding the adolescent in his search for a unique individuality and a personal identity. Considering the Waterman and Waterman (1970) findings, it appears that foreclosure subjects were more comfortable in school and held more positive attitudes toward their educational experiences while the uncommitted, searching, and experimenting moratorium subjects evaluated their educational experience rather negatively. Apparently, the structure of the school, the curriculum, schedules, grades, hall passes, and so on, encourage foreclosure rather than efforts toward self-finding and self-definition, which implies questioning and challenging existing patterns, values, and authorities. One might speculate whether the all-pervasive indifference toward school (Buxton,

1973) and frequent adolescent discontent with education and with teachers is at least in part a result of the lack of concern on the part of many educators with what Erikson and Marcia consider a fundamental developmental issue, namely, the resolution of the identity crisis. It has long been recognized that the problem of the high school dropout is not simply a matter of lack of ability, or even lack of achievement, but a desire for independence, a search without a goal, an expression of inner discontent and restlessness. Youth dissatisfaction with college, students questioning the value of their college education, the increasing pattern of "dropping in and dropping out" of college, as well as the increasing pattern of transferring from one college to another, do make sense in view of Erikson's "adolescent identity crisis" concept and Marcia's assumption that a moratorium requires this kind of Wanderlust and exploration and is an essential prerequisite for the achievement of a mature identity.

Much of youth experimentation with drugs and involvement in the drug scene is motivated by a search for new insights, new experiences, religious revelations, new levels of consciousness, mind expansion, and self-understanding. The drug trip may not provide all of these valued experiences as critics of the youth scene are quick to point out. However, the promise and the possibility is enough to serve as a motivation—often encouraged by peers who have already "been there"—to find a shortcut to the often agonizing search for an answer to the questions "Who am I?" and "What makes me what I am?"

The cry for relevance in the curriculum and in the total educational experience might also be better understood in view of the moratorium issues: developing a sexual identity, finding religious values, selecting career goals, and developing a commitment to a political ideology. The adolescent often has difficulty in seeing the relationship among these burning personal issues and conjugating French verbs, studying ancient Rome, proving the Pythagorean theorem, and examining the finer points of Shakespeare's *Macbeth;* and teachers are often remiss in not making these relationships obvious, even in those content areas where they are most readily apparent. The junior high school student's and even the senior high school student's choices of different courses are limited, and the adolescent has relatively little to say about the curriculum. The curriculum itself could become more closely related to the adolescent's search for self-understanding by including more identity relevant topics. This could include such controversial issues as drug education and sex education, areas in which considerable misinformation exists even among sophisticated youth. Furthermore, such topics as human development, sociology, interpersonal relations, consumer economics, social organization, career opportunities in the future, ecology, sex roles and sex stereotypes, and a study of values could aid adolescents in developing a philosophy of life. All of these topics could be taught in a way that makes them academically respectable, as well as personally meaningful. In their English courses high school students could study the problems of adolescents as reflected in the literature dealing with adolescents (Kiell, 1959; Withman, 1964). In addition, present teaching styles frequently include lecturing, rehearsing, reviewing, drills, quizzes, tests, and assignments—which means that even when these activities are meaningful, they are teacher directed and the learning activities are controlled by the authority of the teacher. Consequently, the high school student too often is placed in a docile and submissive role, so that there is little opportunity to fulfill the needs of the moratorium subjects, and the foreclosure subjects are not encouraged to move out of their developmental stagnation but may be rewarded for foreclosure behavior. Why the need of the moratorium may be satisfied more effectively through joining the Peace Corps or a hippie culture rather than within the traditional setting of the school will be discussed in Chapter 14.

In contrast to Freud's emphasis on the dangers of frustration and the possible contribution of frustration to neurosis, Erikson distinguishes between meaningful frustration and neurotic frustration. Meaningful frustration can serve useful ends as an educational experience and implies that even though the adolescent initially does not see a possible solution to the teacher's question, problem, or assignment—and consequently feels frustrated—he can, with work and perseverance, find the solution by himself. The teacher who has become an effective frustrator does not contribute to neuroses but instead helps his students to develop frustration tolerance. Therefore, parents and teachers might introduce more culturally meaningful but frustrating challenges that the adolescent can resolve with effort. As part of the process of growing up, children must learn to accept some of the inevitable limitations and restrictions that may be frustrating. Erikson objects to a frustration-free educational environment—like Summerhill—in which children's natural tendencies and interests determine the learning activities and the curriculum. An educational policy characterized by the child's questioning his freedom to learn—as implied in the often quoted "Teacher *must* we do today what we *want* to do?" (Erikson, 1968: 127)—can be as detrimental to the establishment of a healthy identity as the traditional emphasis on duty, obedience, self-restraint, and arbitrary rules. Learning occurs more effectively and the development of identity is enhanced in an educational climate that avoids the pitfalls of both these extremes. Youth do benefit from being "mildly but firmly coerced into the adventure of finding out that one can learn to accomplish things which one would never have thought of by oneself, things which owe their attractiveness to the very fact that they are not the product of play and fantasy, but the product of reality, practicality and logic" (Erikson, 1968: 127). Consequently, meaningful ways of frustrating adolescents by challenging them with new ideas, problems, and subjects may increase their efforts to learn and master and, ultimately, contribute to their process of maturing.

In the past, societies through puberty rites, initiation ceremonies, the apprenticeship-journeyman system, confirmation, bar mitzvah, and coming-out parties have provided some fairly clearly defined social roles that gave the individual a kind of identity by providing self-definition and social status. As these social role definitions have virtually disappeared—and as confirmations and bar mitzvahs have become primarily private, religious matters—the individual's search for his own unique identity and for his place in society has become more pronounced, and more of a burden is placed upon the individual. "Some of the adolescent difficulties in Western society may be better understood if one considers the adolescent as the marginal man who stands in a psychological no-man's-land without clear understanding of what is expected of him, struggling to attain adult status" (Muuss, 1970b: 113). The adolescent struggle to attain an identity and achieve adult status can be a frustrating experience, and society, educational institutions, and teachers may well ponder how they can make this experience more meaningful.

5

A *Geisteswissenschaftliche* Theory of Adolescence

Eduard Spranger (1882–1963) late professor of psychology at the University of Berlin was a representative of *geisteswissenschaftliche* psychology.* He was a pupil and follower of the German philosopher Wilhelm Dilthey (1833–1911), the father of *geisteswissenschaftliche* psychology. Dilthey believed that psychology and natural science are not related, because psychological facts that pertain to one person are not likely to pertain to any other person. Laws that related cause and effect, as they do in physics, cannot be obtained in psychology. He consequently believed that each individual is unique and ineffable.

Spranger's *Psychologie des Jugendalters* (1955) has become one of the most widely read books on adolescence in central Europe. Its influence on central European literature in the field is profound and may be compared to the influence that G. Stanley Hall has had in the United States. Spranger was familiar with Hall's and Freud's works. He cited Hall in support of his ideas, but he often challenged, criticized, and modified psychoanalytic assumptions. However, Dilthey's humanistic philosophy had an even greater influence on Spranger's theory. Spranger's approach to development was philosophical, speculative, and, at certain points, even

* *Geisteswissenschaft* has been translated as "cultural science" or "historical humanities," and Allport (1937) translates it as "mental science." Spranger gave as a synonym "philosophy of culture." Since the author knows of no English word that carries the full meaning of the German word *Geisteswissenschaft,* this word will be retained untranslated.

metaphysical. Consequently, he has received relatively little attention from American psychologists, for most of whom psychology is a natural and not a philosophical science.

In the United States some of Spranger's ideas have been expanded by Gordon W. Allport. Actually Spranger is better known in America for his typology (1928) than for his psychology of adolescence, since his "six types of men" provided the theoretical background for Allport's widely used test, "Study of Values."

Spranger set himself the goal of understanding the psychological structure of the developing youth. Consequently, his psychology has been referred to as a "psychology of understanding." The developmental rhythm of the psychological aspects of growing up, rather than mere adolescent behavior and physiological changes, attracted his attention. Spranger did not concern himself with the physiological and medical aspects of pubescence, since he held that psychological functions are not revealed by knowledge of physiological functions, nor, conversely, does knowledge of the mental functions bring about understanding of the growth processes. However, he did not deny a connection between psychological and body functions. He believed that the psychological changes that take place during the adolescent period cannot be explained by the endocrinological changes of pubescence. The investigation of physiological changes of pubescence was seen as the task of a physiological psychology, not of a psychology of understanding. He was concerned with psychological development and the structure of the psyche, which can only be investigated by methods basically different from the methods of natural science used to investigate the physiological changes. Spranger's psychology is based on the methodological principle of *psychologica psychologice* —that is, investigation of psychological issues according to psychological methods.

Spranger's psychology has been classified as structural psychology. His methodological approach is that of understanding psychological structure, rather than causally explaining behavior. He wanted to understand the mental process that is guided by a consciousness of structure. He defined "understanding" as the mental activity that interprets events as full of meanings; however, these meanings can only be understood in relationship to a totality that considers personal perception as well as objective facts. Understanding, even though it is a cognitive process, is not solely intellectual. It also involves appreciation and sympathy, and it is full of feeling. Spranger (1928) does not investigate specific internal experiences such as sensation, feeling, thought, and volition. His structural psychology is defined as that part of psychology which begins with an understanding "of the totality of mental structure." Meaningfully related experiences and acts of the individual are placed at the center of his investigation. It appears that Spranger's structural psychology is more akin to Gestalt psychology and a phenomenological psychology than to the structural psychology of Wundt, James, and Titchner, better known in the United States. Furthermore, since Spranger is mainly concerned with the development of the structure of the "psyche," he identifies his theory: (1) with *developmental psychology;* (2) with *typology.*

Since he investigates the changes that accompany development during adolescence, Spranger's theory is concerned with *developmental psychology.* The youth himself does not fully experience the meaning of his own development. Many of the phenomena of consciousness have a purposeful meaning only if one learns to understand them as developmental phenomena. Adolescence is not only the transition period from childhood to physiological maturity, but—more important—it is the age during which the relatively undifferentiated mental structure of the child reaches full maturity.

Since Spranger is interested in individual differences in structural change during development, he is concerned with *typology.* During adolescent development a more definite and lasting hierarchy of values is established. According to Spranger (1928), the "dominant value direction" of the individual is the profound determiner of personality. Therefore, personality types are classified according to the value direction that is predominant in the individual's personality structure.

Spranger (1955) resolves the controversial issue of whether adolescent development is gradual and harmonious or disturbed and full of stress and strain by asserting that adolescent development may be experienced in different patterns or rhythms. Three patterns of adolescent development can be distinguished.

The first pattern, which corresponds to Hall's idea of adolescent development, is experienced as a form of rebirth in which the individual sees himself as another person when he reaches maturity. This is a period of storm, stress, strain, and crisis, and results in basic personality change. It has much in common with a religious conversion, also emphasized by Hall.

The second pattern is a slow, continuous growth process and a gradual acquisition of the cultural values and ideas held in the society, without a basic personality change.

The third pattern is a growth process in which the individual himself actively participates. The youth consciously improves himself and contributes to his own development, overcoming obstacles and crises by his own energetic and goal-directed efforts. This pattern is characterized by self-control and self-discipline, which Spranger relates to a personality type that is striving for power.

Spranger (1955) takes an interesting position concerning sexual-affectional development during adolescence. He makes an important distinction between "sexuality" and "pure love." Sexuality refers to the conscious sensual body pleasures that result in sexual excitement and desire. "Pure love" refers to the spiritual form of love without a desire for physical contact and stimulation; it is basically aesthetic, not sensual. Pure love is a psychological function depending upon understanding, empathy, and sympathy. Sexuality and pure love originate in different layers of the psychological structure. In a genuine love relationship of mature adults, sexuality and pure love merge into affectional sexuality. But they develop separately and independently during adolescence. It is this division of sexual development into aesthetic and sensual components that results in many adolescent problems. The split between the two aspects of love in the adolescent can go so far that a boy directs his pure love toward one girl and his sexuality toward another. Sullivan, similarly, speaks of the "collision between the intimacy need and lust" (Sullivan, 1953: 268) that the adolescent experiences and that is accompanied by a distinction between people who satisfy lust and those who satisfy loneliness. This division of sexual development into two factors is not unlike the theory of Bühler, who differentiates between the sensual component and the spiritual component of sexuality. Furthermore, this distinction is related to Erikson's idea of searching for an ego-identity during adolescence. Erikson maintained that falling in love at this age is frequently not a sexual experience but an attempt to define one's ego-identity. One's ego image becomes clarified by reflecting on it in the light of a like-minded and loved companion. Pure love relies on the polarity of two different individuals, each of whom needs the other to supplement his own personality in order to define his own relationship to the outside world.

Underlying both Spranger's and Bühler's ideas is the belief that the development of each of the two components during adolescence takes place independently and separately. In Spranger's words, "in the psyche of the adolescent, pure love and sexuality are in the beginning sharply separated in consciousness" (Spranger, 1955: 84). The adolescent can be aware of both forms, but the object of pure love may be different from that of sexuality. This division of the two aspects of sexual development frequently results in a postponement of sexual gratification, since the emotional aesthetic component acts as an inhibitor of sexuality.

The two aspects of sexual development unite toward the end of the adolescent period, preparing the mature person for marriage. From this concept of divided sexual development, Spranger concludes that sexual gratification has to be postponed by inhibition. Inhibition of sexual desires is an important aspect of personality development; precocious sexual experiences result in disharmonious psychological development, since pure love and sexuality are not yet united and sexuality without pure love remains a superficial and shallow experience. Furthermore, since ethical, volitional, inhibitory forces have not yet developed sufficiently, precocious sex experience will further inhibit such development and have far-reaching negative effects on further growth of the personality.

Spranger also sees a dualism between fantasy and reality. The child frequently does not fully comprehend the distinction between the two. The adolescent learns to distinguish between fantasy and reality and now dares to do things that he previously engaged in only in play or fantasy. When he does indulge in fantasy, he recognizes it as such. *oh for christs sake*

Structural development of the psyche of the growing youth is determined by a combination of internal and external factors, with maturational factors being predominant. The three areas in which the structural change of the organization of the psyche can be observed are: (1) discovery of the ego or self, (2) gradual formation of a life plan, and (3) the selection and integration of a personal value system (Spranger, 1955: 46).

In referring to the discovery of the ego, Spranger does not say that the child has no ego experiences. Rather, the child's ego and the world appear to be united. During pubescence this unity is divided, and the juvenile begins to reflect upon himself by directing his attention internally and analyzing himself. The discovery of the internal ego, experienced now as separated from the external world, results not only in loneliness, but also in a need to experiment with one's own undifferentiated ego, in order to again reestablish ego unity. This brings about three effects:

1. A challenging of all previously unquestioned ideas and relationships. Thus, there is a rebellion against tradition, mores, family, school, and other social institutions.*
2. An increased need for social recognition and interpersonal relationships.†
3. A need to experiment with different aspects of one's own ego; trying out and testing one's own personality. The adolescent is puzzled and challenged by the question "Who am I?" Spranger relates the desire of many youths to become actors, as well as their admiration for actors, to this need and suggests the educational use of this attitude.‡

The adolescent has not yet obtained internal harmony and unity. Spranger (1955) suggests as a criterion for the achievement of maturity a relative degree of stability, harmony, self-acceptance, and ego unity. One interesting characteristic of adolescence (adolescents have this characteristic in common with delinquents and schizophrenics, though to a milder degree) is that it has many egos that are in a constant fight for supremacy; the unification of

---

*Gesell (1956) describes the thirteen-year-old as withdrawing from family activities; fourteen as sensitive to parental standards, critical, and easily embarrassed; fifteen as argumentative and remote from his parents.

†Gesell describes twelve as trying to win approval of associates; fifteen finds interpersonal satisfaction outside the home and family.

‡Gesell also describes the frequent identification of youth with actors and actresses and the admiration of youth for actors, especially at the ages of fourteen and fifteen.

the several fighting egos into a single stable psychic structure is considered essential for the attainment of maturity.

Spranger does not limit the idea of the formation of a life plan to the selection of a vocation, but refers in a more general way to a philosophy of life and a life orientation toward the future. While the child lives chiefly in the present, the adolescent rapidly expands his time perspective into both past and future. He sees himself as a growing totality in which each experience becomes part of himself, and each experience is influential in his future development. The life goals that adolescents set for themselves, owing to their vivid fantasy, are frequently too high; the individual could not reach them even with great ability and great effort. This overestimation of one's ability is based on a lack of experience as well as on an inflated self-assessment that is typical of adolescence.*

There is an active attempt to acquire a personal value system with regard to aesthetics, religion, love, truth, power, and money as a reflection of one's own identity. For the child, these aspects of life are not yet differentiated or fully conscious. Youth experiences them in a subjective way, with personal involvement, and frequently with strong acceptance or rejection. These values become filled with personal experiences; they are evaluated in the light of one's own ideas, beliefs, and judgments. The various attitudes of the adolescent are differentiated, but they are still unrelated, just as his own ego appears to be divided.

Spranger is one of the few psychologists discussed here who directs almost all his attention to the period of adolescence. He did not advance a general developmental theory and wrote very little about child development. In only a few pages does he deal with childhood in order to emphasize the totality and wholeness of psychological development and organization. Furthermore, Spranger states that the child "lives in a different world from ours" (Spranger, 1955: 42). The underlying assumption of this quotation is that reality is not a constant factor, but changes with the psycho-

*Even though Spranger does not support his statement with empirical evidence, findings in the United States sustain his assertion. Adults strive "for a more limited set of goals than did adolescents" and seek "a continuously slower and more regular tempo of living" (Blair, 1950: 380). Wylie and Hutchins (1967) found that high school students—blacks as well as whites—overestimated their ability to do schoolwork.

logical organization and development of the person. Therefore, we must conclude that he sees adolescence as a specific developmental period that has unique characteristics different from both childhood and adulthood.

In his theory of adolescent development, Spranger does not attempt to explain cultural differences. He limits his investigation to one specific culture, that of Germany. However, both cultural and individual differences are implicitly assumed. He wants only to develop a psychological picture of the typical adolescent. The individual case must be approached by way of the typical and the general. Science, he feels, should be concerned with the derivation of generalizations. Nevertheless, Spranger (1955) suggests three ways by which an understanding of individuality can be approached:

1. There are great individual differences in adolescent behavior according to the developmental rhythm by which an adolescent experiences the transition from childhood. The three forms that have already been discussed are:
   a. stress and strain development,
   b. gradual, continuous development, and
   c. self-directed and self-controlled development.
2. The three pairs of contrasting modes of experience of the psychological processes are:
   a. the calm and the enthusiastic,
   b. the receptive and the creative, and
   c. the melancholic and the cheerful.
3. Tendencies in the human psyche create or realize values differently. These values differ from individual to individual, but the values or the evaluative attitude of the individual determines his personality. Not until the beginning of pubescence do these mental attitudes become clearly distinguishable. Different forms of values that are realized by the human psyche are described in *Types of Men* (1928). He applies to adolescence a modified form of these types of evaluation and feeling toward life:
   a. The type who is preoccupied with his body and nature, characterized by vitality, health, and a need for power.

b. The aesthetic-enthusiastic type who has a typical adolescent attitude of idealistic exuberance toward life.

c. The ponderer who considers life a problem and is theoretically oriented; this type is not unusual during pubescence.

d. The active type whose main values are progress and success; Spranger identifies this type with a stereotyped form of Americanism.

e. The adventurous type who likes to dominate and yearns for fame.

f. The social type who can give altruistic love, a rare type among adolescents, since youth is too preoccupied in establishing its own ego unity.

g. The ethical enthusiast who can become a rigorous and radical defender of ethical principles.

h. The religious type, also frequent among adolescents, which can take many different patterns. Characteristic of youth is the mystic.

This combination of developmental rhythms, mode of experience, and type of value realization allows for many differences. It helps explain individual variations but does not contribute to the understanding of specific individuals. Though Spranger states that it is his aim to understand the individual, he does not provide the reader with an adequate theoretical way to return from the generalizations of a typical case to an individual case—not even *post hoc*.

Educational Implications

Spranger's theory, like Lewin's, is influenced by the philosophical school of phenomenology. For the phenomenologist the determining factor in behavior is not the objective nature of a situation but the individual's perception of it. To an outsider, a certain kind of behavior might appear irrelevant and illogical, but from the behaver's viewpoint, it could be relevant and appropriate. In opposition to epistemology and in agreement with phenomenology, Spranger holds that even the same objective experience of reality is not constant among different individuals but depends upon subjective factors, such as the stage of development, the value system, the personality structure, the emotional involvement, and past experiences. It is possible for a teacher to comprehend the behavior of the adolescent only if he attempts to understand the adolescent rather than the situation. The teacher trying to understand the situation is only able to see it in the light of his own experiences; he will fail to comprehend the specific relationship between the adolescent and the situation. He must understand the psyche of the adolescent and his subjective perception of the situation. Spranger recognizes that this is a hard task because it requires psychological training. *requires more than that honey*

One characteristic of the transition from childhood to adolescence is a reflective discovery of the self. Self-discovery leads to self-evaluation, and this in turn leads to self-education. No healthy youth considers himself without need for education and improvement. However, through this change in self-concept—from a naïve, childish concept to a reflective, maturing one—the adolescent consciously begins to select those influences to which he will expose himself. Thus, beginning with adolescence, self-education must be distinguished from other-education. No other-education will influence an adolescent if he does not see its value and is not receptive to it. Therefore, in the adolescent period, all education is self-education, since other-education can only become influential if the self has accepted its value.

Teachers ought to be concerned with the adolescent's concept of what constitutes educational values. Implied is the democratic idea that the adolescent should be allowed to choose courses and express his views of the curriculum, since his attitude toward courses can determine what effect they will have on him.

The discovery of the self is further related to striving for emancipation. Since the individual experiences himself for the first time as an entity different from anything else, he has to integrate this newly discovered independence into his behavior. If the school does not take into account this increased need for recognition, respect, independence, and self-determination during the adolescent period, rebellious and negative behavior must be expected.

Spranger maintains that teaching sexual knowledge does not fulfill the hopes of its proponents; it only satisfies sexual curiosity. However, sexual information obtained through the school is better than misleading or partial information from friends, dictionaries, and spurious literature. He argues that sex education does not decrease actual sexual desire. Since the information remains often on an intellectual, rational basis, it does not penetrate into the emotional layers of the human psyche. The influence of sex education in changing behavior remains doubtful. Moreover, sex education may be viewed as sensational and may stimulate sexual fantasy. *oh boy*

Since Spranger had great interest in literature, he analyzed the appeal of certain forms of literature taught in German high schools. He maintained that the literary products of the classical period most frequently included in the curriculum have little appeal, whereas the literature of the *Sturm und Drang* epoch is closest to the adolescent's psychological structure. Similarly, in music there is an appreciation for Beethoven's idealism—and Beethoven is referred to as the "emancipator of music"—before youth is attracted to the classical works of Mozart.

6

Cultural Anthropology and Adolescence

During the late 1920s and early 1930s a number of systematic anthropological field studies of primitive societies opened a new area of thinking about personality development, the socialization process, and human instincts. Two books by Margaret Mead (1901–), *Coming of Age in Samoa* (1950) and *Growing Up in New Guinea* (1953), are relevant to a discussion of adolescence. We will be concerned primarily with the former book, since it is devoted entirely to the adolescent period.

The findings of cultural anthropology constitute a serious challenge to earlier theoretical propositions—especially those of Hall and Sigmund Freud—that held that certain important patterns in the development and behavior of human beings are universal and part of human nature. Since relatively little was known about the social structure of primitive societies prior to these anthropological investigations, earlier theories of adolescence had too readily assumed that the pattern of development found in the most widely studied Western cultures were universal. On the other hand, cultural anthropologists were stimulated in their theorizing and in their investigations by hypotheses derived from psychoanalysis. Consequently, the reciprocal influence of more recent psychoanalytic theory and cultural anthropology has been fruitful and stimulating. The theoretical ideas of these two schools of thought have actually converged to a rather remarkable extent during the past decade. Mutual recognition and research evidence have produced the emergence of theoretical ideas in which the extreme positions of environmental determinism and genetic universalism have yielded to a composite position in which biogenetic factors and environmental forces are weighed more carefully and recognized as mutually interacting. Comparing writings of Erikson (1950) and Mead (1961) we find a degree of accord that one could not have imagined when comparing early psychoanalytic theory with the writings of cultural anthropologists in the late twenties and early thirties. However, in order to facilitate an understanding of the controversial arguments in their historical perspective, we will first consider the early anthropological position, since it has been a challenge and a stimulus to many subsequent developmental theories. The more recent modifications will be considered when appropriate.

Coming of Age in Samoa is an empirical field study; it uses anthropological methodology, but does not contain an explicitly stated theory of adolescent development. However, Ruth Benedict (1887–1948) in "Continuities and Discontinuities in Cultural Conditioning" (1954) does provide us with an explicit theory of development from a cultural anthropological point of view. This theory of cultural conditioning relates directly to Mead's study of adolescence in Samoa. By combining the theoretical writings of Benedict with the empirical study by Mead, we derive a systematic statement concerning the importance of cultural factors in the developmental process. "Cultural relativism"—a term more appropriate to the earlier than to the later writings of Mead—contributes new and important ideas to the understanding of the phenomenon of adolescence. It emphasizes the importance of social institutions and cultural factors in human development and describes the rituals of pubescence as well as adolescent experiences in primitive societies.

Human beings show far greater plasticity and modifiability than lower animals. This accounts for the progress the human species has made as well as for the wide intercultural differences. The biological constitution of man does not determine particular patterns of behavior; germ cells do not transmit culture. Few, if any, human traits are universal; even if there are universal traits, they may not be biogenetically determined. An early form of learned behavior—Benedict (1950) calls it a "cradle trait"—may have become a universal institution, for example, exogamous restriction on marriage.

Benedict (1954) offers a theoretical means of relating the way of life of a given culture to the growth and development of individual personality. She sees growth as a gradual, continuous process. The newborn infant depends for his survival on other people. From this infantile dependence, he must grow into a state of relative independence; as an adult he will have to provide for and protect his offspring who then will be dependent upon him. The pattern by which the child obtains independence varies from one culture to another. In some cultures, such as the American, the difference between a child and an adult is emphasized sharply by social and legal institutions. The change from one mode of interpersonal relationship to another creates discontinuity in the growth process. Lewin (to be discussed in Chapter 7) also accounted for adolescent difficulties in terms of the existing dichotomy between children and adults.

One example of this discontinuity in our society is the emphasis on the sexless nature of the child (or, since Freud, we should say on the social restriction of sex expression in the child) as contrasted with adult sexual activities. The child never, or rarely, sees childbirth, sexual intercourse, and death; pregnancy is camouflaged, evacuation veiled with prudery, breastfeeding hidden, and girls menstruate the first time without knowing what it is all about. The child gets very incomplete information about the life cycle of the sexes.

In contrast, the Samoan child follows a relatively continuous growth pattern. Youth has an opportunity to see birth and death near home, and many have seen a partly developed fetus, the opening of dead bodies, and occasional glimpses of sex activities. The child is not considered basically different from the adult. Sex life is not repressed or inhibited by society, but is considered natural and pleasurable. Perversion, homosexuality, promiscuity, and other sexual activities, which because of their social and moral stigma divert emotional development toward neuroses in American society and may result in unsatisfactory marriage, are relatively harmless in Samoa; they are considered "simply play" and are without moral stigma. In Samoan society, most experiences follow a relatively gradual, continuous line of development without severe interruptions, interferences, or restrictions. By contrast, in Western society many experiences that are approved for adults are restricted or forbidden to children. Attitudes, values, and skills that children have learned must be unlearned when they become adults.

Benedict discusses three specific aspects of discontinuity versus continuity in cultural conditioning. The major changes in Western society occur during adolescence. They are:

1. Responsible versus nonresponsible status role
2. Dominance versus submission
3. Contrasted sexual role (Benedict, 1954: 143).

The difference between continuous and discontinuous behavior in development from nonresponsible to responsible status can be demonstrated by the issue of work and play. In American society, especially in urban areas, work and play are considered separate and distinct. A child makes no important labor contributions to society; he is even forbidden by law to do so. But when young men and women reach maturity, they must compete on an equal basis with older adults. In some primitive societies, development from a nonresponsible to a responsible status role is much more gradual. Play and work are not necessarily separated; they often involve the same activities. Among the Cheyenne Indians, a boy receives a bow and arrow at birth. As he grows, the bows are increased in size. His first contribution of a snow bird to the family meal is celebrated as a feast. The boy's contribution is valued and celebrated even if his father brings home a buffalo. Nor does his status change when he finally brings home a buffalo himself.

In Samoa, the girls, sometimes only six or seven years old, are responsible for caring for and disciplining the younger siblings. Thus, each girl is socialized and develops responsibility by her early involvement in family duties. The boys at an early age learn the simple tasks of reef fishing and canoeing while the girls, after they are released from their duties as nursemaids for their younger brothers and sisters, work on plantations and help carry food to the village. No basic change takes place during the adolescent period; the degree of responsibility increases, and the amount and quality of work increases as the child grows stronger and matures. In our society—especially in urban and suburban communities—the shift from nonresponsible play to responsible work generally occurs during adolescence as a rather sudden shift. It creates a conflict in the adolescent since it requires a redefinition of essential roles.

The difference between submission and dominance is even more extreme in our culture. The child must drop his childhood submission and adopt its very opposite—dominance—in adulthood. Submission to parental authority is often enforced by emotional attachments that are hard to break later. Our emphasis on respect for parents and elders creates strong elements of discontinuity, since the submissive child must himself become a dominant parent. The standard American joke about the henpecked male is an indication of the frequency of the problem and the difficulty involved in making this shift.

During adolescence, a rather sudden shift takes place from submission to dominance. Frequently only a short time elapses between the adolescent's leaving home and founding his own family. At times this change is consciously experienced as a discontinuity by the adolescent who is ready to leave home, but who has received little training for independence. According to Erikson (1950), it is "Mom" who accentuates the difference between child and adult status to the extent that young men and women feel ill prepared for life. In contrast, some primitive societies have patterns of continuous conditioning in respect to submission-dominance. Benedict reports a case among the Crow Indians in which a father boasted "about his young son's intractability even when it was the father himself who was flouted; 'He will be a man,' his father said. He would have been baffled at the idea that his child should show behavior which would obviously make him appear a poor creature in the eyes of his fellows if he used it as an adult" (Benedict, 1954: 145). In Samoan society the six- or seven-year-old girl dominates her younger siblings as their nursemaid, but she herself may still be under the dominance of older sisters. As the child becomes older, she dominates and must discipline more younger children while she in turn is restricted and disciplined by fewer older children. If a youth gets into conflict with his parents, he simply moves to his uncle's house or village without social, moral, or emotional stigma. Parents have only limited influence over their children; discipline is always the job of an older sibling. As a result, Samoan society does not know the intensely emotional conflict between dominance and submission that often erupts during adolescence in our society.

A most important discontinuity in the life cycle is the fact that the child must assume a sexual role leading to parenthood. Benedict does not deny that the contrasting sex role has an important biological source in the distinction between sterility before pubescence and fertility after maturation is reached. However, whether the contrasted sex roles of child and adult are experienced as continuous or discontinuous is not determined by physiological maturation but by social institutions and cultural experiences, since they channel and alter the influence of the physiological factors. Our culture emphasizes the discontinuity of the sexual role. Childhood sexual experiences are frowned upon and restricted, and sex is considered wicked. Until marriage, virginity and sexual abstinence are upheld as social ideals. But on the wedding night, sexual responsiveness is expected. Clinical evidence shows that the young bride frequently cannot make a good sexual adjustment after marriage because she has failed to unlearn the "danger" and "evil" of sex that she learned during adolescence. Benedict defines continuity in the sexual role as meaning "that the child is taught nothing it must unlearn later" (Benedict, 1954: 146). Mead, in describing the Samoan girl as she grows up, gives an example of a continuous pattern of sex expression; the Samoan girl does not have to unlearn anything about sex. She has the opportunity to experiment and to become familiar with sex with almost no limitations except a rigid taboo against incest. Parental indulgence toward masturbation is common. The postpubescent girl expends "all of her interest . . . on clandestine sex adventures" (Mead, 1950: 31). No sex repression is practiced, and she actually postpones marriage so she can enjoy the carefree adolescent period. Sexual maladjustment in marriage is unknown; psychic impotence does not occur. The adolescent does not experience moral conflicts, and what we call "storm and stress" behavior is hardly known in Samoa.

Benedict (1954) assumes that discontinuity in childrearing necessarily results in emotional strain, whereas cultural conditioning that is continuous in nature is marked by smooth and gradual growth. Societies that emphasize discontinuity of behavior are described as "age-grade societies." In these societies, stages in child development can be observed, since different behavior is demanded by the society at different age levels. Children in a certain age-grade are grouped in formal institutions such as school, the Boy Scouts, or informal peer groups. Their activities are organized around those forms of behavior considered desirable for that age level. Individuals often "graduate" from one stage or age-grade with social recognition and public celebrations.

The Adolescent Girl in Samoa

Mead is concerned primarily with the adolescent girl. A brief summary of her description of the transition from childhood to adulthood in Samoan society follows. The Samoan pattern of child-rearing shows no signs of the extreme discontinuity between child-hood and adulthood we see in America. The Samoan child is born into a permissive society, and permissiveness remains an outstand-ing characteristic. When the child becomes an adult, the demands on him do not increase very much; they remain continuous with his past contributions. The adolescent does not experience any sharp break in his activities and social expectations. The personal-ity ideal of Samoa can be described as uncomplaining, cooperative, yielding, avoiding conflict and trouble, with little emphasis on personal prestige and material success. This attitude and the lack of pressure produce comparatively fewer maladjustments and neu-roses than in America.

Life in Samoa is unhurried, casual, and without deep feelings. No one fights for ideals or suffers for convictions. The gifted are held back and the slow coddled; family organization is a matter of expediency and involves no deep emotions and loyalties. The wife may go home to her family and the husband may select a new mate. The injury of adultery can be settled with the exchange of a few mats. Samoan society, in contrast to American society, is homoge-neous and shows little indication of social change. Behavioral cues in interpersonal relationships are less ambiguous in Samoa than in more complex societies. In primitive societies, courtship patterns are frequently clearly established. Consequently, a girl in an en-counter with boys knows rather clearly what effect her smile will have, how boys will react to her laughing, casting down her eyes, or softly walking past the group. In the United States, such a behavior cue has greater ambiguity, and the boys' responses can be predicted with less precision. The girl smiling while passing a group of boys may bring forth a variety of reactions: embarrassment, a casual returning grin, a flirtatious remark, a wolf whistle, a direct advance, or even a follower along the streets—"not because each boy who answers feels differently about the girl, but because each understands differently the cue that she gives" (Mead, 1949: 257). Fewer choices have to be made in Samoa by both the child and the adult, and these choices have less severe consequences and can be reversed more easily. There is only one religion, not dozens as in the United States. There is only one moral standard, which includes very few restrictions. The American adolescent experiences several standards with a multitude of restrictions. One important characteristic is the lack of specialization of feeling in Samoan society. Casual sex relations occur without strong emotional ties and without moral disapproval, but they lack the romantic component that is so characteristic of adolescent love in Western culture. In Samoa "love and hate, jealousy and revenge, sorrow and bereavement, are all matters of weeks" (Mead, 1950: 132). Disciplining is a matter of convenience; it is not systematic. Punishment is administered by the child-nurse, not by the parent. There is a slow increase in responsibilities and a willingness to accept family duties as the child grows older. The young girl begins her work at six or seven by caring for a younger sibling; as she grows older, she learns to weave firm round balls, make pinwheels of palm leaves, open coconuts, tidy the house, bring water from the sea, spread out the copra, weave, and cook. The boy in a similar fashion learns to fish, plant taro, transplant coconuts, take the canoe over the reef safely, husk coconuts, and cut out their meat.

Cultural Anthropology and Some Theoretical Issues

Is adolescence a biological or a psychosocial phenomenon? Cultural anthropologists consistently emphasize the differences in human behavior, social institutions, habits, mores, rituals, and religious beliefs in various societies. Underlying most anthropological research and writing is the assumption that the social environment into which an infant is born plays a tremendous role in his personality development. In other words, cultural anthropologists believe in cultural determinism. Since the economic, ideological, and institutional patterns of societies vary widely, we are justified in speaking of cultural relativism. One of Benedict's (1950) objectives was to help people understand relativity in the patterns of culture.

Though cultural anthropologists emphasize social and cultural environment—critics say they overemphasize it (Ausubel, 1954; Dennis, 1946; Sherif and Cantril, 1947)—they do not deny the influence of biological factors. They just disregard them. This can be demonstrated by Mead's comparison of adolescents in primitive and complex societies. "If we lay aside the purely physical definition of maturation and consider adolescence as a period following childhood during which the individual becomes placed in his society, we are struck at once by the enormous difference in range" (Mead, 1952: 538–539). In the earlier writings of Benedict and Mead the physiological aspects of pubescence have been laid aside.

Since cultural anthropologists assume the plasticity of human nature and the importance of social environment, it follows that they do not consider pubescence to be causally related to adolescence. The social nature of adolescence is indicated by statements such as : "At whatever point the society decides to stress a particular adjustment, it will be at this point that adjustment becomes acute to the individual" (Mead, 1952: 537). Comparison of adolescence in various primitive societies demonstrates that adolescent problems can be solved in different ways and at different age levels, or they may not exist at all. It does not seem reasonable to consider these problems inherent in adolescent development. A few examples from the writings of Mead (1952) and Benedict (1950) dealing with the attitudes of various societies toward menstruation will demonstrate this point:

1. Northern California Indian tribes held the attitude that the menstruating girl was dangerous to the village because she could dry up the well and scare the game.
2. The Yuki Indians in North Central California emphasized the goodness of the menstruating girl; their rituals were mainly

concerned with the improvement of the crops. By lying quiet, the girl could increase the food supply. They emphasized the resources of society rather than the girl.

3. Among the Thompson Indians, a menstruating girl's observance of symbolic rituals and taboos increased her chances for a career and a happy life. She lived in a hut away from other people and performed ritual acts of magic.

4. In the Gilbert Islands the menstruating girl was considered especially prone to enemy magic. By sitting still and facing west, she protected herself from evil.

5. In Samoa no taboos and rituals were connected with menstruation; the girls were not even forbidden to prepare food.

6. The Apache Indian girl's first menstruation was considered a potent supernatural blessing. The priest knelt before her to obtain the blessing of her touch.

These examples demonstrate that physiological maturity, if it is recognized at all, will be recognized in different ways. The social attributes of physiological puberty are part of the traditional cultural pattern.

In the later writings of Mead we find that the earlier extreme position—frequently identified as cultural relativism—has undergone modification and moderation to include some universal aspects of development (Mead prefers to call them "basic regularities") without yielding any of the insight gained from her earlier writings. This new position might best be demonstrated by a few selected quotes from *Male and Female:* "there are basic regularities that no known culture has been able to evade" (Mead, 1949: 143). "In all known societies, we find . . . some manifestation of what psychoanalysts call latency . . ." (Mead, 1949: 109). "The child is not only a *tabula rasa,* but a vigorous, maturing organism with modes of behavior appropriate to its age and strength. But it is not a maturing organism in a glass box . . ." (Mead, 1949: 145).

Is development stagelike or continuous? The answer to this question is not an either/or proposition, since both patterns—a gradual development and a stagelike saltatory form of development—are considered possible.

The controversial issue of stages versus continuity is resolved by the view that social environment, institutions, and the specific pattern of cultural conditioning determine whether development takes place in stages or is continuous. A similar position is taken by social learning theory to be discussed in Chapter 13. According to Benedict the cycle from infantile dependence to adult independence is "a fact of nature and inescapable" (Benedict, 1954: 142); thus it contains an element of discontinuity. But this transition takes place in different ways in various cultures, so that no one way can be considered natural and universal. In Western cultures society reinforces stages of development by social institutions organized around those stages—grades of school, types of schools, and the legal and moral concept of "underage." Graduation from one age level or school to the next brings about socially expected changes in behavior. These changes are frequently discontinuous in nature, especially during adolescence, giving support to a theory of developmental stages. For example, the fourteen-year-old is not allowed to drive a car, whereas the eighteen-year-old is often expected to. If a boy begins dating at ten or eleven, he is considered precocious and parents become concerned; if he does not date when he is seventeen or eighteen, parents also become concerned, wondering whether his sexual development is normal. In Samoa, the unrestricted, unhurried, and noncompetitive pattern of development allows a continual and gradual development without any actual "graduation" and without any far-reaching disturbances or basic changes in behavior as a function of age.

Cultural anthropology challenges the universality and general validity of any stage theory. "Theories of developmental stages would also suffer serious revision if submitted to primitive tests. Not only the cruder theories of the inevitable stress and strain at physiological puberty, or of a 'collecting stage' go by the boards, but many smaller variations occur" (Mead, 1933: 918).

Mead in her more recent writings postulates that menstruation does constitute a dramatic experience and an unmistakable indication of the attainment of a new social status. "The girl's first menstruation marks a dividing-line between childhood and womanhood" (Mead, 1949: 176). For the boy no such specific experience exists, and his pubescence is characterized by a long series of slow developmental changes.

How are cultural and individual differences explained? Mead asserts that personality development is "jointly influenced by hereditary, cultural, and individual life-history factors" (Mead, 1942:

55). Cultural anthropologists, even though they do not deny hereditary factors, neglect them in their earlier theoretical consideration and do not supply any systematic concepts by which to incorporate heredity into anthropological theory.

Culture is more homogeneous in primitive societies; one can expect greater similarities in the behavior of adolescents, since they have limited opportunities to make choices. Their behavior can be predicted more easily than that of youths in a modern Western city, whose individual differences would be greater because of (1) heterogeneity of culture, (2) rapidity of cultural change, and (3) diversified cultural and hereditary background. In primitive society, certain forms of behavior can be predicted through knowledge of the cultural pattern; in a modern city, the behavior of a given individual is less directly conditioned by the total culture than by subcultural and family patterns. It is better understood through a case-history approach.

Certain patterns of educational practices are related to patterns of personality development in primitive societies. Cultural anthropologists assume considerable homogeneity in the educational pattern of a given primitive society. But anthropological studies have shown that great differences exist among societies in methods of childrearing, forms of cultural conditioning, and the kind of restrictions and limitations enforced upon youth. The particular cultural pattern of childrearing accounts for intercultural differences. Mead (1942) rejects the early psychoanalytic notion that a few outstanding events in childrearing, such as weaning, toilet training, and thumb-sucking, determine character development. She asserts that the total cultural pattern and the nature of social interaction—especially the continuity or discontinuity of cultural conditioning—are the important factors in the development of personality. Specific aspects of childrearing in a culture selected for detailed study by anthropologists are not selected because a preconceived theory assumes that they are determinants of personality, but because they are outstanding and striking features of the given culture. These outstanding patterns of childrearing may be quite different in the socialization process of other societies.

Mead credits biogenetic inheritance with more importance as a determining factor in human development in her later writing than she did in *Coming of Age in Samoa*. Biological inheritance as a developmental factor may help in accounting for considerable variation of intercultural and intracultural differences. Even in highly inbred and isolated groups with a great deal of uniformity in patterns of childrearing, she found remarkable "differences in physique and apparent temperament" (Mead, 1949: 133). Furthermore, she hypothesizes that the same constitutional types that are found in our society are likely to be found—in different proportions—in most, if not all, societies.

Stimulated by Gesell's growth studies (to be discussed in Chapter 9), Mead (1951) compared and contrasted the growth pattern and sequence of Balinese infants with the pattern Gesell reported for children in New Haven, confirming some of his findings and challenging others. She raises a theoretical question as to the extent to which innate patterns of maturation are interfered with, altered, or supported by cultural factors. Mead's later position appears to deviate from her earlier Samoan findings: ". . . any alternative to following the developing child's manifestations of its mammalian ancestry and generic humanity, has been conceived as a distortion of the human being by cultural pressures" (Mead, 1954: 175).

As the more recent psychoanalytic concepts have been expanded to include social determinants, cultural anthropological theory has moved from an early position of "cultural relativism" to a broader theoretical position that takes biogenetic factors into consideration. Though the two schools of thought place emphasis on different determinants, they have become highly compatible and complementary.

Educational Implications

Though the Samoan way of life contrasts sharply with life in America as well as with life in "most primitive civilizations," Mead (1950) draws far-reaching conclusions, with important educational implications, from her study of Samoan culture.

In her later writings, Mead includes among the factors responsible for adolescent difficulties in American society "the contradictions and unevenness of physical puberty" (Mead, 1961: 37). However, her emphasis is on social factors. Since certain cultural conditions in the United States produce stress, strain, anxiety, and emotional instability in the adolescent, Mead suggests modification of these conditions through social planning.

In complex Western societies, which are characterized by a rapid rate of social and technological change, adolescents are confronted with many alternatives. Consequently, problem situations involving genuine choice arise more frequently than they do in primitive societies, and the possibility of an inappropriate choice increases. Adolescent difficulties in complex societies relate to "the presence of conflicting standards and the belief that every individual should make his or her own choices, coupled with the feeling that choice is an important matter" (Mead, 1950: 154). This conflict of choice is facilitated by the fact that physiological puberty occurs earlier now than in the past and that a number of other forms of behavior —dating, going steady, wearing lipstick, dance parties, and so on —have slowly moved down to earlier ages (Muuss, 1970a). At the same time, the expectations for prolonged formal education are increasing to the extent that an ever-increasing number of parents with children of school age expect their children to go to college. The earlier imitation of "adultlike" behavior, on the one hand, and the extended period of education, on the other hand, have increased the duration of social adolescence and created a "mass adolescent culture pattern" characterized by conformity to peer-group standards and unresponsiveness to parental values and expectations. Mead feels that the junior high school in particular has contributed to adolescents' increased anxiety* about their growth pattern and appropriate sex behavior. The slow-maturing male is especially vulnerable to anxiety during this period. Owing to the differential growth rate of boys and girls, he is forced into association with members of the opposite sex at a time when he is not yet psychologically or physiologically ready for that kind of relationship. Instead of developing deep personal friendships and associations with members of his own sex, which would help him in developing his own masculine identity, he learns to distrust his male companions as competitors in the dating process. Consequently, boys and girls begin too soon to depend too much on each other "for social and intellectual companionship" (Mead, 1961:

---

*Cattell (1961) found that anxiety reaches its peak at about fifteen and only returns to such height again in old age.

44). Mead feels that this immature and early heterosexual interaction, which junior high schools invite and the peer group expects, contributes to negative attitudes and hostility between the sexes. It lays "the basis for hostility to females on the boys' part and, on the girls' part, pressure toward marriage combined with contempt for males" (Mead, 1961: 38).

The emphasis in our society on installment-plan buying, conspicuous consumption, and early vocational success has brought about a basic shift in attitude from the saving of money, postponement of desires, and pursuit of long-range goals to an emphasis on immediate consumption and an enjoyment of the gratifications that the present provides. This shift to the immediate consumption of goods has been accompanied by a similar shift in attitude with respect to the consumption of sex. This places an increasing demand on the adolescent boy whose sexual desires are strong, but who has not yet learned to control them. The desire for the immediate consumption of sex brings him into conflict with the moral values of society. He can satisfy his desire through marriage, but early marriage will conflict with the continuation of his education. Parents are frequently willing to "finance" or "subsidize" the early marriage of their children, thus making their prematurely gained independence in one sphere a cause of their dependency in the economic sphere. Mead hypothesizes that premature domesticity may prevent the full development of the "higher mental capacities" in both sexes. A student needs to explore the world, stimulate his curiosity, and find out who he is. The emotional commitment and the domesticity of early marriage may inhibit the desire to test, explore, discuss, mediate, and repudiate ideas and the intellectual maturity resulting from such processes. Self-finding, role exploration, and search for an identity must precede the dependency of intimacy and marriage according to Erikson. The major motive of the married student often becomes "to get through," "to get established," "to make money," and not to experiment, explore, and search for knowledge.

With Erikson (1950) and other contemporary writers, Mead maintains that the major task facing adolescents today is the search for a meaningful identity. This task is immeasurably more difficult in a modern democratic society than in a primitive society. The behavior and values of parents no longer constitute models, since they are outmoded as compared with the models provided by the mass media. Furthermore, the adolescent in the process of freeing himself from dependency on parents is not only unresponsive, but frequently antagonistic to their value system. Since he has been taught to evaluate his behavior against that of his age-mates, he now discards his parents' value system and exchanges it for the standard of his peers. Rapidity of social change, exposure to various secular and religious value systems, and modern technology make the world appear to the adolescent too complex, too relativistic, too unpredictable, and too ambiguous to provide him with a stable frame of reference. In the past there has been a period, which both Erikson and Mead call a "psychological moratorium," an "as if" period during which youth could tentatively experiment without being asked to show "success" and without final emotional, economic, or social consequences. The loss of such a period of uncommitted experimentation, during which youth can find itself, makes it difficult to establish ego-identity. As a substitute for psychological identity, youth utilizes peer group symbols to establish a semi-identity by way of special clothes, special language, and special attitudes toward the world; in the past these were symbols of identity of deprived and/or semicriminal groups. Even education has become functional and "success" oriented. Consequently, the goals and values of adolescents are directed toward success, security, immediate gratification of desires, conformity, and social acceptance with little room for experimentation, idealism, utopianism, and personal martyrdom. "Failure to adopt our educational and social system . . . may be held responsible for some of the sense of self-alienation, search for negative identities, and so forth, characteristic of this present group of young people" (Mead, 1961: 49).

Mead discusses the possibility of a "return to nature" in the Rousseauistic sense, but she rejects it because it presupposes a total change of our social structure and way of life. Although a communal living pattern and a Thoreauvian way of life among youth who are dissatisfied with the rigid structure of school, college, and society reflect this "return to nature" philosophy, Mead rejects a return to more primitive forms of life as a realistic solution for parents of an adolescent. While it is true that in Samoan society children witness, with no negative effect, reproduction, birth, illness, and death, the same experiences provided in an American family could do more harm than good, since society considers these experiences inappropriate and taboo for children.

However, Mead does advocate greater freedom and less emphasis on conformity to family, peer group, and community expectations so that the adolescent can realize his creative potential. "We can attempt to alter our whole culture, and especially our child-rearing patterns, so as to incorporate within them a greater freedom for and expectation of variations" (Mead, 1951: 185). This alteration can be achieved by a combination of freedom and training in educational practice that is based both on an understanding of the students' "maturational psychodynamics" and adequate insight into the patterns of culture.

Mead criticizes the American family for its too intimate organization and its crippling effect on the emotional life of the growing youth. She believes that too strong family ties handicap the individual in his ability to live his own life and make his own choices. She suggests that "it would be desirable to mitigate, at least in some slight measure, the strong role which parents play in children's lives, and so eliminate one of the most powerful accidental factors in the choices of any individual life" (Mead, 1950: 141). However, even though she objects to the pattern of the American family that produces conformity and dependency in its children, she considers the family a tough institution and demonstrates that it is nearly universal. Mead knows of no better way to produce wholesome individuals than through a tolerant family system in which "father says 'yes' and mother says 'no' about the same thing" (Mead, 1947: 330), and in which the adolescent can disagree with his parents without a resulting loss of love, self-respect, or increase of emotional tensions.

Mead demands more emphasis on mental and physical health in the classroom. Making choices is an important aspect of growing up in America and of maintaining mental health, especially at that period of development when sexual urges begin to play a more important role, but when society does not condone sexual behavior. The adolescent will be increasingly confronted with conflicting choices, in sexual as well as in other matters. This choice situation is complicated by a lack of a definite, generally accepted social canon in American society, and the advice received from parents, teachers, peers, and the lure of the commercial are frequently in conflict. Consequently, many choice situations produce anxiety during adolescence. To help youth in overcoming this dilemma, a special educational effort ought to be made to train children and adolescents to consider alternatives and consequences when confronted with a choice situation. "Children must be taught how to think, not what to think" (Mead, 1950: 16).

Finally, returning to Benedict's theory of continuities and discontinuities in cultural conditioning, the educational implications become quite obvious: our educational practices at home as well as in school should emphasize continuity in the learning process so that the child becomes conditioned to the same set of values and behavior in childhood that will be expected from him in adulthood. The child should be taught nothing that he will have to unlearn in order to become a mature adult. The implementation of this idea is obviously difficult in our modern and complex society as it is today. Many social roles are defined by age and by social expectations. Changes in behavior, often constituting a discontinuity, are expected as the individual moves from elementary to high school, from college into the labor market, and from denial of sexuality before to sexual responsiveness following the wedding.

Leta Hollingworth's Emphasis on the Continuity of Development

A theory of adolescent development that has become quite influential, especially in the United States, was advanced by Leta Hollingworth (1886–1939) in her book *The Psychology of the Adolescent* (1928). She was even more pronounced than were Mead and Benedict in her attack on Hall's idea of adolescence as a period of inevitable storm and stress. She dismissed his works as of little scientific or practical value. On the other hand, Hollingworth was strongly influenced by some of the earlier works of cultural anthropologists, as indicated by the chapter on "The Pubic Ceremonies" in her book. Hollingworth emphasized the idea of continuity of development and the gradualness of change during the adolescent period. "The child grows by imperceptible degrees into the adolescent, and the adolescent turns by gradual degrees into the adult" (Hollingworth, 1928: 1). This challenged the idea that there were distinct stages and sharp dividing lines among the different "epochs," "stages," and "phases of development." Hollingworth's concept of continuity of growth and development is in sharp contrast to Rousseau's and Hall's claims that adolescence is a new birth. Hall had said that during adolescence development is more "saltatory"; new, previously nonexistent functions arise while other psychic functions undergo reconstruction, and "every trait and faculty is liable to exaggeration and excess" (Hall, 1916: xiii–xiv). A quotation from Hollingworth may clarify the dichotomy between her viewpoint and Hall's. In speaking about prepubescent youth, she advanced the idea that from it

> . . . is evolved by imperceptible degrees the pubescent girl or boy of thirteen or fourteen years; and therefore by degrees still very gradual, though somewhat more noticeable, the total growth is achieved, till we have at last the matured human adult. . . . The quality of the organism is a constant, which shows itself from the beginning to the end of the individual life. . . . This widespread myth that every child is a changeling, who at puberty comes forth as a different personality, is doubtless a survival in folklore of the ceremonial rebirth, which constituted the formal initiation of our savage ancestors into manhood and womanhood [Hollingworth, 1928: 16–17].

She asserted that the sudden change in social status that resulted from puberty initiation rites and ceremonies of primitive people has become confused with the biological changes of organic development. In her somewhat extreme position she maintained that there is no connection between the biological changes and the changes in social status that she attributed to social institutions and ceremonies.

It is interesting to note the difference between Hollingworth's idea of development and that of cultural anthropologists. Hollingworth considered development as being gradual and continuous, and she rejected as folklore and myth the idea of storm and stress and personality change during adolescence. Benedict, even though she maintained that development is gradual and continuous by nature, if not interfered with, claimed that stages can be culturally induced by discontinuities in childrearing methods and educational practice. Benedict argued that developmental stages are due to the specific pattern of American culture and are not universal, as some of the older stage theories had asserted. Mead, in agreement with Benedict, asserts that "the adolescent in America stands at the point of highest pressure and difficulty, just as another set of forces places her at the lowest point of pressure in Samoa" (Mead, 1952: 538).

Other theories have taken issue with Hollingworth's point of view. Allport challenges her idea of continuity of development and accuses her of risking "the error of underestimating the frequency with which radical alterations of personality do occur in the period of *Sturm und Drang*" (Allport, 1937: 209). Spranger had already suggested earlier that there are three different patterns of developmental rhythm that may accompany pubescence in different individuals and presumably in different societies. In the first of these developmental patterns, the adolescent period is characterized by instability and disturbance, which corresponds to Hall's "storm and stress" concept. In the second pattern, which corresponds to Hollingworth's conceptualization, the adolescent does not experience a "storm and stress" period but rather a continuous, undisturbed development of his internalized personality and his social world. In the third pattern, development occurs in spurts, but the adolescent is striving toward important life goals and is able to guide himself, thus actively contributing to his own growth, as Piaget would suggest.

7

Field Theory and Adolescence

Kurt Lewin (1890–1947) was a pupil of the early Gestalt school of psychologists at the University of Berlin. He was also influenced by Freud's psychoanalytic theory, particularly in regard to motivation in human behavior. However, Lewin's theory of adolescence is conceptually quite different from any of the theories discussed so far. Lewin's field theory—especially as it relates to social psychology and learning theory—is widely known and frequently discussed in the psychological literature, but comparatively few references are made to his theory of adolescent development, which is explicitly stated in "Field Theory and Experiment in Social Psychology" (1939). His field theory explains and describes the dynamics of behavior of the individual adolescent without generalizing about adolescents as a group. His constructs help to describe and explain, and if the field forces are known, to predict the behavior of a given individual in a specific situation. In a sense, the field theory of adolescence is expressed explicitly and stated more formally than other theories of adolescent development. At the same time, however, Lewin's theory opposes strongly those conceptual schemes that require placing the phenomenal world in rigid and mutually exclusive categories.

Lewin assumed the "lawfulness" of all psychological events, even those that occur only once. He maintained that general psychological concepts and laws derived on the basis of frequency of occurrence created a dilemma, since these laws are abstracted from many individuals and are true in terms of probability only. Such laws may or may not apply to a specific individual. Therefore, there is no way back from these generalizations to a particular individual except by way of probability.

Developmental Concepts of Field Theory

One of Lewin's (1939: 34) core concepts is the law "that behavior (B) is a function (f) of the person (P) and of his environment (E), $B = f(PE)$, and that P and E in this formula are interdependent variables." How a child perceives his environment depends upon the stage of his development, his personality, and his knowledge. An unstable psychological environment during adolescence brings about instability in the behavior of the individual. Therefore, to understand a child's behavior, one must consider him and his environment as a constellation of interdependent factors. The sum total of all environmental and personal factors in interaction is called the "life space" (LSp), or the "psychological space." Behavior is a function of the life space and not only of the physical stimuli, $B = f(LSp)$. The life space includes physical-environmental, social and psychological factors, such as needs, motives, and goals, all of which determine behavior. To demonstrate the dynamics of the life space, Lewin introduces two constructs that are to represent the situation of a particular individual at a particular time in a particular environment:

1. A map or geometrical representation of the life space, in which the person, available goals, and possible barriers between an individual and his goals are depicted (Figure 3).
2. A representation of the forces that act upon the individual and bring about locomotion toward or away from a goal.

Within the life space, objects or goals can have positive (attraction) or negative (repulsion) valence. If goals allow the fulfillment of needs and desires, they have a positive valence; barriers that interfere with the attainment of a goal have a negative valence. If the attracting and repulsing forces are in balance, a person experiences conflict. If the forces are not in balance, they produce locomotion and the individual moves, psychologically speaking,

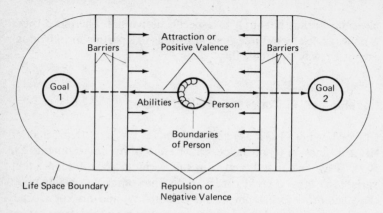

FIGURE 3. An individual's life space in a conflict situation.

toward or away from the goal. When several forces act simultaneously, the locomotion is called a "resultant." A barrier between an individual and his goal may increase the individual's efforts to reach the goal, but it may also result in frustration.

In Figure 3 the person (P) is strongly attracted to the goal (G1), such as passing a course or getting a good grade in high school. However, to reach this goal various barriers having negative valences—for instance, quizzes, exams, papers, and reports, which require effort and time—must be overcome. If another attractive goal (G2), wanting to earn money, is operative at the same time and also requires overcoming barriers—namely, mowing the lawn, washing the car, and so on—the adolescent may experience conflict if the forces are in balance. Actual behavior would be determined by the strength of the forces, as one individual may be more attracted to earning money, or less repulsed by mowing the lawn, whereas another individual may be more interested in passing the course, or may actually enjoy writing the required paper.

The psychological field, or the life space, includes the individual with his biological and psychological dimensions as well as the environment with its social relations and physical objects. Since person and environment are seen as a constellation of interrelated factors, this theory achieves harmony among the many aspects of development by combining biological, sociological, environmental, and psychological factors in the concept life space. Field theory has successfully integrated the biological and sociological factors, which are frequently considered contradictory (for example, the nature-nurture issue). Lewin made explicit his position on this issue in several of his publications: "the social aspect of the psychological situation is at least as important as the physical" (Lewin, 1946: 793); "the psychological influence of environment on the behavior and development of the child is extremely important" (Lewin, 1931: 94); "psychology in general [is regarded] as a field of biology" (Lewin, 1935: 35). "Psychological ecology" is seen as the biological science that deals with the relationship between the organism and its environment or, as Lewin states the issue, "the relationship between psychological and non-psychological factors" (Lewin, 1951: 170). Thus he attempts to combine biological, social, and environmental forces into one system, and he accomplishes this with the construct of the life space, which can be readily illustrated as a map of the objects, goals, and valences that are operative.

In infancy, a child's life space is unstructured and undifferentiated; the child depends on outside help and external structuring of his environment by other people. An individual's space of free movement is limited by "(a) what is forbidden to a person, (b) what is beyond his ability" (Lewin, 1936: 219). As the child grows older and as the life space increases in structure and differentiation, he learns to depend more and more on himself. Fewer restrictions are placed on his freedom to move, and his ability to deal effectively with the increased life space grows. To acquire maximal differentiation of his life space, he must have the freedom to advance into new regions, to explore and include new experiences. Lack of freedom of movement will place restrictions on the child's attempt to expand his life space; psychological rigidity of personality will result. Conversely, if the life space, especially in early childhood, remains unstructured, the personality will lack integration and organization. Thus Lewin not only emphasizes the child's developmental need for independence, which was pointed out by Rank, but he also adds the idea of a developmental need for a kind of dependency that provides the child with structure and guidance toward favorable personality development. The importance of the dependency need and the structure in the home contributing to the socialization of the child is a major concern of social learning theory discussed

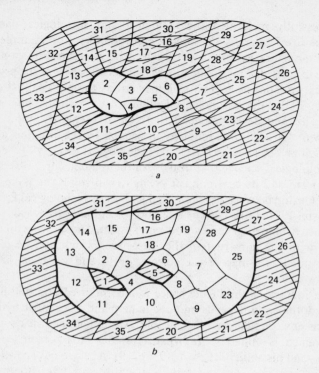

FIGURE 4. Comparison of the *space of free movement* of child and adult. The actual activity regions are represented. The accessible regions are blank; the inaccessible shaded. (*a*) The space of free movement of the *child* includes the regions *1–6* representing activities such as getting into the movies at children's rates, belonging to a boy's club, etc. The regions *7–35* are not accessible, representing activities such as driving a car, writing checks for purchases, political activities, performance of adults' occupations, etc. (*b*) The *adult* space of free movement is considerably wider, although it too is bounded by regions of activities inaccessible to the adult, such as shooting his enemy or entering activities beyond his social or intellectual capacity (represented by regions including *29–35*). Some of the regions accessible to the child are not accessible to the adult, for instance, getting into the movies at children's rates, or doing things socially taboo for an adult which are permitted to the child (represented by regions *1* and *5*).

From Kurt Lewin, The Field Theory Approach to Adolescence. *American Journal of Sociology,* 1939, *44,* 868–897. Reproduced by permission from The University of Chicago Press.

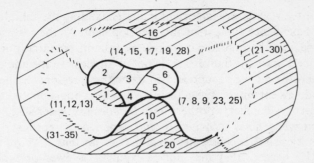

FIGURE 5. The *space of free movement* of the *adolescent* as it appears to him. The space of free movement is greatly increased, including many regions which previously have not been accessible to the child, for instance, freedom to smoke, returning home late, driving a car (regions *7–9, 11–13,* . . .). Certain regions accessible to the adult are clearly not accessible to the adolescent, such as voting (represented by regions *10* and *16*). Certain regions accessible to the child have already become inaccessible, such as getting into the movies at children's rates, or behaving on too childish a level (region *1*). The boundaries of these newly acquired portions of the space of free movement are only vaguely determined and in themselves generally less clearly and sharply differentiated than for an adult. In such cases the life-space of the adolescent seems to be full of possibilities and at the same time of uncertainties.

From Kurt Lewin, The Field Theory Approach to Adolescence. *American Journal of Sociology,* 1939, *44,* 868–897. Reproduced by permission from The University of Chicago Press.

in Chapter 13. Research findings reported by Harris (1958) support this idea. Studies were made of the feelings, attitudes, and ideas of adults who, as children, attended the University of Minnesota Nursery School in the late 1920s. Those who had been reared in structured situations were decisive, confident, self-accepting, and achievement-oriented. Those raised in an unstructured home situation were indecisive, distrustful, pessimistic, and perceived success and failure in terms of good or bad luck.

The space of free movement—that region in the physical and psychological life space that is accessible to an individual—differs from person to person both in scope and nature, thus providing for a conceptualization of different experiences and thereby explaining individual differences. But even more important are the restrictions that limit free movement. Individual differences in forbidden and permitted regions are important in understanding the achievement of independence and personality development. As the adolescent's life space increases, many more regions become potentially accessible (see Figure 5). But often it is not at all clear to the adolescent whether or not he is supposed to enter these regions. Sometimes the adolescent enters such a region when he is not supposed to and experiences conflict; at other times he does not enter such a new region when he is supposed to and experiences reprimand. The difficulty arises because these regions are no longer "beyond his ability"; because they may not be explicitly allowed or explicitly forbidden, they are part of his space of free movement but remain undefined and unclear. If they are forbidden, he realizes that they are not forbidden for some of his peers, and he hopes that his own restrictions will soon be lifted. Consequently, the definition and redefinition of the space of free movement in the adolescent's life space may take innumerable hours of discussion and argumentation between him and his parents. This uncertainty of the undefined space of free movement illustrated in Figure 5 is the psychological construct by which field theory explains some of the unpredictable aspects of adolescent behavior. Many of the undefined regions in Figure 5 are "new psychological situations" in the sense that Barker uses this term in the second part of this chapter.

Lewin speaks of developmental stages, but his conceptualization of stages is quite different from the stages of Freud, Erikson, Gesell, and Piaget. Lewin's stages relate to differences in the scope of the life space and the degree of life space differentiation. In accordance with the all-inclusive definition of the life space, these developmental differences are concerned with the psychological environment as well as with the individual, his body, his goals, and his self-perception. According to Lewin, the differences between developmental stages manifest themselves in the following ways:

1. An increase in the scope of the life space in regard to
   a. what is part of the psychological present
   b. the time perspective in the direction of the psychological past and the psychological future
   c. the reality-irreality dimension
2. An increasing differentiation of every level of the life space into a multitude of social relations and areas of activities

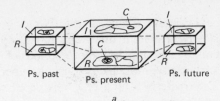

FIGURE 6. The life space at two developmental stages. Figure 6a represents the life space of a younger child. Figure 6b represents the higher degree of differentiation of the life space of the older child in regard to the present situation, the reality-irreality dimension, and the time perspective. C, child; R, level of reality; I, level of irreality; Ps Past, psychological past; Ps Present, psychological present; Ps Future, psychological future.

From Kurt Lewin, Behavior and Development as a Function of the Total Situation. In L. Carmichael (Ed.) *Manual of Child Development.* © 1946 by John Wiley & Sons, New York. Reproduced by permission.

3. An increasing organization
4. A change in the general fluidity or rigidity of the life space [Lewin, 1946: 797–798].

Figure 6 illustrates the change in life space as a function of age, comparing the child's (a) life space with that of an adolescent (b). Several important developmental differences become obvious from this comparison. (1) The main difference is the increased differentiation in the life space of the adolescent as compared to the undifferentiated and unstructured area of the child's life space. Both the child and his perception of the environment become differentiated and structured in the developmental process. This holds true in respect to many different aspects of development, such as language skills, social relations, and emotions, as well as the child's understanding of his world. Change in the differentiation of the life space occurs slowly at certain times and more rapidly at other times. Slow changes result in harmonious periods of development, whereas rapid changes are more likely to result in periods of crisis. Adolescence is characterized by a relatively rapid change in the structure of the life space, and the rapidity of the growth of the life space during adolescence may be responsible for the so-called adolescent crisis. (2) The comparison between (a) and (b) makes clear that the time perspective has expanded, since it now includes a more distant future and a more distant past. Such change in time perspective is a fundamental aspect of development; it has far-reaching consequences for education, the curriculum, and vocational planning. The adolescent develops the ability to understand the past, adopt a new outlook toward the future, and plan his own life more realistically. (3) Since the life space differentiates and the time perspective expands, the reality-irreality level also takes on new dimensions. The reality-irreality dimension is an important concept of Lewin's (1946) theory. "Irreality" refers to fantasies, dreams, wishes, fears, and certain forms of play. The young child is not able to distinguish clearly between wishes and facts, hopes and expectations. As the child grows older, his understanding of reality enables him to distinguish with increasing accuracy between truth and falsehood, perception and imagination. One characteristic of the adolescent is that he has learned to distinguish between reality and irreality. Spranger also observed that adolescents learn to differentiate between reality and fantasy.

Kurt Lewin's Theory of Adolescent Development

Fundamental to Lewin's theory of development is the view that adolescence is a period of transition in which the adolescent must change his group membership. While both the child and the adult have a fairly clear concept of how they fit into the group, the adolescent belongs partly to the child group, partly to the adult group, without belonging completely to either group. Parents, teachers, and society reflect this lack of clearly defined group status; and their ambiguous feelings toward the adolescent become obvious when they treat him at one time like a child and at another time like an adult. Difficulties arise because certain childish forms of behavior are no longer acceptable. At the same time some of the adult forms of behavior are not yet permitted either, or if they are permitted, they are new and strange to the adolescent. The adolescent is in a state of "social locomotion," since he is moving into an unstructured social and psychological field. Goals are no longer clear, and the paths to them are ambiguous and full of uncertainties —the adolescent may no longer be certain that they even lead to his goals. Such ambiguities and uncertainties are illustrated well by the boy asking or hesitating to ask for his first date. Since the adolescent does not yet have a clear understanding of his social status, expectations, and obligations, his behavior reflects this uncertainty.

A life space—as illustrated in Figure 3—has different regions that are separated by boundaries with varying degrees of permeability. For example, the adolescent is confronted with several attractive choices that at the same time have relatively impervious boundaries. Driving a car, smoking pot, dropping acid, having sexual relations are all possible goals with positive valence, and thus they become a part of the adolescent's life space. However, they are also inaccessible because of parental restriction, legal limitations, or the individual's own internalized moral code. Since the adolescent is moving through a rapidly changing field, he does not know the directions to specific goals and is open to constructive guidance, but he is also vulnerable to persuasion and pressure. Unfamiliar situations cause crises that can produce withdrawal, sensitivity, and inhibition as well as aggression, inappropriate emotional outbursts, rebellion, and radicalism. Consequently, because of a lack of cognitive structure, the adolescent frequently is not sure whether his behavior will lead him toward or away from his goal. This concept of "lack of cognitive structure" helps explain the uncertainty in adolescent behavior.

The self-image of an individual depends upon his body. During the normal developmental process body changes are so slow that the self-image remains relatively stable. The body image has time to adjust to these developmental changes so that the individual knows his own body. During adolescence changes in body structure, body experience, and new body sensations and urges are more drastic so that even the well-known life space of the body image becomes less familiar, unreliable, and unpredictable. The adolescent is preoccupied with the normality of his body and how his body is perceived by others; he is concerned about and may actually be disturbed by his body image. He spends considerable time studying his own image in the mirror and is concerned about the development of primary and secondary sex characteristics in relationship to age-mates. This is understandable; obviously, the body is especially close to and vital to one's feelings of attractiveness, stability, security, and one's sex role. Negative feelings about one's own body are related to a negative self-concept (Rosen and Ross, 1968) and may lead to emotional instability that can change one's orientation toward life. Because of these various uncertainties adolescent behavior is characterized by an increased plasticity of personality that can lead to personality changes and even religious conversions.

The change in a child's life space from being limited in scope but relatively structured to the increased but often unknown regions of the adolescent's life space includes not only more extensive social relationships, a new body image, and expanding geographic surroundings, but also an increased perception of the future and a better understanding of his own past.

Field theory defines adolescence as a period of transition from childhood to adulthood. This transition is characterized by deeper and far-reaching changes, a faster rate of growth, and differentiation of the life space as compared with the preceding stage of late childhood. The transition is also characterized by the fact that the individual enters a cognitively unstructured region that results in uncertainty of behavior. Transition from childhood to adulthood is obviously a universal phenomenon, since children become mature adults in all societies. However, the shift from childhood to adulthood can occur in different patterns. It can take the form of a sudden shift, such as has been observed in primitive societies in which the puberty rites end childhood and signify the beginning of adulthood. Mead reports, for example, that for the Manus girl, puberty "means the beginning of adult life and responsibility" (Mead, 1953: 107). There can also be a gradual shift, especially if the children's group and the adult group are not as clearly separated and defined as they are in our society. Thus development would be continuous and the adolescent crisis would be mild. This appears to be the case in Samoan society discussed in Chapter 6. If the transition period is prolonged and if the children as a group are clearly distinguished from adults, as is the case in Western societies, the adolescent finds himself in a social situation in which his group belonging is not clearly defined. The adolescent in such an in-between situation is referred to by Lewin as the "marginal man," and the adolescent's in-between standing is represented in Figure 7 by the overlapping area (Ad) of the child region (C) and the adult region (A). The assumption of the marginal man concept is that the adolescent no longer belongs to the social group of children and does not want to be considered a child; yet he is not yet accepted into the social group of adults, and to the extent that this in-between situation is operative in his personal life space, his behavior will reflect this marginality. Being a marginal man implies that the adolescent may at times act more like a child, often when he wants to avoid adult responsibilities; at other times, he may act more like an adult and request adult privileges. Parents and teachers, too, may interpret the marginal man situation in their own way; however, they are more likely to remind the adolescent to be mature, grown-up and adultlike when the issues involve responsibilities, chores, work, and study. They perceive their offspring as "still so young" and "immature" when it comes to adult rights and privileges. Such a situation is most characteristic of youth in Western society, and it is partly responsible for some of Western society's "adolescent difficulties." The marginal man, topographically speaking, stands on the boundaries that separate two groups. "They are people who belong neither here nor there, standing 'between' the groups" (Lewin, 1948: 179). Marginality, even in other social situations, increases social tensions. A minority group member may find himself in such a situation when he attempts to establish a close personal relationship within the majority group—that is, by changing his group belonging. The psychological problems confronting the marginal man are both internal—instability, uncertainty, and self-hate—and external—a constant conflict over group belonging and a lack of role definition, with ostracism by either group possible.

From these basic assumptions about the nature of human development, Lewin (1939) derives a number of statements that de-

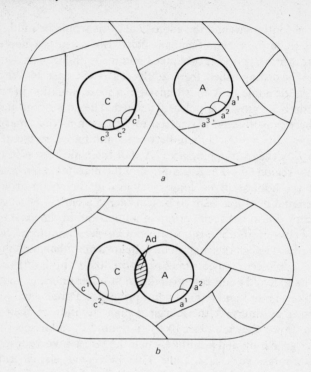

FIGURE 7. The adolescent as a marginal man. (a) During childhood and adulthood the "adults" (A) and "children" (C) are viewed as relatively separated groups, the individual child (c^1, c^2) and the individual adult (a^1, a^2) being sure of their belonging to their respective groups. (b) The adolescent belonging to a group (Ad) which can be viewed as an overlapping region of the children's (C) and the adults' (A) group belonging to both of them, or as standing between them, not belonging to either one.

From Kurt Lewin, The Field Theory Approach to Adolescence. *American Journal of Sociology,* 1939, *44,* 868–897. Reproduced by permission from The University of Chicago Press.

scribe, explain, and if the field forces are known, predict adolescent behavior:

1. The adolescent may show shyness and sensitivity, but at the same time aggressiveness may occur, mainly because of the unclearness of the situation and the disequilibrium in the adolescent's life space.

2. As a marginal man, the adolescent experiences a continuous conflict among different attitudes, values, ideologies, and life styles, since he is shifting his orientation from the childhood group to the adult group, but he really does not belong to either. Therefore, he experiences lack of social anchorage, except in relationship to his peer group.

3. These conflicts in values, attitudes, and ideologies result in increased emotional tension.

4. There is a predisposition in the adolescent to take radical positions and to change behavior drastically; consequently, one can find radical, rebellious attitudes and actions side by side with sensitivity and withdrawal tendencies.

5. "Adolescent behavior" can be observed only if and to the extent that the structure and the dynamics of the life space involve the following: (1) expansion and differentiation of the life space; (2) marginal man standing in relationship to childhood and adult groups; (3) biologically determined changes in the life space, as a result of body changes. The particular type of behavior that emerges and the degree of "adolescent behavior" depend greatly on the strength and nature of these conflicting forces. Above all in importance is the amount of difference between—and the factors that separate—adult society and child society in a particular culture.

The question of universality of the adolescent phenomenon is one of statistical frequency. Lewinian field theory (1935) considers this question irrelevant as well as the question of whether heredity or environment is the greater influence on development. They are irrelevant because knowing that a certain phenomenon, such as adolescence, occurs 100 percent, 80 percent, or 60 percent of the time does not give any insight into the dynamics of the developing individual. Nor does it show the relative influence of physical-development, social, and emotional factors, or how they oppose and influence each other.

What is . . . important to the investigation of dynamics is not to abstract from the situation, but to hunt out those situations in which determinative factors of the total dynamic structure are most clearly, distinctly, and purely to be discerned. Instead of a reference to the abstract average of as many historically given cases as possible, there is a reference to the full concreteness of the particular situations [Lewin, 1935: 31].

The dynamic aspect of adolescent behavior, not the statistical frequency of one event or another, is the concern of field theory.

According to Lewin, specific characteristics of individuals cannot be classified in categories of overt behavior. Field theory moves away from classification systems; it assumes that there are great individual differences and sees as its objective the systematic explanation of these differences. Sensitivity to environmental influences varies greatly among people. The speed with which the differentiation and structurization of the life space takes place also varies considerably in different people. Therefore, we must expect great individual variations in behavior. Furthermore, since sensitivity as well as rate of change in the life space increases during the adolescent period, we must expect that behavior changes also will differ widely and probably more noticeably than at other times.

Moreover, field theory assumes not only individual differences, but cultural differences as well. Thus, while the life space varies from individual to individual within a given culture, the differences from culture to culture are even greater. Two aspects that will be relatively stable within a given culture but quite different from culture to culture are (1) the ideologies, attitudes, and values that are recognized and emphasized, and (2) the way in which different activities are seen as related or unrelated (for example, religion and work are more closely related in Mennonite society than in American society as a whole) (Lewin, 1942).

Another factor that may account for cultural differences in adolescent behavior is the varying length of the adolescent period from culture to culture and from social class to social class within a culture. Furthermore, the degree to which the child group and the adult group are differentiated in a given culture has far-reaching consequences for adolescent behavior. The more clearly they are separated, the more difficult the transition.

Roger Barker's Somatopsychological Theory of Adolescence

Roger Barker and others expanded and elaborated Lewin's theory of adolescent development in "Somatopsychological Significance of Physical Growth in Adolescence" (1953). Barker applies field theory to show the effects of physiological changes on behavior during adolescence. His goal is to develop hypotheses that provide insight into the dynamics by which changes in physiological structure influence behavior. Barker bases his hypothesis of a somatopsychological mechanism on these assumptions:

1. Adolescents are moving toward the social status, physical maturity, strength, and motor control of adults. But they are not yet adults; they are in an intermediate position between adults and children. They are in a marginal or transitory period, to use Lewin's terms.
2. Body dimensions, physique, and endocrinological changes occur at an accelerated speed, as compared to the preadolescent years.
3. The time and speed of changes in physique vary greatly among individuals, and these differences are more noticeable than during any other period of development. They are not only more noticeable but also more consequential, as the research on early and late maturation clearly demonstrates.
4. There are great differences within a given individual in the degree of maturity attained by different parts of the body. This phenomenon of asynchronous body growth has been described by Stolz and Stolz (1944) and is emphasized in Zeller's (1951, 1952) theory.

We can predict two psychological situations from these known facts about adolescent physical development: first, "new psychological situations" will arise during adolescence; and second, experiential psychological situations will take place in which "overlapping of the psychological field" occurs.

Lewin stated that great cultural differences in adolescent behavior can be explained in terms of whether the child group and the adult group are two clearly distinguishable social groups or one undifferentiated social group with easy locomotion from one segment to the other. Barker continues this argument by assuming that in the United States the child group is clearly separated from the adult group, for whom different forms of behavior are accepted. Children have a social position equivalent to that of a minority group; this increases the difficulty of moving from one group to the other. The possibility of moving from one social group to the other is determined informally by one's physique: looking like an adult makes it easier to get adult privileges. Formally, adult privileges and responsibilities are determined by law and come at a legally established age.

Barker applies the properties of the "new psychological situation" to adolescence in this way:

1. In a new psychological situation, the course of action to be followed to reach a certain goal is unknown. This means that a given individual cannot accurately predict what behavior will bring him closer to the desired goal. Lewin (1942) describes this situation in detail, comparing it to moving into a strange town.

2. In an unknown situation, the valence is positive and negative at the same time, because the individual does not know whether a certain kind of behavior will bring him closer to or further away from his goal.

3. In an unknown situation, "the perceptual structure is unstable" (Barker, 1953: 30), the psychological dynamics that result from an unknown situation are unclear, indefinite, and ambiguous. Small changes in the perceptual field of a given individual may change the total field.

From these considerations Barker derives behavioral characteristics that can be observed in an individual if he operates, as the adolescent does, in a new psychological situation in which directions are unknown (Assumption #1).

a. The behavior will not be parsimonious as it was in the familiar situation in which the direction was known and the individual responded by habit, selecting the simplest route to his goal. In the new and unknown situation, he again must respond by exploration and trial and error to reach his goal. He will pursue a course of action until he finds that it does not bring him closer to the goal. Then he will begin another course of action and repeat this trial-and-error process until he reaches his goal. Awkwardness and timidity in dating behavior of early adolescence is an illustration of such a situation.

b. Since a person cannot foresee the consequences of a course of action, frequent errors will make him cautious. But, in addition to caution, this exploratory situation also produces a tendency toward radical and extreme moves. The discrepancy in adolescence between ideals and aspirations on the one hand and actual achievements on the other has been reported frequently both on theoretical (Spanger, 1955) and on empirical grounds (Wylie and Hutchins, 1967). Adolescents are quicker in providing verbal solutions to basic social problems than are more experienced adults. This is due partly to the increased time perspective and a desire to grow up, to achieve, and to succeed, which invites the making of long-range goals, and is also partly due to the inability to foresee obstacles and consequences of actions.

c. The unknown in the new situation, since it offers resistance to locomotion, is actually experienced as a barrier to the goal. Frustration builds up; aggressive, emotional, and disruptive behavior must be expected as a result.

Similarly, Barker derives behavioral characteristics from the assumption that the "valence is simultaneously positive and negative" (Barker, 1953: 36) (Assumption #2).

a. Positive valence will bring an advance toward the goal; negative valence will bring about a withdrawal. Since both are present simultaneously, the adolescent will be in conflict, trying to advance and withdraw at the same time. Consequently, emotionally disruptive behavior may occur, especially if the goal is important.

b. If the positive or negative valences shift, the individual will advance or retreat accordingly.

c. If in a given situation the valence is simultaneously positive and negative, the adolescent will be on the lookout for cues; he will move cautiously, trying to "feel" whether his behavior leads to success or failure.

From the third definition in which the new psychological situation was characterized as "perceptual structure is unstable" (Barker, 1953: 36), Barker derives the following behavioral characteristics (Assumption #3).

a. Behavior will depend on the perception of the situation. Since the adolescent's perceptual structure is unstable, his behavior will be unstable and vacillating. The first adolescent realization of the contradictions between the values taught by adults and the failure of adults to live and succeed by their own beliefs presents a new psychological situation that may change the child's outlook toward life, since he cannot easily reconcile a discrepancy between the ideal and the real.

b. The less stable the situation, the more the individual depends upon small and sometimes unimportant cues. Behavior can be influenced easily; the adolescent has little resistance to suggestion. This is especially true for suggestions coming from the social group he wants to belong to. Peer group conformity is the psychological response to living in an unstable situation. The high degree of uniformity observed among adolescents can be explained as an attempt to structure the field, which is experienced as unstable by the individual.

The alternative overlapping situation refers to the uneven rate of maturity of different organic or functional aspects of adolescence. For example, an adolescent may show signs of emotional immaturity, but he may look like an adult. Or an adolescent may have a child's physique but already have had a voice change. While Lewin emphasizes that the adolescent is the marginal man in social group belonging, Barker stresses the ambiguous situation that results from overlapping in body growth, emphasizing the somato-psychological significance of development. His hypothesis is this: because of the rapidity and ambiguity of their physical changes, adolescents are in a marginal situation; their behavior often is determined at the same time by childhood and adult values and expectations. This lack of consistency in value orientation accounts for the problems involved in so-called adolescent behavior.

Barker says there are three aspects in the overlapping situation:

1. *Congruence.* ". . . two or more overlapping psychological situations differ in the degree to which the behavior in each is congruent" (Barker, 1953: 39). The degree to which forms of behavior in a certain overlapping situation differ or agree makes a further breakdown necessary. In the first instance, the "overlapping conso-

nant situation," the behavior required to reach two or more goals is practically identical. An example from the adolescent world would be the behavior needed to learn to box and develop muscular strength. Learning to box systematically makes muscles strong. The forces involved will "strengthen instead of weaken each other" (Lewin, 1938).

In the second overlapping situation, the actions taken to reach the one goal do not interfere with the behavior needed to reach the second goal; they are compatible. For example, an adolescent can get a high school education and make friends. But going to school does not automatically result in making friends, in the way that boxing increases strength. Barker (1953) calls this the "overlapping compatible situation."

In the third instance, we have a situation in which behavior necessary to reach one goal interferes with, but does not completely disrupt, behavior required to obtain another goal—say, getting an education and supporting a family. This is the "overlapping interfering situation."

Finally, we have the situation in which the behavior necessary to obtain one goal is incompatible with that required to reach another goal, for example, to drive a car in traffic and kiss a girl. This is the "overlapping antagonistic situation."

The adolescent frequently finds himself in one of the latter two situations when his desires, ambitions, and aspirations reach into the adult world, where age, law, limited experience, and parents interfere.

2. *Potency.* The concept of potency represents the relative influence a particular factor or goal in a given psychological field has upon behavior, as a result of an overlapping situation. Thus, learning to box and wanting to develop physical strength are, probably, subordinate to other goals in the life space and have a relatively low potency. Conversely, it may be assumed that if an adolescent supports a family and continues his education, both factors consume a relatively large segment of his life space and have a relatively high potency. "The relative potency is important for group membership in case of belonging to several overlapping groups" (Lewin, 1938: 202). It is not primarily the fact that the adolescent belongs to several groups that causes adjustment difficulties; it is his uncer-

tainty concerning his group loyalties. He may have to choose between old childhood friends or belonging to the "in-group." Also, the relative importance of the family over the peer group during the transition years is not always clear, and sometimes this uncertainty creates conflict.

3. *Valence.* Of further importance in an overlapping situation is the valence each of the goals holds for the individual. From the examples given, any one of the two possible forms of behavior could have a relatively large or small valence in comparison to the other. In Lewin's terminology, the valence a goal has can vary. For example, for one individual making friends can be far more important than getting an education; for another person making friends is secondary to getting an education. The behavior and attitudes of these two individuals would differ greatly. "Potency" refers to the relative influence of one goal as compared with all other goals, whereas "valence" refers to the actual attraction or repulsion of one given goal. In the case of the adolescent, generally speaking, adult privileges have a higher positive valence than those of childhood, which frequently have a negative valence.

Educational Implications

The adolescent and his problems are related to his change in group belonging. He no longer belongs to the child group and is no longer considered a child. Nor does he yet belong to the adult group and receive its privileges, even though adult activities may have a positive valence for him. Thus, he is in a stage of social locomotion; he is transferring from one group to another but does not belong to either one. He is a "social outcast," to use a somewhat extreme term. This condition necessarily makes him more dependent upon his own age group for support, inspiration, fellowship, and idols than either children or adults are dependent upon their age groups. These insights gained through field theory may be used as psychological arguments in favor of the junior high school, since this is the age group in which the accelerated change in body maturity and the shift in group belonging is most obvious. Counterarguments concerning the psychological effects of the junior high school are advanced by Mead and were presented in the previous chapter.

An important factor in adolescent development is the enlargement, differentiation, and conceptualization of the time perspective. The young child lives mainly in the present; the past and the future include only a few days or weeks and have relatively little effect on his behavior. As a child grows older, and especially during the adolescent period, he develops a time concept that makes the past significant to him. He can now understand historical occurrences in their chronological sequence. Lewin's concept of the enlargement of the time perspective during adolescence coincides with the teaching of history at the onset of adolescence and has been supported by research studies. But the time concept expands not only into the past but also into the future, which now becomes meaningful for the child. He begins to plan his life, set his goals. He has to make choices in his training and prepare for a vocation. This bespeaks the necessity for vocational guidance.

Adolescence is a period in which reality and irreality should be clearly distinguished, even though irreality will not necessarily disappear completely from the thought of the adolescent. It is important for the educator to emphasize the understanding of reality and to confront the adolescent with facts when his responses become fabrications based on fantasy or irreality.

The adolescent's social awareness of group belonging undergoes great change, as do his body and body image. The child "knew" his body or showed little interest in it, but sexual maturity disturbs the adolescent, and the new dimensions, qualities, and functions of his body sometimes threaten him. Thus, a very close and vital part of his life space, his own body, becomes foreign and produces tension. Since body image is a fundamental region in the life space, this change leads to confusion, conflict, and uncertainty of behavior. Education probably will not be able to overcome all the difficulties related to body change, but it can at least prepare the adolescent boy and girl for these changes by helping them understand human growth and by giving them knowledge of the great normal variations in physical development.

The infant and the child must have their life space structured by their parents and other adults. But as they grow older, the restrictions and limitations should be removed slowly so that the young adult is allowed to structure his own world. From an educational point of view, this means that the adolescent should be encouraged to develop independence and responsibility by setting his own goals and choosing his own methods to reach them.

Field theory presents the total situation, with all the aspects that make up the child's life space. If teaching is to be successful and produce the maximum amount of learning, the activities involved should have a positive valence for the student. Field theory holds that success in teaching depends on all of those conditions of learning that have been singled out by one or another educational theory—the social atmosphere, the amount of security, the interest and meaningfulness of the material, its psychological appropriateness for the developmental level of the learner, and the atmosphere in which the material is taught.

Lewin suggested, as do other phenomenologically oriented psychologists, that what is more important psychologically speaking is the subject's perception of an event, rather than the objective reality. This implies that a teacher must make a genuine effort to understand the student's perception of the situation—that is, to try to empathize with his point of view. An illustration is the not uncommon observation that two students perform about the same on an examination and both receive a B grade. However, their psychological experience of success or failure is not so much dependent on the objective reality of their performance, but on their expectation. The student who expected an A is disappointed and perhaps even angry. The student who feared a C or worse is encouraged and feels elated. Understanding behavior is only possible through a reconstruction and understanding of the perceptual field of the behavior. Facts acquired in this way may be quite different from those obtained by an objective approach. Psychoanalysis, clinical psychology, Gestalt psychology, and field theory have applied this method within its natural limitations. Understanding the other person is also an important issue in Spranger's psychology of adolescence. However, the phenomenological viewpoint raises the question whether it is possible to see the world or a particular issue as another person sees it.

8

Social Psychology and Adolescence

Allison Davis' Concept of Socialized Anxiety

Allison Davis (1902–) in "Socialization and Adolescent Personality" (1944), defines "socialization" as the process by which an individual learns and adapts the ways, ideas, beliefs, values, and norms of his culture and makes them part of his personality. He sees development as a continuous process of learning socially acceptable behavior by means of reinforcement and punishment. Acceptable and unacceptable behavior are defined by each society, or its socializing agents, the subgroups, social classes, or castes. Cultural behavior is acquired through social learning. Understanding the effects of social learning on adolescents is the crucial issue in Davis' theory.

Since punishment, threats, and withdrawal of love are used to foster the development of acceptable forms of behavior and inhibit the expression of undesirable forms, they are frequently anticipated in new learning situations. This anticipated fear of punishment as a result of repeated social reinforcement brings about what Davis calls "socialized anxiety," which becomes an important factor in facilitating the socialization process.* Socialized anxiety is adaptive in nature and culturally useful. The child learns to aspire to socially approved behavior and to avoid behavior that is punished.

---

*Davis sees the first source of anxiety in the cleanliness training of the child.

However, what is approved and what is punished are dependent on his age, sex, race, and social class. Socialized anxiety must be distinguished from neurotic anxiety, which is nonadaptive and irrational. Socialized anxiety serves as a motivating and reinforcing agent in the socialization process: it brings about, in Mowrer's (1939) words, "anticipation of discomfort" and becomes a behavior-controlling mechanism. During adolescence, it becomes internalized and increasingly independent of its reinforcing or socializing agents. It is Davis' (1944) hypothesis that the effective socialization of adolescent behavior is dependent upon the amount of adaptive or socialized anxiety that has been implanted in an individual. If an individual's socialized anxiety becomes strong enough, it will serve as an impetus toward mature, responsible, normal behavior. It is implied that if socialized anxiety is too weak or too strong, the attainment of mature behavior is less likely.

The goals of socialization differ not only from culture to culture, but also from social class to social class within a given culture, as demonstrated by social psychologists such as Davis and Havighurst. Consequently, social anxiety becomes attached to various forms of behavior depending upon the expectations, values, and definition of what is normal in a given social class. For example, the middle-class child acquires moral values, needs, and social goals different from those of either the lower- or the upper-class child. Furthermore, since the middle class is more concerned with normality, success, morality, and status, the amount of socially instilled anxiety is greater than in the other classes. It is characteristic of middle-class youth that his social anxiety increases with the onset of adolescence, since he faces new developmental and behavioral tasks, such as preparation for work and heterosexual adjustment. Furthermore, as he becomes increasingly aware of his own social needs—having prestige, friends, being accepted by the peer group, relating to the opposite sex—he becomes more sensitive to social cues and social pressures. Since he depends greatly upon social acceptance, prestige, and status, his social anxiety increases. This produces an increased striving for socially desirable goals. "Adolescents with a strongly developed social anxiety, therefore, usually strive for the approved social goals most eagerly and learn most successfully" (Davis, 1944: 208).

Lower-class adolescents behave differently from those in the middle class in such areas of socialization as sex expression, attitudes toward long-range goals, aggression, and formal schooling. The lower-class adolescent has been exposed to socializing agents whose attitudes toward these areas are quite different from those of the middle class. He does not develop the kind of socialized anxiety that motivates his middle-class counterpart to achieve and to postpone immediate pleasure for long-range goals. Furthermore, he has learned by trial and error that he is not likely to receive the rewards available to middle-class adolescents even if he studies his lessons, is a "good little boy," and avoids the sexual and recreational activities of his peers. "This means that the culture determines (1) what the goal-responses are for a given adolescent, (2) the degree to which the goal-responses are available to him. With regard to a great many goals, what is rewarding to a middle-class adolescent is not at all so to a lower-class adolescent" (Davis, 1944: 209).

Robert Havighurst's Developmental Tasks of Adolescence

In Robert Havighurst's (1900–   ) book *Developmental Tasks and Education* (1951) the emphasis shifts from the social motivation that guides the behavior of the individual, namely social anxiety, to the criteria by which society defines the attainment of certain stages of development; however, these criteria are related to the needs of the organism. "A developmental task is midway between an individual need and a societal demand" (Havighurst, 1951: 4). Developmental tasks are defined as skills, knowledge, functions, and attitudes that an individual has to acquire at a certain point in his life; they are acquired through physical maturation, social expectations, and personal efforts. Successful mastery of these tasks will result in adjustment and will prepare the individual for the harder tasks ahead. Failure in a given developmental task will result in a lack of adjustment, increased anxiety, social disapproval, and the inability to handle the more difficult tasks to come. A rather important aspect of the concept of developmental tasks is its sequential nature; each task is the prerequisite for the next one. Furthermore, there is for at least some of these tasks a biological basis and, consequently, there is a definite time limit within which a specific task must be accomplished. Inability to master a task within its time limit may make later learning of that task much more difficult if not impossible. In other words, there is a "teachable moment" for many developmental tasks. Through its socializing agents and methods of reinforcement and punishment, society attempts to help the individual learn those developmental tasks at their proper age levels. Psychologically speaking, the teachable moment is the correct time for teaching and learning a given task. This time element is determined by maturation, social pressures and demands, and motivation. These three factors should be considered in curriculum planning, if the student is to learn most effectively and with the least waste of energy by both the teacher and the student.

It is Havighurst's assumption that the specific nature of the developmental tasks differs from culture to culture, the degree of difference depending on the relative importance of biological, psychological, and cultural elements in a given task. If the cultural element in a task is dominant over the biological, then greater differences in the nature of that task are likely to be observed from culture to culture.

Havighurst (1951) describes the nature of the task; the biological, psychological, and cultural bases; the differences in the upper, middle, and lower classes in America; and educational implications. The developmental tasks for adolescence (from about twelve to eighteen) are:

1. Accepting one's physique and accepting a masculine or feminine role. FUCK OFF
2. New relations with age-mates of both sexes.
3. Emotional independence of parents and other adults.
4. Achieving assurance of economic independence.
5. Selecting and preparing for an occupation.
6. Developing intellectual skills and concepts necessary for civic competence.
7. Desiring and achieving socially responsible behavior.
8. Preparing for marriage and family life. DTO
9. Building conscious values in harmony with an adequate scientific world-picture (Havighurst, 1951: 30–55).

The achievement of these tasks might be taken as an indication that adulthood and maturity have been achieved. However, a new set of developmental tasks awaits the "Early Adulthood" period, just as a set of "Middle Childhood Tasks" preceded those listed previously.

A study by Schoeppe and Havighurst (1952) demonstrates that good achievement on one developmental task is positively related to good performance on another task at the same age. They also found that the performance in any one of these areas is positively related to future performance in that area. Furthermore, the early period of adolescence, between ten and thirteen, is crucial for socialization in that changes in level of performance were found before thirteen, but relatively little change was observed between thirteen and sixteen.

Developmental tasks 1, 2, and 8 listed previously have an obvious biological basis and should therefore be found in every society, even though the specific behavior may vary somewhat because of social mores. The biological basis in 3, 5, and 6 is less obvious, but nevertheless present. These adolescent tasks exist in every society, though the behavior involved may differ greatly from one society to another. Developmental tasks 4, 7, and 9 have no biological basis and therefore are characteristic of some societies, but not of others. Havighurst included them because he is especially concerned with adolescence in the United States, where these tasks are required in order to meet the Early Adulthood Tasks.

Havighurst, in the formulation of his theory of developmental tasks, draws upon several theories of adolescence that emphasize only certain aspects of adolescent development. He credits Williams (1930) with the original idea of specific tasks that are most important for the adjustment of boys and girls of this age group: "(1) to become emotionally independent of the family and (2) to achieve a good relationship with age-mates of the opposite sex" (Havighurst, 1951: 1) (Havighurst's tasks 2 and 3). Also, Rank in his theory of adolescence puts great emphasis on the achievement of emotional independence (task 3). For Adler, the acceptance of the feminine or masculine role takes on great importance, especially for girls (task 1). For Freud, sexual adjustment, as expressed in developmental tasks 2 and 8, seems to be fundamental. Spranger emphasizes the building of a conscious value system (task 9). Erikson's concept of ego-identity is reflected in tasks 1, 3, and 7. Lewin's concept of increased organization and differentiation of the adolescent's life space encompasses tasks 2, 3, 5, and 7. Obviously Havighurst's developmental tasks theory is an eclectic one combining previously developed concepts and constructs.

9

Arnold Gesell's Theory of Adolescent Development

Arnold Gesell's (1880–1961) theory of adolescent development is a natural and integral part of his general developmental theory. His three best known works, *Infant and Child in the Culture of Today* (1943), *The Child from Five to Ten* (1946a), and *Youth: The Years from Ten to Sixteen* (1956), constitute a trilogy describing human growth and development from birth to adolescence. A systematic statement of Gesell's general theory of development can be found in his "The Ontogenesis of Infant Behavior" (1946b). Gesell's biologically oriented theory of predetermined maturation reflects the strong influence of Hall's theory of development. Gesell drew certain parallels between the evolution of the human race and the ontogenesis of the growing child, returning in a way to Hall's theory of recapitulation. He assumed, as did Freud, that development is biological in nature; however, he rejected the idea that unconscious motives direct and form actions, emotions, and personality structure. Gesell's emphasis on overt observable behavior and the more tangible aspects of personality is reflected in his definition of personality as "the total psychic individual as manifested in action and attitude" (Gesell, 1956: 32). Gesell was mainly interested in the behavioral manifestations of development and personality, rather than their structure.* His constructs of growth gradient as revealed in stages and cycles of development are like certain developmental theories advanced in central Europe, which will be discussed in Chapter 10.

In the introductory chapter of *Youth,* Gesell refers to his subjects as "adolescents" as well as "youths." However, in an earlier publication (1946a), he states, as did Hall, that adolescence is a period from about eleven to twenty-four; the term "youth" refers only to the earlier half of the adolescent period.

Gesell's study of growth and development is fundamentally normative. In his trilogy, he described the overall pattern of developmental trends and the "norms" of behavior in their chronological sequence. One can compare a given child with this schedule of development in order to assess the degree of precocity or immaturity. However, critics have pointed out that there are certain dangers in relying too much on normative descriptive data, especially when the concern is with a particular individual. A parent cannot really compare his own child's development to tables of averages without considering the great diversity and variability in human behavior and development. Lack of awareness of the difference between an average and an individual can result in much anxiety, since the average is too closely associated with "normality" and any deviation from the average, "abnormality." These not uncommon difficulties of a normative descriptive approach stem from the well-known and conclusively proved principle that there are great individual differences in onset, rate, and nature of almost all developmental phenomena. Children may deviate widely from the average without being "abnormal." Gesell (1943) was aware of this criticism; anticipating it, he devoted a whole section to "The Uses and Misuses of Age Norms." Nevertheless, he proceeded normatively and described the twelve-year-old as if twelve-year-olds had highly specific generalizable characteristics and as if

*Gesell's comments on the three levels of reality that embrace the mental life are similar to Aristotle's three-layer concept of the human soul. Gesell's three levels of reality are: "1. the vegetative functions of respiration, alimentation, elimination; 2. the world of things, in time and space; 3. the world of persons, in home and community" (Gesell, 1943: 20). However, whereas for Aristotle the lower layers of the soul had to develop before the higher could develop, Gesell saw the organism as an integrated unit, with all three levels growing simultaneously. The "mind does not grow on the installment plan" (Gesell, 1943: 20).

twelve-year-olds in general were substantially different from eleven- and thirteen-year-olds.

Gesell's Theory of Development

The concept of growth, both mental and physical, forms the core of Gesell's theory. He saw growth* as a process that brings about changes in form and function; it has its seasons and lawful sequences. To reveal these sequences, seasons, and principles of development was Gesell's objective. He emphasized that "mental growth is a patterning process; a progressive *morphogenesis* of patterns of behavior" (Gesell, 1940: 7). Growth is a process of progressive differentiation and integration. It is the concept that unifies "the dualism of heredity and environment," since environmental influence stimulates, modifies, and supports growth (Gesell, 1946b: 316). However, environmental factors do not generate the sequence of growth. This is brought about by maturation—the appearance of functions, abilities, and skills without the influence of special training or practice. Maturation is considered the intrinsic component of the more comprehensive term "growth." The relationship between growth and maturation can best be described in Gesell's own words:

> Growth is a process so intricate and so sensitive that there must be powerful stabilizing factors, intrinsic rather than extrinsic, which preserve the balance of the total pattern and the direction of the growth trend. Maturation is, in a sense, a name for this regulatory mechanism [Gesell, 1933: 232].

Furthermore, "maturation is mediated by genes" (Gesell, 1956: 27). Biology determines the order of the appearance of behavioral traits and developmental trends. For example, the infant raises his head first, then his trunk; he sits before he stands; he babbles before he talks. Gesell's theory assumes that there is an inborn biological force that determines the sequence of the occurrence of basic developmental phenomena, motor control, skills, abilities, and behavior patterns.

*Gesell used the terms "growth" and "development" interchangeably.

Even though Gesell spoke of an "inherent maturational mechanism," the term "maturation" is not connected to or identified with specific physiological processes. Genetic factors guide and control the direction and sequence of the maturation mechanism. The concept of maturation implies that the individual masters certain forms of behavior with no known direct external influence. Gesell (1929, 1941) demonstrated the genetically determined concept of maturation in studies of identical twins. The developmental principle that results from these studies—that maturation is an essential prerequisite for learning—has been verified by others. Gesell summarized: "There is no conclusive evidence that practice and exercise even hasten the actual appearance of types of reaction like climbing and tower building. The time of appearance is fundamentally determined by the ripeness of neural structures" (Gesell, 1929: 114). Although the appearance of maturationally acquired skills can be demonstrated more easily with infants and young children, Gesell (1933) applied this principle to development in general, including adolescence.

Gesell rejected as early behavioristic the idea that infants are alike at birth and that differences are due to conditioning. He advanced the following idea to reconcile his normative descriptive approach with the principle of individual differences: The child is born a unique individual with an inherited pattern of growth, but also with great plasticity. Two factors account for individual differences:

1. The "genetic factors of individual constitution and innate maturation sequence" (Gesell, 1956: 22),
2. The "environmental factors ranging from home and school to the total cultural setting" (Gesell, 1956: 22). This latter process he called "acculturation."

Both processes interact to form a particular individual growth pattern, but since maturation is of primary importance, "acculturation can never transcend maturation" (Gesell, 1943: 41).

Although development is basically a continuous process of patterning, there are fluctuations in the acquisition of specific functions. Growth takes place according to the principle of reciprocal interweaving in neuromotor development (1939). These developmental fluctuations and trends, corresponding to the ancient process of human evolution, are illustrated by the mechanical model of a spiral. Gesell (1933) spoke of a "process of continuous differentiation." Development takes place in sequential patterns or cycles. It oscillates along a spiral course of development toward maturity. The child progresses as he acquires specific functions until he reaches a certain degree of mastery. Then he reverts to earlier forms of behavior before he is able to surpass his previous performance. Plateaus may occur at either the high or low point of the developmental spiral. This theory helps explain why children return to earlier forms of development and why, for a time, they seem to be unable to accomplish those skills they were able to do well at an earlier age. Gesell perceived this downward gradient as nature's way of giving the child an opportunity to consolidate his abilities and potentialities for further development. The developmental spiral of interchanging upward and downward gradients is a growth mechanism of self-adjustment. This concept of downward gradient is like Freud's concept of regression, with one basic difference: psychoanalytic regression has a pathological aspect because it takes place when a person is unable to master a new situation. Downward gradient is an important, necessary, and natural part of the developmental process, since it provides the organism with rest and consolidation so it can move on to higher forms of achievement.

The concept of gradient of development may also be applied to adolescence. But the downward gradient cannot be demonstrated in adolescents as easily as it can with acquisition of the simple motor skills in early infancy. Growth gradients for the adolescent are well-defined stages of maturity by which the youth advances toward more complex and more mature functions. Gesell warned that growth gradients do not constitute a psychometric scale, but rather a theoretical construct that explains the growth process and helps identify and assess levels of maturity.

Gesell's Description of the Pubescent and Adolescent Period

Gesell, like Lewin, considered adolescence the crucial transition period from childhood to adulthood. The beginnings of adolescent behavior appear at approximately eleven and final maturity is reached in the early twenties. The adolescent's central task is to find himself. The period is approximately two years shorter for girls, because they develop faster. The more important changes occur in the first five years of adolescence. This is the time span Gesell (1956) called "youth" in his book on adolescence.

In the description of adolescent maturity profiles, maturity traits, and trends, Gesell drew his conclusions from a selected population segment in one geographic area of the United States. His subjects came from the high-average to superior ability range of the school population, and many of them planned to go to college. In the light of insight gained from cultural anthropology and social psychology, this is a serious limitation. But because of the postulated biological nature of development, Gesell considered many of the important and broad developmental principles, trends, and sequences to be universal. He described the innate maturational sequence and the pattern of growth as "more or less characteristic of the human species" (Gesell, 1956: 22–23).

Gesell did not systematically distinguish between pubescence and adolescence. He believed that biology controls not only changes in growth, glandular secretion, and the development of primary and secondary sex characteristics, but also abilities and attitudes; for example, "the instinctive basis of reasoning ability is repeatedly shown in the adolescence of individuals . . ." (Gesell, 1956: 181). Again, when he discussed the characteristics of sixteen-year-old girls, he stated: "the girls instinctively stressed interpersonal relationship" in describing their future husbands (Gesell, 1956: 253).

Gesell did not see adolescence as necessarily turbulent, erratic, and troublesome, as Hall pictured it in his "storm and stress" concept. He considered it a ripening process, though not without irregularities. Furthermore, the age levels he used to define the different stages of development were only considered as approximates, with a slow process of change from one level to the next and some overlapping.

Gesell objected to a purely functional psychology and to a purely theoretical developmental system; he used maturity profiles to describe the characteristics of each age level. The concepts and ideas presented in the following synopsis are from *Youth: The Years from*

Ten to Sixteen (1956), and all direct quotes refer to this book unless otherwise indicated.

The Ten-Year-Old. Gesell described the ten-year-old as being in a state of equilibrium. Ten may be considered a golden age of developmental balance; the child is able to accept life and the world with ease. Ten is fond of his home, recognizes authority, has confidence, and is obedient. He enjoys family activities such as picnics. He is also fond of friends and joins groups and organizations. He is intrigued by secret societies and other forms of secretiveness. However, his sociability is limited to his own sex. The ten-year-old boy might say, "We sort of hate girls," and the ten-year-old girl might retort, "We are not interested in boys *yet.*" Care of clothes is at a low point; so is body care. However, educationally, the ten-year-old is assimilative. He has a sense of fairness, and it is important for him that his teacher be fair. With the age of ten childhood culminates its subcycle and adolescence is in the making.

The Eleven-Year-Old. The eleven-year-old is in the foothills of adolescence. Gesell, in analogy to Lewin's new situation and new field, said that the terrain is new; the organism is in a state of change; even physiological functions undergo far-reaching reconstruction. This shows up in impulsiveness and moods, anger and enthusiasm, negativism and argumentativeness, quarreling with siblings and rebellion against parents. In agreement with the basically biological orientation of his theory, Gesell saw some of these symptoms as almost instinctive manifestations of those biological changes that mark the dawn of adolescence.

The Twelve-Year-Old. By the age of twelve much of the turbulent behavior of eleven has disappeared. Twelve becomes more reasonable, more companionable, and more sociable: "Twelve is predisposed to be positive and enthusiastic rather than negative and reticent" (p. 105). He is trying to grow up and does not wish to be considered a baby. He achieves some independence from his home and from his parents, and is now influenced more by his peer group. The twelfth year demonstrates integration of personality. His basic personality traits are reasonableness, tolerance, and humor. He is ready to take his own initiative and enters self-chosen tasks with enthusiasm. Twelve becomes aware of his appearance, especially under the influence of the crowd; he wants to wear what the crowd wears. There is a change in boy-girl relationships. Ten's antagonism toward the opposite sex has faded away. "No twelve year old party can be guaranteed immune from some sort of kissing game—a most natural expression for Twelve" (p. 122).

The Thirteen-Year-Old. The chief characteristic of the thirteen-year-old is his thrust inward. He is reflective and enters a period of introversion. Thirteen becomes his own critic and seems to be overconscientious. He worries frequently and from time to time withdraws into himself. He is sensitive to criticism, quite aware of the emotional state of others, and, generally speaking, is fascinated by the term "psychology." At this age, he indulges in detailed criticism of his parents and also in searching self-appraisals. He has fewer friends than twelve, and those friends that he does choose have many things in common with him. Great changes in body structure and body chemistry affect his behavior in many ways: posture, motor coordination, voice change, facial expression, and related tensions and attitudes. These changes increase his awareness of the fact that he is growing up. Somatic events are related to fluctuations in mood from despair to self-acceptance.

The Fourteen-Year-Old. The general developmental trend now reverses itself from a thrust inward to a period of extroversion characterized by energy, exuberance, and expansiveness. A degree of integration affects both his interpersonal relationships and his self-concept. Thus he achieves a degree of self-assurance that makes him feel content and relaxed. His sociability is expressed by a great interest in people and an understanding of personality differences. Fourteen is fascinated by the word "personality" and likes to compare and discuss personality traits. His friendships are built on identical interests and compatibility of personality traits. We may describe the fourteen-year-old's preoccupation with the intricacies of human personalities as "an instinctive amateur form of applied psychology" (p. 178). Interest in his own personality is also demonstrated by his frequent identification with heroes and characters in movies and literature; he may exclaim, "That's me. That's me all over" (p. 180).

The Fifteen-Year-Old. The fifteen-year-old cannot be "readily summed up in a simple formula" (p. 214). The description of the fifteen-year-old emphasizes individual differences, but some generalizations are made. The most important is a rising spirit of independence that manifests itself in increased tensions, with occasional blowups and hostility in parental and school relationships. The fifteen-year-old is neither antischool nor antihome, but since he is now starting to think about founding his own home and family, he wants to outgrow parental control. He wishes to have free time and free choice and may show defiance of external control. Furthermore, he is increasingly self-aware and perceptive. This shows itself in perfectionistic tendencies, self-criticism, and a beginning of self-control. Fifteen is in a vulnerable maturity zone; he can be led into behavior problems and delinquency which, along with his spirit of independence, may bring about an urge to leave school and home.

The Sixteen-Year-Old. Sixteen, the last age described, is characterized as mid-adolescence and as the prototype of the preadult. Self-awareness, self-dependence, and personal social adjustment have now achieved a remarkable degree of balance and integration. Emotions are generally controlled. He is cheerful, friendly, outgoing, and well adjusted. The rebellious spirit, so characteristic of the fifteen-year-old, has given way to a sense of independence based on self-confidence; it has lost its rebellious component. Sixteen is oriented toward the future; the girls already have matrimonial plans. There is much companionship between boys and girls, but, generally speaking, it is still on a nonromantic basis.

The developmental principle underlying these descriptions appears to be that growth occurs not in a straight, gradual, continuous pattern, but in fluctuations and oscillations. These descriptions also imply a stage theory that, rather oddly, is spaced by time intervals that approach our calendar year rather than by physiological changes or psychological characteristics. However, we observe a progression from immature to more mature stages, culminations of development, and partial reversion to less mature stages.

In spite of Gesell's emphasis on the "continuity of the growth cycle," the descriptions of age levels show some lack of gradualness and steadiness that is theoretically not fully accounted for. Emphasis is placed on cycles, subcycles, and stages, and Gesell attempted purposely "to sharpen the contrast" between personality structure and behavior in one age level and the next. "The tight, withdrawn ways of Thirteen have loosened up at fourteen. A profound change has occurred, not only within Fourteen but also in his impact upon the world around him" (p. 182). An example of behavioral change is the contrasting boy-girl relationship at eleven, twelve, and thirteen. For the twelve-year-old, Gesell reported strong interest in the opposite sex with kissing games, regular dancing groups, and first dates. "Some boys who were not interested in girls at eleven and won't be at thirteen enjoy a short period of genuine interest in girls at twelve" (p. 127). Gesell used many such examples to highlight the difference between the preceding and the succeeding age-stage.

These differences in behavior, and even in personality structure, which in Gesell's descriptions so clearly distinguish one age group from another only twelve months older, appear to be unrealistic and mystical. Development appears to be more continuous than Gesell's theory admitted. Even more mystical is Gesell's description of the kinship and similarity found between children and youth in the same stage of development but in a different subcycle. Gesell impresses upon his reader again and again the similarities of children at various age levels in different subcycles of development. "The 8-year-old is indeed an elaborated and elaborating version of the 4-year-old" (Gesell, 1946a: 159). Also: "Then as Two becomes Two-and-a-half and as Five becomes Five-and-a-half or Six, a change occurs—a change in the same direction in each case. Behavior 'loosens up,' perhaps even 'goes to pieces'; life becomes charged with equally attractive, yet incompatible, dual alternatives; 'No' and 'Mine' become prominent items of vocabulary" (p. 18). A more specific example of this kind of emphasis on the similarities between various subcycles is his observation that freckles are especially evident at both six and twelve; he does not mention them at five and eleven nor at seven and thirteen, almost as if six and twelve had greater similarities with each other than with the age level that preceded or followed each of them.

Educational Implications

Since, in Gesell's theory, maturation is an internal ripening process and growth cannot be facilitated by external factors, it is frequently assumed that time alone will solve most of the minor problems in the majority of children. Difficulties and deviations will be outgrown. This permissive attitude turns up in Gesell's support of infants' self-regulation of sleep and self-demand for food. Gesell advises against the use of emotional methods of discipline and recommends that mothers make the baby "with all its inborn wisdom a working partner" (Gesell, 1943: 57). His philosophy of child care lies somewhere between the authoritarian and the laissez-faire approach and attempts to combine a belief in self-regulation with developmental guidance. He like Rousseau believed in the wisdom of nature and emphasized that the educator must take his cues from the child.

Gesell identifies this idea of cultural guidance with democracy, and relates the future of democracy to an understanding of the principles of child development. "Indeed the further evolution of democracy demands a much more refined understanding of . . . children than our civilization has yet attained" (Gesell, 1943: 11). Since he attempts to bring about this understanding among parents, his writing appeals to the lay public rather than the academic world. Understanding of children must be anchored in understanding the processes of growth, maturation, and acculturation. By applying the idea of innate growth potentialities, the realization of which he sees as an inalienable right, Gesell makes growth into a philosophical political concept. The child embodies a "spirit of liberty" based on the developmental principle that "growth tends toward an optimum realization" (Gesell, 1933: 230). Environmental factors alone prevent optimal development—an idea more radically expressed by Rousseau. A developmental philosophy of child care based on empirical research has far-reaching consequences for a democratic society. "The new biological doctrines of growth have vast social implications—implications for child guidance, for mental diagnosis, for health supervision, for the conduct of education, and for the very arrangements of our ways of living" (Gesell, 1948: 10). Gesell compares the influence his biological psychology will have to the impact of Darwin's theory of evolution.

Gesell maintains that the school curriculum should be founded on a psychology of development rather than on a psychology of learning. Furthermore, he hopes that with increased knowledge of development, the laws of learning will "be reformulated in terms of the biology and physiology of development" (Gesell, 1946: 298). This belief follows from his emphasis on the interdependence of maturation and learning. Gesell demonstrated with identical twins that successful learning cannot take place until the maturational level appropriate for the particular kind of learning is reached. Consequently, a school curriculum should be based on psychological knowledge of the nature and sequence of maturation. The cultural pattern of teaching and learning must be adapted to the genetically determined growth pattern.

In considering the educational implications of specific age zones, we must emphasize the pupils' attitudes toward school and learning and their behavior in school. But this information may also indicate maturational trends and thus have bearing on curriculum development. The discussion will be limited to ages ten to sixteen.

Ten seems to be especially well suited for the educational processes; he is assimilative, loves to memorize, and is more inclined to identify facts, rather than correlate, conceptualize, or generalize. His attention span is short, but his interest varies widely. He is sociable and needs social organizations. If the community does not provide healthy outlets for this social need, youth will form its own gangs.

The restless, seething, and explosive form of behavior that characterizes the eleven-year-old will manifest itself in the classroom too. He will wriggle in his seat, but his exuberance will be followed by pronounced fatigue. A rather unorthodox suggestion for overcoming this fatigue is half-day school attendance. Eleven is highly competitive and especially enjoys group competition. Gesell suggests nonacademic activities such as music, art, shop, and dramatics for his spontaneity and creativeness.

Twelve's sociability results in an increased interest in group work. The group may become so important that he loses his own identity and conforms to group norms. His greater independence from adults and longer attention span make him less in need of supervision. He shows a remarkable increase in conceptual thinking, and can define such abstractions as time, space, life, law, loyalty, crime, and justice. His ability to classify and generalize also shows considerable improvement. He likes to debate and can become involved and enthusiastic in defending or advancing the "right" idea.

Thirteen becomes more reflective and evaluative; he remains cooperative and is more careful in selecting the right words, phrases, and ideas. He criticizes his own performance and may limit his argument by adding "I think." He has a better sense of responsibility and is more dependable in his work, but he is also absent-minded. Now, for the first time, he distinguishes between liking the teacher and liking the subject. Since he is getting interested in hobbies, he needs extracurricular activities. His interests now include world affairs, political history, the solar system, nuclear science, and the weather. He shows interest in the different branches of science; psychology seems especially fascinating.

Fourteen attempts to improve his command of language and enters the ideational realm. His tendency toward sociability becomes of greater importance than his academic interest. He is curious about himself and his personality traits; this makes guidance and counseling especially important. Gesell suggests a school unit just for fourteen-year-olds, because fourteen is the pivotal year in the cycle of human development.

Fifteen shows a craving for independence that may make him rebel against school, especially if he feels controlled and restricted. The need "to be on his own" may make him want to leave school and home. Participation in community experiences are suggested for this age. He is susceptible to peer group influences and may be quite a challenge to the teacher. But if he meets his need for independence, the teacher can produce integration of knowledge and high achievement.

Sixteen shows the first signs of a mature mind and the maturity traits are balanced and integrated. His attitudes toward school, teacher, learning, and himself improve. He begins to "buckle down," works on his own, and accepts responsibility. Gesell's description of the cycle breaks off at sixteen, even though this is not the end of the adolescent period.

10

Central European Stage Theories of Adolescent Development

Ernst Kretschmer's Typology Applied to Adolescent Development

Ernst Kretschmer (1881–1964) is better known for his typology of personality, which associated body configuration of somatotype with psychiatric disorders, than for his theoretical contributions to developmental psychology. The developmental applications of Kretschmer's theory are actually made by some of his followers: Conrad, Stratz, and Zeller. The basic assumption underlying their theory is that similarities exist among certain adult personality types and some of the outstanding characteristics of various developmental periods. Kretschmer (1951) investigated the relationship between the physical constitution of his psychiatric patients and their mental illnesses. The findings of his studies have been received rather skeptically in the United States, since additional investigations produced results that were less definitive. However, the interest in the relationship between somatotype and personality or temperament has remained high, and the closely related studies investigating the relationship between early and late maturation and personality traits are reviewed in detail in most adolescent development texts.

Kretschmer had observed that schizophrenic tendencies occurred frequently in people with linear or "leptosome" or "asthenic" body type and that schizophrenia was not uncommon in the person with an athletic body type. On the other hand, manic depressive tendencies or personality patterns characterized by al-

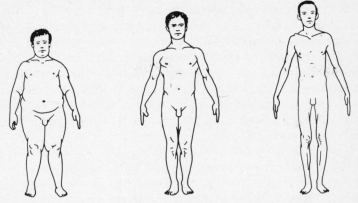

FIGURE 8. The endomorphic (left), mesomorphic (middle), and ectomorphic (right) body types according to Sheldon.

Adapted from Sheldon, 1940.

ternating periods of elation and sadness appeared more frequently among individuals with a stocky or "pyknic" body constitution. Kretschmer's typology postulating three basic types of body constitution has been extended through the work of Sheldon (1940) in the United States and Parnell (1964) in England.

Kretschmer's pyknic type corresponds to Sheldon's endomorphic type in which the body has a tendency toward shortness, roundness, softness, and fat depositions. The personality traits most commonly associated with pyknic or endomorphic somatotype are those of the friendly but nonassertive fat man: food-oriented, comfort seeking, dependent, poor in sports and in risk-taking behavior, sociable but lacking in leadership qualities. Since the personality is based on a concern with the viscera, Sheldon uses the term "viscerotonic type" to describe the personality most commonly found in the endomorphic somatotype.

Kretschmer's athletic type is referred to as mesomorphic by Sheldon; the body appears to be hard, muscular, energetic, and strong boned. Sheldon describes the personality of the mesomorphic body type as somatotonic, and the individual is action- and power-oriented. The somatotonic type is the social leader—the individual is popular, self-assured, aggressive, dominant, daring, and ambitious. He seeks adventure, excels in gross motor activity and loves risk-taking. The muscular athletic adolescent tends to mature early, so that the social advantages of the body type and the developmental acceleration reinforce each other. In addition the mesomorphic body type has the advantage of being closest to an aesthetic and social ideal. Consequently, the individual receives more positive social responses from both sexes and gains in social status. Among adolescents it is the preferred body type for both sexes (Staffieri, 1973).

Kretschmer's leptosome-asthenic or Sheldon's ectomorphic type is fragile, slender, and linear in body build. His personality is cerebrotonic and described as introverted, shy, low in energy, detached, inhibited, nervous, and neither daring nor assertive; he is sometimes referred to as the self-punishing type who avoids attracting attention to himself. Adolescents give the ectomorphic body type an unfavorable evaluation. The ectomorphic adolescent frequently matures late and experiences the combined disadvantages of his somatotype and his late maturation.

Conrad (1941), accepting Kretschmer's findings concerning the relationship between body constitution and character, describes the "cycloid" adult type as relatively childlike in his behavior and outlook toward life and, conversely, late childhood as a "cycloid period." Early adolescence he describes as a developmental phase with "schizoid" characteristics—that is, he postulated psychological disorganization. Since the developmental phase of adolescence is determined partly by the already present personality, partly by the characteristics of that developmental phase, the degree of adolescent disturbance depends on the degree of congruency of personality type and developmental type. Since adolescence is a "schizoid" developmental period, the schizoid personality is likely to experience a rather disturbing period and, in extreme cases, dementia praecox. The cycloid individual may experience only mild forms of disturbance when going through the developmental period of pubescence, since his personality type and developmental type may well balance each other.

Stratz (1923) has related Kretschmer's idea concerning somatotype and personality type to the growth pattern of the body. He finds that the childhood period, which was described as having cycloid characteristics, is a period of "filling out" and weight increase not due to growth. Similarly, Stratz related the preadolescent growth spurt, which he calls a period of "increase in height," to the schizoid characteristics of early adolescence. A temporary growth tendency toward an asthenic body type and a disposition toward inwardness and social withdrawal should be expected in early adolescence.

Oswald Kroh's Developmental Theory of Stages and Phases

Oswald Kroh (1888–1955), late professor at the University of Berlin, was concerned with the psychological aspects of consciousness as manifested at different age levels. He claimed that he was able to identify mental strata. These strata have nothing in common with the morphological-physiological brain structure, which theories of stratification of personality use as their model. Although Kroh has become best known through his work on the phenomenon of eidetic imagery,* the main emphasis in his work has been on developmental psychology.

There was a tendency in German psychological writing, before Kroh's early publications, to describe and investigate psychological functions, such as attention, memory, thinking, emotions, and volition, as independent aspects of the developmental process. Kroh (1944, 1951), however, agreed with organismic and Gestalt theory that the principle of wholeness has validity for human development. Through the concept of phase structure, Kroh advanced the idea that it is always the whole personality that develops, but the child's experiences and behavior differ during different stages of the developmental process.

Kroh observed two developmental trends; both deal with the mental content and structure of consciousness. In the first trend, the emphasis is on the expansion of the child's concept of the world. This trend begins with the physiognomic world view and unreflected expressions of the small child. It expands to the child's expression and application of magical thoughts and mystical expe-

---

*Eidetic imagery refers to the ability to recall mental images, usually visual, with a great deal of accuracy, clarity, and vividness (photographic memory).

riences. Then he goes through a period of realistic perception of the world. Finally, he reaches a deeper understanding and a philosophy of life that must be considered a symptom of maturity.

The second developmental trend emphasizes the child's action. It begins with reflex action, motor control, and purposeful action, moves on to anticipated planning of work, trial-and-error approaches in solving practical problems, and finally comes to the point of causal cognition and creative production.

Kroh's (1951) theory of phases of development appears to be widely accepted in central Europe, especially in the fields of school psychology and the psychological foundations of curriculum planning. According to his theory, development occurs in distinguishable rhythms, from which a law of psychological development follows. He divides the period of development into three "stages," each of which is subdivided into three "phases." Each stage is built upon the previous one, and each has certain definite challenges that must be mastered in order to ensure normal development. The similarity to Havighurst's (1951) developmental tasks is obvious. Every stage in this process has its special purpose and meaning for achieving maturity. From an educational point of view no stage or phase should be neglected; on the contrary, education should be concerned with the implementation of the meaning of each stage. This point might be demonstrated by the case of German children during the war who experienced destruction, evacuation, separation, and threats to their very existence, and who lacked possibilities for harmonious play development. In postwar camps, these children, grown into adolescence, demonstrated a need for play on a level far below what would be expected for their age. They behaved as if they were making up for some of the lost or unfinished childhood play activities (Arnold, 1954).

Kroh's (1944, 1951) three main stages of development are: (1) infancy and early childhood, characterized by a physiognomic world view; (2) elementary school years, with a realistic world view; and (3) adolescence, with the beginning of a theoretical world view and the attainment of maturity.

The three main stages are separated from one another by negativistic periods during which the child acts "in spite." During these negativistic periods qualitative changes take place, old characteristics diminish, and new ones come into existence. These changes result in a restructuring of the psyche and bring about a loosening or disintegration of the psychic structure. This disintegration results in an increased lability of external behavior and an increased internal insecurity. The first period of negativism occurs during the third and fourth years of life and the second during the twelfth year of life, marking the end of childhood and the beginning of adolescence.

Each of the three stages is subdivided into three phases. The first stage includes the period from birth to the beginning of the first period of negativism. The three phases of this first stage are (1) a primitive mode of life in which reflex actions are frequent, (2) contact with the external world manifested in the first smile and the recognition of faces, and (3) the beginning of intellectual functions, speech, and locomotion. Similarities between the nature of Kroh's stages and those of Piaget (Chapter 11) are obvious.

The child reaches the second stage by way of the first period of negativism. This stage, which includes kindergarten and the elementary school years, is a period of realism. Kroh describes the three phases of the second stage of development as: (1) "fantasy-like realism," with fantasy and affective impressions not yet clearly differentiated; (2) "naïve realism," in which the earlier synthetic view is superseded by a more analytic way of thinking; and (3) "critical realism," with the child beginning to reflect on experiences and observations, to think more logically, and to understand consistent relationships between natural events.

The transition from childhood to adolescence is brought about by a second period of negativism, during which the child rebels against authority and withdraws from social interaction. Rebellion against parental authority may be viewed as the breaking of the umbilical cord of emotional dependency.

Kroh refers to the third stage, which corresponds to adolescence, as the "time of maturation." It is characterized by a theoretical apperception of the world. This period begins a year later for boys than for girls, and lasts longer for them. Onset and length of the period are determined partly by geographical location, culture, and socioeconomic status, as well as sex.

The first phase of the third stage is characterized by a labile and often depressive mood. Changing interests, moodiness, internal restlessness, and hypersensitivity are frequently covered by a veneer of external indifference; along with this is a reflective attitude toward one's own personality and a search for one's self.*

In the second phase, the relationship to the external environment again becomes more positive, corresponding to Bühler's "positive phase." There is a strong preoccupation with the mental functions and the character of people. The ability for abstraction develops and the individual's value system begins to form. In the third phase, a more realistic planning of life goals begins and a new orientation toward the social world takes place; this also includes heterosexual adjustment. Kroh's theory of development was further expanded by Remplein, and parts of it will reappear in the discussion of the theory of personality stratification.

Wilfried Zeller's Genetically Determined Changes in Body Gestalt

Medical psychology offers a different approach to the problem of adolescent development. Wilfried Zeller of Berlin has become known for his research on the relationship between body gestalt and the developmental process. Much of his work is analogous to the earlier growth studies by Shuttleworth, Shock, and Stolz in the United States, except that Zeller postulates a more invariable theoretical relationship between changes in body constitution and changes in psychological functions. He assumes that every stage of psychological development is paralleled by a specific body gestalt that is characteristic of the particular stage and that corresponds to it. Kretschmer's theory of the relationship between body type and character influenced Zeller. But Zeller studied a different aspect of the problem and produced elaborate normative data concerning body growth to support his theory. Like Gesell, he assumed genetically determined changes in body gestalt. His best known work is *Konstitution und Entwicklung* (1952) ("Constitution and Development"), in which he states his theory and cites his empirical evidence. He describes and distinguishes the following stages and changes:

*The first phase has a certain degree of commonality with Gesell's description of the eleven-year-old, the second phase, with his account of the twelve-year-old.

1. The body gestalt of the small child
2. The transitional period; first change in body gestalt
3. The body gestalt of the elementary school child
4. Prepuberal phase of physiological inhibition
5. First puberal phase; second change in body gestalt
6. Second puberal phase and maturity.

Zeller claims that this developmental process is applicable to every body type and can be found in every culture. However, he does not supply evidence to support this claim of universality.

The child's body gestalt undergoes basic changes for the first time when he is between five-and-a-half and six-and-a-half, at the time when he first enters school. At this time many children lose their deciduous teeth and get their first permanent teeth; this is one of the more obvious developmental phenomena that Zeller cites in support of his theory that a basic change in body structure takes place. However, there are many other more subtle indications of the first change in body gestalt. Zeller's method of identifying changes in body gestalt in combination with school maturity tests have provided useful criteria for answering the question of whether a child has reached "school maturity."

The second change takes place at the beginning of pubescence and has been compared with a metamorphosis. This change includes the appearance of the secondary sex characteristics and basic changes in glandular productivity; it ends with reproductive maturity of the sex organs. The internal secretion of hormones influences development, especially during the pubescent period. Before the beginning of the first puberal phase, the corticotropic hormones of the anterior lobe of the pituitary gland are dominant. Beginning with the second puberal phase, the gonadotropic hormones—estrogen produced by the ovaries and androgen produced by the testes—become more influential. In the final phase of maturity, the hormones produced by the adrenal glands control the changes. This account of hormonal changes appears to be in agreement with similar, more detailed accounts reported by Ausubel (1954) and Greulich (1944).

In Zeller's system, the child reaches "school maturity" about the time he completes the first change in body gestalt. He reaches "work maturity" during the second puberal stage, at the age of fourteen or fifteen. Daily school attendance is no longer required in Germany, and most boys and girls leave school at this time and enter the labor market.

The change in body gestalt is qualitative as well as quantitative; it cannot be measured solely in inches and pounds. For this reason he relies on anthroposcopic as well as anthropometric methods. The former are more intuitive in nature than the latter. Zeller describes body changes with these words: "The body not only increases in height, but at the same time differentiates itself; it obtains a new gestalt quality, which cannot be assessed by objective methods of measurement only, but rather has to be obtained through intuitive methods of observation" (Zeller, 1952: 65). From his data, he advances a theory of synchronism between somatic and psychological development. The two periods of change in body gestalt bring about not only changes in body structure, but also changes in psychological structure. The latter results in a different attitude toward the world. In assessing cases of deviant development, Zeller (1951) points out that severe forms of physical deviation indicate psychological deviation or disturbance as well.

The periods between changes in body gestalt have a comparatively quiet and predominantly quantitative pattern of growth and development. This quiet period has been found by many other investigators. Stone and Church (1973) introduced the concept "growth latency" for the relative quiescence in physical development. It is also apparent that Zeller's period of the body gestalt of the elementary school child corresponds to Freud's latency period. A rather short and insufficiently described phase takes place in prepuberty when the growth increment begins to decrease. It ends for girls at the age of about ten-and-a-half and for boys at twelve. Zeller asserts that the beginning disharmony of the body gestalt is an indication of the first puberal phase. It is characterized by a sudden increase in psychosexual impulses and by increased lability, easy exhaustion, and increased nervousness. The pubescent youth now shows a critical attitude toward the social world—especially toward his parents—and an increased interest and preoccupation with his own internal psychological world. This description seems to correspond to Kroh's second period of negativism, Gesell's description of the eleven-year-old, and even more closely to Hildegard Hetzer's (1948) concept "negative phase." Hetzer used Zeller's findings and assumptions. She attempted to relate body gestalt to psychological aspects of development from an educational point of view. Zeller's and Hetzer's theories complement each other, the former emphasizing the physiological, the latter the psychological aspects of development.

The first puberal phase in girls reaches its greatest disharmony and crisis at about the onset of menstruation. This is also the time when girl's legs are longest in proportion to their trunks. Zeller uses this ratio as an index to determine the corresponding level of development in boys; he assumes that boys' legs are relatively longest at about the time they produce their first spermatozoa. Stolz and Stolz (1944) have observed and described the same phenomenon and speak of the "degrees of asynchrony of development as between leg length and stem length. . . ." Menstruation in girls and greatest trunk-leg ratio in boys mark the beginning of the second puberal phase. During this phase, annual growth rapidly decreases until it reaches zero; that, of course, is physical maturity. With the decrease in annual growth, the trunk-leg ratio becomes normal, and a general harmony of body structure is reestablished.

Motor coordination also goes out of harmony during the first puberal phase, but returns during the second phase. The graceful movements of childhood disappear during the first phase; movements become impulsive, clumsy, awkward, and abrupt. During the second phase, coordination and harmony return. Zeller's detailed account of the sequence of appearance of secondary sex characteristics is similar to the sequence discussed in Chapter 1.

Heinz Remplein's Theory of Stratification of Personality

A recent trend in psychological thinking in central Europe concerns the layer structure of personality. Theories of stratification of personality follow a model that is similar to Plato's and Aristotle's idea of the layers of the soul. The model is not unlike Freud's id-ego-superego structure. However, since most theories of personality stratification claim allegiance to comparative anatomy and a genetic history of brain development, little credit is given to Freud. These theories are biologically oriented; they perceive the individual as a whole. The term "stratification" is taken from geology, but in psychology the relationship between the strata is dynamic, not static. The philosophical background for a psychological theory of personality stratification is provided by Nicolai Hartmann's ontology: four interrelated layers encompass the universe—the inorganic, the organic, the psychological, and the rational. Each has its own categories and laws.

Proponents of a theory of stratification maintain that experimental evidence* demonstrates that psychological functions are embedded in specific brain layers (Gilbert, 1951). The more vital and affective mental functions are located in the old brain (cerebellum or paleoencephalon), while the new brain (cerebrum or neoencephalon), in which the cognitive volitional functions originate, acts as an inhibitor or controlling agent. A direct relationship between the structure of the brain and personality is the core assumption of most theories of personality stratification.

Philipp Lersch (1898–) has developed a widely known and influential theory of personality stratification. Without suggesting any explicit relationship to the anatomical model of the brain, Lersch (1951) assumes a three-layer structure of personality: the vital vegetative ground, the endothymic ground, and the personal superstructure. Only the latter two are part of the psychological structure. The vital vegetative ground is the deepest layer of the organism; it includes body functions and processes and is somatic rather than psychological. The feelings and needs related to this vital vegetative ground are the conscious experiences and the automatic functions of the organism such as breathing, digestion, circulation of blood, and endocrinological changes.

The endothymic ground is the lowest psychological layer. It rests upon the vital vegetative ground and supplies the higher layer, the personal superstructure, with energies and alternatives for action. It comprises the deeper, irrational, less obvious, less controllable, and often unconscious aspects of the personality, such as feelings, emotions, moods, desires, drives, and passions.

---

*"One relevant discovery is that emotional responses by the thalamus and hypothalamus are obliterated when injury is suffered by these parts of the old brain, and this finding reveals them as areas controlling emotion and emotional expression. Cats decorticated by Bekhterev would purr and spit, and decorticated dogs would go into fits of rage on the slightest irritation" (Gilbert, 1951: 5).

The personal superstructure encompasses the conscious ego functions, mainly cognition and volition. It also contains those functions that can inhibit, suppress, organize, direct, and redirect endothymic motives and needs. "Will power" is the conscious effort of the ego to direct endothymic needs and experiences into forms of acceptable behavior. The ego is experienced as the initiator of thought processes and the executor of motivations and drives. It permits them to manifest themselves in behavior.

Heinz Remplein (1914–   ), a pupil and follower of Lersch, advances a developmental theory of personality stratification that modifies Lersch's ideas. Remplein's (1956) theory of development is also an extension of Kroh's earlier theory of phases and stages of development as they relate to the development of psychological strata.

Remplein accepts Lersch's three layers of human personality, but he changes the organization and the meaning of each layer. Lersch's lowest layer, the vital vegetative ground, becomes in Remplein's theory part of the psychological processes that are related to body functions: (1) instincts for preserving life, such as breathing, hunger and thirst, sex, and aggression; (2) body needs for comfort, such as rest, sleep, activity, play, pain avoidance, danger avoidance, heat and cold avoidance, elimination; (3) those psychological functions that depend on body organs, such as sensation, perception, and associative memory; and finally (4) those automatic processes that become conscious only if interfered with, such as digestion, respiration, circulation, and body temperature. The human being has the vital needs stratum in common with the animal world.

Lersch's endothymic ground becomes Remplein's endothymic stratum. That stratum is the point of origin of emotions—fantasy, interests, attitudes, admiration, love,* passion, hate, doubt, and hope, for example—which are not directly dependent upon body organs and body functions. Lersch's personal superstructure becomes in Remplein's theory the personal stratum, the stratum of the ego functions—cognition and volition. Here are the "egocentric psychic activities" (Gilbert, 1951: 7) that dominate, select, and

*The separation between sex and love corresponds to Spranger's distinction between sexuality and pure love; the former comes from the lowest layer of personality, the latter from a higher layer.

direct the drives, motives, and energies of the lower stratum into specific forms of behavior.

Remplein's stratification theory of development assumes that the newborn infant is "living out of the old brain" (Gilbert, 1951: 5) without any mental life. Most of his behavior is reflexlike, concerned mainly with satisfaction of vital needs. The new brain, with its cognitive and volitional functions, matures slowly. It takes a long time before the cortex can function as a controlling and inhibitory organ. Remplein does not consider development as a continuous, gradual increase of the psychological system and its functions. Rather, he sees it as new layers being superimposed on old ones (Remplein, 1956). Human development cannot be described as the gradual superseding and domination of the older brain strata by newer ones. The maturing, new strata interpenetrate the older ones, retaining some of their independence while leaving a measure of independence to the older layers. Among all the theories discussed, Remplein's makes the strongest plea for a stagelike form of development. Remplein states the developmental principle thus: "The totality of the psychological structure, as well as that of the body, does not change gradually by way of continuous growth, but stage-like, in such a form that times of increased acquisition of new functions and knowledge are followed by periods of rest, consolidation and maturation of the acquired skills" (Remplein, 1956: 75).

In early infancy, the vital needs stratum develops first; at this point the endothymic and the personal strata are still "thin layers" and follow chronologically in the maturing process. Before the vital needs stratum has developed completely, the endothymic stratum begins its development. It is followed by the personal stratum. Remplein sees development as a rhythmical pattern of interaction of all brain strata. The process begins with the vital needs stratum operating from the old brain, and producing a vegetative form of life. The endothymic layer soon ripens and expands, resulting in an uncontrolled affective form of life. It is soon followed by development of the personal layer. But the new layers do not stop the older ones from continuing their development.

The primitive vital stratum of infancy does not retain its qualities when the higher strata begin to supersede it. They influence and change it by adding new functions. These new functions take over leadership from the older ones in the psychological apparatus. This is analogous to the genetic history of brain development, in which the instinctual action in primitive animal life gives way to increased adjustability and intelligence in higher animal life. In the human being, only a few instincts survive, but there is a greater ability to adjust to new situations.

The full period of development can be divided into three different stages:

1. Early childhood, which extends from birth to the beginning of the first period of negativism; it covers the first two years of life.
2. Middle and late childhood, which covers the period from the first to the second period of negativism (roughly, ages three to thirteen).
3. Time of maturation, which extends from the second period of negativism until the end of adolescence (roughly, ages twelve to twenty-two).

Between each stage and the next is a period of negativism that manifests itself in a disintegration of the psychological structure. It results in lability of emotional mood and insecurity of behavior.

Each stage is subdivided into three phases, as in Kroh's theory. The first stage, early childhood, is dominated by the development of the vital needs stratum. Many functions of this layer, such as reflex actions and somatic and sensual feelings, are present at birth. So is the ability to register satisfaction at the fulfillment, or dissatisfaction at the nonfulfillment, of needs such as hunger, thirst, activity, rest, sleep, comfort, and elimination. During the second phase perception is developed. The third phase, including approximately the second year of life, shows an increased differentiation of perceptual functions in the vital needs stratum, resulting in the ability to distinguish size, form, brightness, and color of objects. In the endothymic stratum, memory and fantasy come forth. So do object-directed emotions such as anger, imitation, astonishment, amazement, and fondness. The personal stratum begins to function with the early use of language, acts of practical intelligence, and simple choice.

The transition from the first to the second stage is of great importance for further total development. This negative period is marked by an increased supply of vital energy with an increased lability of mood stemming from the lowest psychic stratum. The ego in the personal layer is discovered, and the child first experiences self-determination and the ability to choose consciously. By acting in spite and showing negative tendencies, the child's personal stratum asserts its leadership over the two lower psychic strata.

During the first phase of the second stage, the endothymic stratum expands by developing new emotions, such as jealousy, envy, malicious joy, love, and interest as well as a new drive to form, achieve, and create. In the personal stratum, the ego is developing goal determination of behavior and an insightful subordination of volition in the objective context of reality. The second phase of the second stage comprises the last three years of the first decade of life. During this period we can observe eidetic imagery stemming from the endothymic stratum. Endothymic motivations become stronger, influencing interest and a positive attitude toward learning. Conviction and doubt are added to the feelings during this period. The personal stratum now develops teleological thinking directed toward an end. Volition increases in intensity and allows prolonged concentration. The child's world view becomes more realistic and is oriented toward objectivity.

The third phase of the second stage—late childhood, the time from about ten to thirteen—is the prepuberal phase. In the vital needs stratum an increased drive for activity combines with a feeling of strength and wantonness. This results in an urge to scuffle and fight, reinforcing self-assertive motives. The endothymic layer produces a drive to acquire, which is connected with an interest in collecting things. Interests become more specialized and differentiated, and the child seeks to learn more about them. We see increased ability for abstraction, logical reasoning, and causal understanding in the personal stratum. This extinguishes the child's magical and fantasy perception of the world. Withdrawal from the external world into the internal self prepares the child for the coming changes of puberty.

Remplein (1956) considers the second period of negativism, separating childhood from adolescence, as the first phase of maturation. In the vital needs stratum, new drives arise—the drive to wander and seek new adventure, the drive to join peers and form gangs, and sexual urges—and the belligerence and activity drives further increase in strength. The general emotional tone becomes labile, with a tendency toward moodiness and unhappiness. These changes penetrate the personal stratum, bringing about a desire for self-determination, independence, and new experiences. The sexual drive from the vital layer increases sexual interest in the endothymic stratum. Remplein sees an obvious relationship between the psychological phenomena of adolescence and changes in the endocrinological secretions. For example, the interplay among the pineal gland, thymus, and gonads accounts for the sequence of growth spurt and reproductive maturity; the beginning of the secretion of gonadotropic hormones is at least partly responsible for increased sexual interest and drives. Body changes result in a disturbed body image. They are related to psychological instability and self-reflective tendencies. It is suggested that sensitivity, moodiness, and enthusiasm may be related to puberal changes. However, like Spranger, Remplein is interested mainly in the psychological aspects of development. The regulation of the hormonic secretion stems from the vital needs stratum and is part of nature's plan for development. Body changes as well as the new desire for freedom and independence bring about increased sensitivity, unwillingness, impatience, anger, rebelliousness, hostility, and even temper tantrums. The adolescent's personal stratum develops abstract thought processes, logical memory, and an internalized critical reflection on his own psychic life.

During the second phase of the adolescent stage, new energy impulses originate in the endothymic stratum, and an increased need for independence is combined with values and ideals. There is a strong desire to experiment with the liberated ego. Therefore, the adolescent evaluates old values and ideals and frequently rejects them in the light of his newly acquired self-concept. The personal stratum supports these emancipating tendencies with a newly arising desire for self-education and active participation in personality formation. Thought processes become separated from behavior as thinking becomes more and more a function of planning behavior.

The third phase of adolescence brings the developmental cycle to an end with the attainment of maturity. The sexual drive of the vital needs stratum is integrated with the affective love of the endothymic stratum, which is now directed toward a partner. Attitudes toward external life and internal self unite and stabilize. In the personal stratum, development increases and strengthens volitional energies and depth of thought. Remplein (1956) observes a searching for the meaning of life and the rounding out of a philosophy of life. With the attainment of self-security and self-esteem, energies and interests are released from their earlier attachment to the internal processes of growth and maturation. They now can be utilized in the striving for goals in the external, objective world. There is new motivation for self-realization, achievement, and productivity. Social maturation is also achieved, and other people are considered both on the level of personal love and on a general level of social adjustment and social conformity.

Remplein's theory of personality stratification—like Hall's, Gesell's, and Kroh's theories—assumes that in a general way ontogeny recapitulates phylogeny. The process of the new brain developing and dominating the old brain takes place not only in the evolution of the species, but functionally the same process occurs in individual development. The recapitulation of the evolution of the animal world starts during the prenatal period and is nearly finished at the time of birth. The first stage, that of early childhood, corresponds roughly to the earliest form of human development. A rudimentary form of pubescence follows the first negative phase; this idea is also postulated by Freud's oedipal situation and Bühler's concept of "little puberty." The second stage, including middle and late childhood, is a repetition of primitive man. In some primitive societies, youth attains full adult status when physiological maturation is reached. Civilized man has a prolonged period of maturation beyond pubescence, namely, adolescence, after which the individual enters adulthood. Both early and late childhood and corresponding stages of development of the species are preceded by a negativistic phase and end with a sort of puberty.

Remplein's (1956) theory of development is based on a genetic concept of brain development. Only a biological maturational process could produce such a uniform and well-defined pattern of stages and phases of development. However, he maintains, an innate disposition depends upon environmental and psychosocial factors to bring about development. "Innate disposition and environment belong inseparably together, one without the other is unthinkable.

There is no development without innate disposition but there also is none without environment, and any theory which makes one of these two sides of development an absolute is one-sided and mistaken" (Remplein, 1956: 16).

Remplein holds that innate disposition limits the influence of environmental forces on developmental processes, forms of behavior, and personality characteristics. But these limits are not the same for all characteristics; some resist environmental influences, whereas others are more open to them. Those innate dispositions that are necessary for the survival of the species are, generally speaking, resistant to environmental influences. The animal instincts, for example, fall into this category, while those qualities that have arisen late in the phylogenetic development, such as special abilities, are more open to environmental influences.

Remplein—whose theories are similar in many ways to Gesell's —speaks of innate character traits, innate homosexual tendencies, innate language differences between boys and girls, innate speed and rhythm of development, innate tendencies to perceive either analytically or synthetically, and even an innate disposition for conscience; his biological, genetic emphasis is obvious. He summarizes the controversial issue between nature and nurture: ". . . the innate disposition provides a potential, the environmental factors are responsible for the realization of this potential" (Remplein, 1956: 18). There can be no doubt that Remplein strongly emphasizes the innate disposition and that the developmental theory of stratification, even though it tends to compromise, is more biological than psychosocial.

Remplein strongly advocates the idea that an individual must experience fully all the stages and phases of development in order to become a mature person, since each of them has its specific developmental purpose. Consequently, educational efforts should aim not only at the development of the personal stratum and its cognitive functions, but also at a healthy development of the lower affective strata. An intellect based on an unstable and immature motivational and emotional foundation cannot be accepted as a legitimate educational goal.

Play activity during the first years is a functional preparation for more formal training later. Premature pushing beyond the developmental expectancies, though it may produce momentary results, involves dangers: the psychological energies are used up too early, and development stagnates at a relatively early age. Remplein cites the fact that "miracle children" frequently did not achieve anything extraordinary as adults. Education must take developmental rhythm into account. It must organize the curriculum so that it corresponds to the natural plan of development. For the adolescent, this would mean opportunities for self-determination, self-education, self-realization, self-control, abstract and logical thinking, social interaction and planning, and the building up of a personal concept of values and a philosophy of life.

Remplein's ideas about the nature of maladjustment are of special educational value. Maladjustment comes from a wrong or deficient interrelationship between the strata. It results if the newly developing strata fail to integrate properly with the older ones, or if the older ones are unwilling to submit to the higher order and retain their independence (Freud's id-impulse-driven personality). The psychological structure is especially vulnerable to maladjustment during the two negative periods, since during these periods innate disposition as well as environmental influences may disturb adjustment and foster neurotic tendencies. Periods of negativism are characterized by an internal disintegration of the psychological structure, which permits a restructuring and reorganization of the relationships among the psychological strata. For example, during the first negative period integration of the vital needs stratum and the endothymic stratum must be achieved, with both subordinate to the newly arising personal stratum. However, the behavioral phenomena connected with such a disintegration and reorganization of the psychic structure—negativism, emotional lability, disobedience, and excessive self-assertion—are frequently misunderstood and unfavorably received. Remplein cites three forms of maladjustment that can be accounted for by unfavorable experiences in the negative period:

1. Rebellion, in which characteristics of the negative period remain operative beyond the expected time. Disobedience, rebellion, and destruction become permanently established in the personality.
2. Withdrawal, characterized by an escape from reality into fan-

tasy. This occurs if a child is unable to break away from the lower stratum.

3. Regression, a return to earlier forms of behavior, with a greater dependency on the mother.

Education must help in overcoming these problems by finding a sound compromise between rigid forms of discipline and overindulgence. Both tend to increase the possibility for neurotic development. Parents must learn that negative behavior during certain periods is part of the developmental process and should not be "broken."

11

Jean Piaget's Cognitive Theory of Adolescent Development*

Jean Piaget's (1896–   ) contribution to the understanding of human development is reflected in the increasing attention that psychologists—especially those with a cognitive orientation—devote to his theory. In his earlier work, Piaget emphasized cognitive development in infancy and early childhood. Two of his early books, *The Origins of Intelligence in Children* (1952) and *The Construction of Reality in the Child* (1954), are primarily devoted to the period of development from birth to age two. Only in his more recent research has Piaget moved up the developmental scale and given more systematic attention to the period of adolescence. This trend is particularly reflected in *The Growth of Logical Thinking from Childhood to Adolescence†* (1958).

Piaget worked as an assistant to Binet in Paris while the latter was developing his intelligence test. Though Piaget showed limited interest in the psychometric and statistical aspects of test construction, he became fascinated with the thought processes the children revealed in attempting to solve the test problems. The Geneva group still feels that standardized questions frequently lead to stereotyped and uninteresting answers (Inhelder, 1966) and use a

---

*Chapter 11 is a revision and extension of an article by the author, "Jean Piaget's Cognitive Theory of Adolescent Development," *Adolescence* 1967 Vol. II, pp. 285–310.

†Reference will be to Piaget and his theory even though Bärbel Inhelder is the senior author of this volume, which offers the major source material for this chapter.

"clinical method" for data gathering that reveals thought processes rather than knowledge. Piaget's preoccupation with qualitative changes in children's thought processes may be seen throughout his work. However, the lack of statistical analysis of his data has caused frequent criticism.

Even though Piaget takes a comparatively independent position among contemporary psychological theorists, he has been influenced by a number of people. Philosophically, he has been influenced by Kant's epistemology and by Bergson's metaphysics. Piaget appears to be familiar with Freud's theory, since he makes occasional references to Freud in his work. Freud's influence is much more noticeable in Piaget's early work up to 1930, but has declined since. Piaget does not share Freud's interest in the subconscious, in conflicts, in behavior dynamics, and in the affective aspects of human development. Instead, he focuses his research upon the conflict-free and rational side of human development and emphasizes thought processes and the structure of intelligence. Nevertheless, Piaget's concept of "egocentrism," which characterizes the language, thought, and morality of the young child, is compatible with Freud's concept "id."

In certain respects, Piaget (1947b) appears to be closer to Gestalt psychology than to any other theory. His kinship with Gestalt psychology is especially clear in his emphasis on the patterns of organization, the structural whole, and the total system. Piaget is concerned, as are the Gestalt psychologists, with the relationship between the parts and the whole. However, he disagrees with several of their assumptions. For example, Gestalt principles do not seem to be useful in explaining the "logical operations in thought" that Piaget attempts to discover. Furthermore, he emphasizes structural changes as a function of development, while Gestalt psychology maintains that the "laws of organizations" and "perceptual structure" are independent of age.

Piaget, who has been characterized as a "zoologist by training, an epistemologist by vocation, and a logician by method," is best known for his contribution to developmental psychology. He regards himself as an interdisciplinary thinker. Consequently, his methodology as well as his theoretical conceptualizations are quite unique and have been assimilated by the mainstream of psychological thought very slowly. The following discussion of Piaget's developmental theory can only highlight the most essential concepts of his theory of cognitive growth.

The Major Developmental Concepts of Piaget's Theory

Piaget's theory of development has two dimensions that, even though closely interrelated, can be analyzed separately: the stage-dependent theory and the stage-independent theory (Flavell, 1963a). The stage-dependent theory consists of four basic stages: sensorimotor, preoperational, concrete operational, and formal thought, which will be discussed in detail later. In addition, Piaget has developed a system of interrelated developmental concepts, such as schema, structure, operation, assimilation, accommodation, adaptation, equilibrium, and equilibration. These cut across his stage theory and are as applicable to early motor development as they are to the logical thought processes of the adolescent. Piaget has been taken to task for specifying four discreet stages in his theory by critics who overlook the underlying continuity of development that becomes manifest in these concepts.

The first two concepts of the stage-independent theory, schema and structure, appear to be almost interchangeable. A schema is a generalized or established behavior pattern of meaningful and repeatable habits, such as the sucking schema, and initially relates to inborn reflexes. As the child continuously interacts with his environment, the reflexes become broadened and modified and they combine with other schemata. Schemata, therefore, are not static but are continuously growing and are even referred to as mobile schemata. Piaget uses the schema concept mainly when he speaks of early motor behavior patterns, such as the prehension schema, walking schema, sensorimotor schema. When referring to adolescence, he uses concepts such as cognitive schema, anticipatory schema. It is in the latter instance that schema and structure become synonymous, except that schema is the behavioral equivalent of the internal structures. The structures are the organizational properties of thought that determine the nature of the child's behavior, especially his more complex cognitive responses. Thus, the theory focuses on the qualitative changes of intellectual structure from birth to maturity. Each structure is built upon its predecessor. The integration of old into new structures provides the continuity for development (Flavell, 1963b).

According to Piaget, when schemata and structures have developed to the extent that they can be used as interrelated logical systems, they become operations. Consequently, operations are more complex and more differentiated than schemata and begin to approximate a logical model. It is possible to apply operations to a much wider range of related problems, since an operation is not dependent upon a specific stimulus but implies a meaningful understanding of the structure of the problem. Memorized formulas that a student applies to a series of identically stated math problems correspond to schemata. In contrast, operational thinking is able to identify a problem even in a different context and can understand the relationship of each of the figures to the whole problem so that the reliance on a formula becomes unnecessary. To the extent that operations have become meaningful parts of the total structure they show resistance to forgetting, while schemata have a more specific nature and are more easily forgotten. These operations in thought to which Piaget devotes considerable emphasis in his theory have two characteristics.

1. Operational thought is reversible. Logical operations in mathematics or physics can be reversed by cancelling an operation. The operational child understands that subtraction can cancel the process of addition. The addition of $6 + 7 = 13$ can be cancelled by its reversal $13 - 7 = 6$. One can also reverse an operation by reciprocity and return to the starting point. A clay ball can be made into a clay sausage and again be reversed into the original form of a clay ball.
2. Operational thought is associative. Thought is not limited to one route, but has the flexibility and the freedom to pursue a goal by way of detours and by way of a variety of approaches. The arithmetic problem 25×25 can be solved in a number of ways: $(25 \times 20) + (25 \times 5)$; or $20^2 + (2 \times 20 \times 5) + 5^2$; or $25 \times 100 \div 4$; and so on.

The dimensions of preoperational and operational thought constitute the two fundamental dividing classes in the stage-dependent theory of Piaget. Since such systems of logical operations, reversibility and associativity of thought, do not emerge until about the age of seven, Piaget speaks of the child prior to this age as the preoperational child who relies on perception and intuition. After age seven, the child enters the operational stage of development. Operations are seen as internalized actions that constitute a system of organized and related responses and correspond to the operations of mathematics and logic. Piaget speaks of logical operations, such as addition, multiplication, and reciprocity, using mathematics and logic as his models for the analysis of the thought of the operational child.

The three essential variables responsible for development in general and for the formation of mental functions in particular are:

1. The maturation of the nervous system
2. Experiences in interaction with physical reality, and
3. The influence of the social environment.

The maturation-learning model of development, however, constitutes only a general background for Piaget's equilibration-equilibrium model, which places major emphasis on dynamic interaction with the physical and social environment.

Cognitive adaptation to the environment takes place by way of assimilation and accommodation. Environmental experiences are first assimilated. That is, the experience encountered is structured or restructured to fit into the present intellectual organization. To intellectually assimilate "reality is to construe that reality, and to construe it in terms" of one's existing cognitive structure (Flavell, 1963a: 48). Accommodation refers to the process of change that the existing cognitive structure utilizes in order to incorporate the new experience. Piaget seems to have borrowed this model from biology. The organism assimilates food by chewing, swallowing, and breaking it down. Food is restructured to fit the biological need of the organism. The organism accommodates food by incorporating (digesting) it into its own structure; as a result, the organism is restructured; it has more energy, and it grows. Assimilation and accommodation are complementary processes and through their continuous interaction they bring about conceptual adaptation and growth. Indeed, it is through these very processes that the intellectual structure grows and expands. When a balance between assimilation and accommodation has been accomplished, a state of equilibrium exists. Equilibrium is the harmony between sensory information and accumulated knowledge, or harmony between the individual and his environment. As new sensory information disturbs existing incomplete or incorrect knowledge, the equilibrium is thrown out of balance and a new assimilation-accommodation process begins. After endless repetitions of a behavior sequence, equilibrium is reestablished at a higher level and structure is changed. The accommodation of a new experience produces modifications in the structure and the schema. Thus, the theory allows for continuous progressive development. Assimilating and accommodating environmental experiences lead slowly to cognitive growth. This interplay is referred to as the equilibration of structure process. In contrast to purely maturational theories, Piagetian theory views the child as an active participant in his own development.

The concept of equilibration is essential in Piaget's definition of intelligence as a "form of equilibration . . . toward which all cognitive functions lead" (Piaget, 1962: 120). Equilibrium is defined as a compensation for an external disturbance. Intellectual development becomes a continuous progression from structural disequilibrium to structural equilibrium. Intellectual operations never function in isolation, but are regulated by organizing principles that relate to a total system. Consequently, Piaget frequently draws parallels from his work on moral judgment, reasoning, language and thought, and cognitive structure, and relates various facets to the total system. "It is possible to discern synchronized structures of operational development manifesting themselves in such different fields as logic, space, time, etc." (Inhelder, 1966: 304).

Piaget's Stages of Development

Piaget's theory of development originally focused on infancy and childhood and only recently has it systematically included adolescence. The interrelationship of the whole system makes it necessary to discuss briefly the essential characteristics of the early stages of development. The preadolescent and adolescent periods, which are characterized by operational thought, will be developed in detail as the primary focus in this chapter. An excellent and much more detailed discussion of the preoperational stages of development can be found in *Intelligence and Experience* by Hunt (1961). The following stage-dependent theory has to be perceived in the light of the developmental concepts discussed previously.

The *sensorimotor stage of development* (0–2 years), described in great detail by Piaget, is subdivided into six developmental phases. The first phase (0–1 month), *reflexes,* consists primarily of exercising inborn reflexes, such as the sucking schema. During the second phase (1–4 months), which Piaget calls the *primary circular reactions,* the reflexes are replaced by voluntary movements. The child may tirelessly practice a schema, such as grasping, since he is motivated by "function pleasure." In the third phase (4–8 months), *secondary circular reactions,* the infant can pursue objects and events outside himself. He may follow the slow movement of an attractive toy, or, if through trial and error he grasps a cord and makes a bell jingle, he may repeat the sequence. That he can reproduce such a series of events is evidence of the beginning of intentionality and even an incipient form of goal-directed behavior. The fourth phase (8–12 months), that of *coordination of secondary schemata,* is characterized by the emergence of means-ends relationships. The child reaches for a plastic container in order to obtain an animal that is inside. As the concept of "object permanence" emerges, a child will search for a key hidden under a blanket. During the fifth phase (12–18 months), that of *tertiary circular reactions,* the concept of object permanence becomes more stable. The child will search for and find the object even through a series of displacements. The last of the six phases (18–24 months) is that of *internalization of sensorimotor schemata.* The child begins to use foresight and symbolic representation in solving sensorimotor problems. For the first time, he may try to see whether a hole is big enough before attempting to push an object through.

The second period of development (2–7 years), the *preoperational stage,* is a transition period from the predominantly autistic and egocentric stages of early childhood to the early forms of social behavior, sociocentric speech, and conceptual thought, which become more obvious toward the end of the preoperational stage. The preoperational stage is subdivided into two distinguishable phases. The first, *extracting concepts from experiences,* covers the years from two to four. The child must extract concepts on the basis of direct sensory experiences—that is, he is at the mercy of his own perception. Reality is what he perceives; there are no alternatives open to him. When a chocolate bar is broken up, there appears to be more chocolate than in the whole bar. During this phase, the child's language develops at a phenomenal rate. From rather rudimentary forms of language development at the age of two, the child develops language skills that by four years make it possible for him to communicate his thoughts. The words he hears and uses are associated with objects, events, and relationships.

The second, more advanced phase (4–7 years) of the preoperational stage is that of *intuitive thought* or intuitive use of concepts. The differentiation from the previous phase is a fine one; the judgment of the child is still intuitive and subjective, but deals with somewhat more complex configurations than in the previous stage. The child can now manipulate experimental objects more effectively and his ability to communicate is enhanced by language development. Therefore, it becomes possible for him to make more systematic interrogations. Nevertheless, accurate judgment is limited by three factors:

1. Basically, he is still dependent on sensory experiences.
2. He still does not consider two or more dimensions at the same time, but focuses on one aspect and, consequently, overlooks the others.
3. He does not rearrange or reorganize information in his mind.

Because he is too dependent on his sensory impression, he does not yet comprehend the principle of conservation: that a given quantity remains the same, even though the organization of that quantity has changed. Neither does he think in terms of a hierarchy of classes and supraclasses. He may maintain, "We are not in Maryland. We are in Baltimore."

At approximately age seven or eight, a major shift in the child's conceptual development takes place; he begins to perform *concrete operations.* This period (7–8 to 11–12 years) is referred to as the *operational stage in logical thinking.* Chronologically, the period of concrete operations constitutes the preadolescent period.

According to Inhelder and Piaget (1958), egocentrism in language, thought, and moral judgment is characteristic of the preoperational stage of development and declines with increasing age as a result of socialization. There is, however, an interesting exception to this general developmental trend, which is quite relevant to an understanding of the early adolescent. Piaget uses the term "vertical décalages" and postulates that certain operations reoccur at different periods of development. As the child experiences new heights of cognitive functions, he also experiences new bursts of egocentrism. The first and most pronounced period of egocentrism occurs toward the end of the sensorimotor stage. The second burst of egocentrism appears toward the end of the preoperational stage and is reflected in a "lack of differentiation both between ego's and alter's point of view, between the subjective and the objective" (Inhelder and Piaget, 1958: 343). The final form of egocentrism occurs at the transition from the concrete to the formal stage as a result of enlarging the structure of formal operations. This high level egocentrism takes the form of a naïve but exuberant idealism with unrealistic proposals for educational, political, and social reforms, attempts at reshaping reality, and disregard for actual obstacles. "The adolescent not only tries to adapt his ego to his social environment but, just as emphatically, tries to adjust the environment to his ego" (Inhelder and Piaget, 1958: 343).

During the operational stage, the child learns to master logical operations using material with a concrete content. The major limitation still evident is his inability to think abstractly about a problem. Since concrete operations can now be performed mentally, overt trial and error becomes unnecessary. For the first time, the child begins to think in accordance with a logical model of reasoning. He develops an awareness of the principle of conservation, so that he now realizes that pouring the same quantity of water into differently shaped containers does not increase or decrease the amount of water. Changing a clay ball into a sausage or flattening it out into a pancake does not change its mass, weight, or volume. The concept of conservation of mass is established first, weight is of intermediate difficulty, and the concept of conservation of volume, the most difficult to grasp, emerges toward the end of the concrete operational stage.

An understanding of the principle of conservation leads directly to an awareness of reversibility. Reversibility is defined as "the permanent possibility of returning to the starting point of the operation in question" (Inhelder and Piaget, 1958: 272). The child can construct a bead chain in which the original pattern is reversed. Awareness of the concept of reversibility is critical to operational thought. "An operation is an action capable of occurring internally and of which ... the essential characteristic is its reversibility. Cognitive activity becomes operational when it acquires a mobility such that an action (or transformation) can be annulled in thought by an inverse action or can be compensated for by a reciprocal action" (Inhelder, 1966: 302). The ability to return to the starting point of an operation constitutes an important gain in the intellectual growth of the child. The operational child can use various approaches to the solution of a problem without becoming committed to any one as the only one.

The child now becomes concerned with the relationship of the parts to the whole. Understanding and classifying the parts help him in gaining a better concept of the whole. His ability to hold several pieces of information in mind and to reverse his thinking allows for an understanding of a hierarchy of classes and supra-classes. He may become preoccupied with a system of classifications.

Another schema that appears at the beginning of the operational stage is the "operation of serializing." In the test situation, the child is asked to rank in order a series of objects, such as wooden dolls or sticks, according to their size or weight. Such an operation of serializing is similar to the classification of a hierarchy, since it involves an understanding of the structure of the whole. "There is no class without classifications; there is no symmetric relation without serialization" (Piaget, 1962: 126). The child in the concrete stage is able to order the objects according to their size or weight as long as they are presented to him concretely; it is not until adolescence that such an operation can be performed mentally on an abstract level. Furthermore, the child can now visualize a series of positions, such as the sequential steps through which a stick would have to fall before it would come to rest in the horizontal. Such a continuum of a series of positions is difficult for the child to comprehend in the preoperational stage.

At the same age that concrete operations become possible, the child's language, which has been predominantly egocentric until the age of seven, becomes primarily sociocentric. There is a genuine

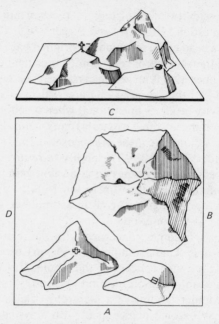

FIGURE 9. The three differently shaped mountains used to study the child's ability to identify the perspectives from positions B, C, and D when he is located in position A. From Jean Piaget and Bärbel Inhelder, *The Child's Conception of Space.*

Reproduced by permission from Routledge & Kegan Paul, London, and Humanities Press, Inc., New York.

effort to understand other people and to communicate thought objectively. "The child really exchanges his thoughts with others, either by telling his hearer something that will interest him and influence his actions, or by an actual interchange of ideas by argument or even by collaboration in pursuit of a common aim" (Piaget, 1957: 33). Critics have challenged the idea that a noticeable shift takes place at this particular age, but they tend to agree that with increasing age the proportion of egocentric speech decreases while sociocentric speech increases.

Language as well as the child's thought processes become less egocentric. The child can place himself in the situation of another person and take another's point of view. When confronted with a model of three differently shaped mountains, he can identify correctly what they look like from other angles. He can rotate objects in his mind and might spontaneously ask, "What does the other side of the moon look like?"

Piaget identifies the properties of "concrete operations" and applies the term "elementary groupings," or "group-like-structure," to the different ways in which the child's thought processes can manipulate classes and relations. Since Piaget sees a direct relationship between logic and the child's cognitive processes, the concepts he introduces are conveyed in terms of the operations of logic and mathematics. An important set of four concrete operational groupings follows:

1. *Combinativity.* Two or more classes may be combined into one larger, more comprehensive class of the same grouping. All men and all women = all adults. Logical relationships such as A is larger than B and B is larger than C may be combined into a new statement that A is larger than C. The ability to combine subclasses into supraclasses is essential to the understanding of a hierarchy of classifications.

2. *Reversibility.* Every operation is reversible. Every mathematical operation has an opposite that reverses it. Supraclasses can be taken apart, so that the effect of combining subclasses is reversed. All adults except all women = all men. The degree of reversibility of the child's thought processes is an important indication of the child's cognitive development.

3. *Associativity.* The child whose operations are associative can reach a goal in various ways; he can make detours in thought, but the results obtained by these different routes remain the same. For example, $(3 + 6) + 4 = 13$, and $6 + (3 + 4) = 13$.

4. *Identity or nullifiability.* An operation that is combined with its opposite becomes nullified. Illustrations of nullifiability in thought are: $3 - 3 = 0$; $5x \div 5 = x$; all Americans except those who are Americans equals no one; I drive one mile west and I drive one mile east = I am where I started.

Primary groupings make combinativity, reversibility, and associativity in thought possible and thus aid the child in achieving an equilibrium that is considerably more mobile and flexible than that of the preoperational child. Thus, the approach to problems is no longer intuitive or impulsive but rational; however, reasoning is not yet integrated into a single total system of interrelated propositions.

The final stage of cognitive development in Piaget's theory is the *stage of formal operations,* which is characterized by the use of propositional and combinatorial operations. The only major source available dealing with adolescent cognitive development is *The Growth of Logical Thinking* (1958). In this book the stage of formal operations has been subdivided into two distinguishable substages that carry the prosaic names III-A (11–12 to 14–15 years) and III-B (14–15 years onward). This division of the adolescent period at the age of fourteen to fifteen implies—just as at the ages of seven to eight and eleven to twelve—another restructuring and disequilibrium, which then leads to a higher level of equilibrium and intellectual structure during late adolescence. In this division, the early substage III-A appears to be a preparatory stage in which the adolescent may make correct discoveries and handle certain formal operations, but the approach is cumbersome and he is not yet able to provide systematic and rigorous proof. In the substage III-B the adolescent is capable of formulating more elegant generalizations and advancing more inclusive laws; most of all he is able to provide spontaneously more systematic proof, since he can use methods of control. Piaget does not ascribe theoretical names to these stages. The difference in approach and reasoning of the adolescent in substages III-A and III-B may be illustrated by actual responses.

In one of the experiments, "The Law of Floating Bodies . . . ," the subject is presented with a great variety of objects and his problem is to distinguish those that float on water from those that do not float and to provide proof for his assertions.

Jim (12; 8) classifies floating or sinking objects according to whether they are *"lighter or heavier than water."*—"What do you mean?"— *"You would have to have much more water than metal to make up the same weight."*—"And this cover?"— *"When you put up the edges, there is air inside; when you put them down, it goes down because the water comes inside and that makes more weight."*—"Why does the wood float?"— *"Because it is light."*—"And that little key?"— *"No, this piece of wood is heavier."*—"So?"— *"If you measure with a key* [= with the weight of a key], *you need more wood than lead for the weight of the key."* —"What do you mean?"— *"If you take metal, you need much more wood to make the same weight than metal"* [Inhelder and Piaget, 1958: 38].

The subject at substage III-B, in contrast, sees the problem more specifically in terms of units of measurements that are provided and that he uses spontaneously. Furthermore, he more precisely appreciates that the weight of the object in relationship to the weight of the water that it replaces determines whether it floats or sinks. There is reduction in trial-and-error reasoning and the proof is provided with greater elegance and precision as indicated by the following protocol:

Lamb (13; 3) correctly classifies the objects that sink: *"I sort of felt that they are all heavier than the water. I compared for the same weight, not for the same volume of water."*—"Can you give a proof?"— *"Yes, I take these two bottles, I weigh them. . . . Oh!* [he notices the cubes] *I weigh this plastic cube with water inside and I compare this volume of water to the wooden cube. You always have to compare a volume to the same volume of water."*—"And with this wooden ball?"— *"By calculation."* —"But otherwise?"— *"Oh, yes, you set the water level* [in the bucket]; *you put the ball in and let out enough water to maintain the original level."* —"Then what do you compare?"— *"The weight of the water let out and the weight of the ball"* [Inhelder and Piaget, 1958: 44].

It becomes obvious that the reasoning from substage III-A to substage III-B becomes increasingly more abstract and shows a higher degree of mastery of the formal operations. Since Piaget postulates a direct correspondence between the structure of logic and the structure of the adolescent's cognitive operations, there is a developmental approximation of the operational thought processes of the adolescent to the formal system of modern logic. The significance that Piaget attaches to the change from concrete operations to formal operations is even reflected in a change in the symbols of logic; for example, A + B for concrete operations changes to the logical symbols "p ∘ q" for the same formal operation. Changes in thought processes are directly related to maturational changes in the cortex that accompany puberty. While the child at the concrete operational stage becomes able to reason on the basis of objects, the adolescent begins to reason on the basis of verbal propositions. He can make hypothetical deductions and entertain the idea of relativity. "Formal thought reaches its fruition during adolescence. An adolescent, unlike the child, is an individual who thinks beyond the present and forms theories about everything, delighting especially in consideration of that which is not" (Piaget, 1947b: 148). He not only thinks beyond the present, but analytically reflects about his own thinking. His theories may still be oversimplifications of reality. Nevertheless, most adolescents in substage III-B have social and political theories and at least some have religious, philosophical, and scientific theories. This preoccupation with theory can even be applied to girls' dreams of their future husbands, which are frequently quite "theoretical," as is their concept of married life (Inhelder and Piaget, 1958).

In his thoughts, the adolescent can leave the real objective world behind and enter the world of ideas. He controls events in his mind through logical deductions of possibilities and consequences. Even the direction of his thought processes changes. The preadolescent begins by thinking about reality and attempts to extend thoughts toward possibility. The adolescent, who has mastered formal operations, begins by thinking of all logical possibilities and then considers them in a systematic fashion; reality for him is secondary to possibility. "The most distinctive property of formal thought is this reversal of direction between *reality* and *possibility;* instead of deriving a rudimentary type of theory from the empirical data as is done in concrete inferences, formal thought begins with a theoretical synthesis implying that certain relations are necessary and thus proceeds in the opposite direction. . . . This type of thinking proceeds *from* what is possible *to* what is empirically real" (Inhelder and Piaget, 1958: 251). This reversal of the direction of thought between reality and possibility constitutes a turning point in the development of the structure of intelligence, since it leads to an equilibrium that is both stable and flexible.

An illustration may serve to contrast the preadolescent reasoning based on concrete operations with adolescent reasoning based on verbal propositions. The nine-year-old can arrange a series of dolls according to their height and can even supply each doll with a stick of corresponding size from a series of different size sticks. He can do this even if the sticks are presented in reverse order. But not until the formal operations appear can he solve a similar, but verbal, problem: "Edith is fairer than Susan; Edith is darker than Lilly; who is the darkest of the three?"

Piaget distinguishes between the concrete elementary or primary groupings discussed earlier and formal or second degree groupings that are characteristic of the formal stage. He also refers to these groupings as operations to the second power or the proposition-about-proposition attribute. Implied in the proposition-about-proposition concept is the idea that the adolescent thinks about his own thought in a reflective way. Turning to a description of the formal operational schemata of adolescence, one ought to be aware that the adolescent thinks operationally without having a basic understanding of the kind of formal logic by which Piaget analyzes adolescent thought processes. The attainment of operations is not an all or none proposition. Between the ages of eleven to twelve and fourteen to fifteen considerable modification, systematization, and formalization of thought processes can be observed. The complexity of problems that can be handled effectively increases substantially during these years and reaches an equilibrium after fourteen or fifteen when substage III-B begins.

Formal operations allow the adolescent to combine propositions and to isolate variables in order to confirm or disprove his hypothesis. He no longer needs to think in terms of objects or concrete events, but can carry out operations of symbols in his mind. The first grouping to be discussed constitutes a combinatorial system of operational schemata characterized by propositional operations. He can make logical combinations in the following ways:

1. *Combine by conjunction.* "Both A and B make a difference." The subject was asked to determine why certain objects float and others do not. In solving this problem the subject has to realize that "both weight and volume make a difference" before he can comprehend the notion of density, which emerges once the relationship between weight and volume is understood. As long as he attempts to explain the phenomenon of floating or sinking on the basis of either "weight" or "size"—as the concrete operational subject frequently does—he fails to make the correct generalization.

2. *Combine by disjunction.* "It's got to be this or that." In order to solve a given problem, variables have to be identified and tested individually so that a hypothesis can be confirmed or rejected. In

one of the experiments, the subject is presented with a simple pendulum. The variables that can be manipulated are: the length of the string, the weight, the point at which the weight is released, and the force of the push. The problem is to discover what factors affect the frequency of the oscillation. Once the subject reasons, "It's got to be this or that" (length of string or weight), he begins to approach the solution hypothetically. By experimenting with each of these two variables independently, he discovers that weight is irrelevant, but that the length of the string is the important variable.

3. *Combine by implication.* "If it is this, then that happens." Once a relevant variable has been identified, a more specific explanation can be tested and stated. "If the string is short then the swing is fast; if the string is long then the swing is slow." That is in essence what one of Inhelder and Piaget's (1958) sixteen-year-old subjects concluded, even though he initially believed that all four variables were involved.

4. *Combine by incompatibility.* "When this happens, then that does not." In the pendulum experiment, increasing and decreasing the weight does not change the oscillation of the pendulum and thus serves to eliminate a hypothesis that is incompatible with the actual observation. A common assumption in this experiment is that weight does make a difference. Consequently, the ability to combine by incompatibility appears in this instance relatively late in the operational stage.

Initially, in substage III-A the adolescent cannot yet reason out the whole range of intrapropositional combinations, which means that he can not produce systematic proof of his response by way of the schema "all other things being equal." It is only at substage III-B that the subject can spontaneously use this method. He now is capable of holding all other variables constant and can change systematically one variable at a time to study the effects. As his thought processes simulate the controls of a scientific experiment, his proofs become more rigorous and his generalizations gain in precision.

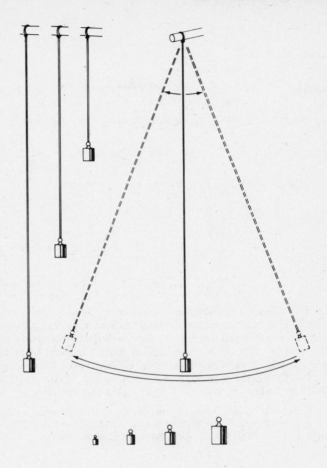

FIGURE 10. The pendulum problem utilizes a simple apparatus consisting of a string, which can be shortened or lengthened, and a set of varying weights. The other variables which at first might be considered relevant are the height of the release point and the force of the push given by the subject.

From *The Growth of Logical Thinking from Childhood to Adolescence,* by Bärbel Inhelder and Jean Piaget, © 1958 by Basic Books, Inc., Publishers, New York and Routledge & Kegan Paul, Ltd., London. Reproduced by permission.

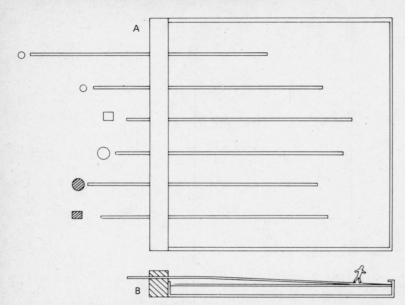

FIGURE 11. Diagram A illustrates the variables used in the flexibility experiment. The rods can be shortened or lengthened by varying the point at which they are clamped (see B for apparatus used). Cross-section forms are shown at the left of each rod; shaded forms represent brass rods, unshaded forms represent non-brass rods. Dolls are used for the weight variable (see B). These are placed at the end of the rod. Maximum flexibility is indicated when the end of the rod touches the water.

From *The Growth of Logical Thinking from Childhood to Adolescence*, by Bärbel Inhelder and Jean Piaget, © 1958 by Basic Books, Inc., Publishers, New York and Routledge & Kegan Paul, Ltd., London. Reproduced by permission.

Contrasting the responses of two adolescents in an experiment that involves five distinct variables may illustrate the reasoning of subjects in substage III-A with subjects in substage III-B who apparently are capable of using the schema "all other things being equal."

The apparatus consists of a vertical holder with clamps from which different rods can be horizontally suspended; the holder stands in a large basin of water. The subject is to determine the flexibility of the rods and especially under what circumstances they would touch the water. The flexibility of the rods is dependent on the following variables:

1. The material (steel and brass)
2. The length of the rods (they can be shortened or lengthened)
3. The thickness of the rods (7mm.^{2}, 10 mm.^{2}, 16 mm.^{2})
4. The cross section or form (round, square, and rectangular)
5. The weight attached to the suspended end of the rod (100 gr., 200 gr., 300 gr.)

The problem is to determine under what circumstances the rod touches the water level and to provide proof for the assertions made.

Pey (12; 9) speculates that if the rod is to touch the water it must be "long and thin." After several trials, he concludes: *"The larger and thicker it is, the more it resists."*—"What did you observe?"— *"This one* [brass, square, 50 cm. long, 16 mm.^{2} cross section with 300 gram weight] *bends more than that one* [steel; otherwise the same conditions which he has selected to be equal]: *it's another metal. And this one* [brass, round] *more than that one"* [brass, square; same conditions for weight and length, but 10 and 16 mm.^{2} cross section].—"If you wanted to buy a rod which bends the most possible?"— *"I would choose it round, thin, long, and made of a soft metal"* [Inhelder and Piaget, 1958: 56–57].

The ability to combine the results of each pair of comparisons leads to an understanding of the "structured whole" and—in contrast to the one-by-one comparisons of earlier stages—implies the operation of formal thought. Such an approach is "under construction" in substage III-A, but it does not become operational until substage III-B and makes the process of verification much more convincing as evidenced by the following protocol:

Dei (16; 10): "Tell me first [after experimental trials] what factors are at work here."— *"Weight, material, the length of the rod, perhaps the form."*—"Can you prove your hypotheses?"—[She compares the 200 gram and 300 gram weights on the same steel rod.] *"You see, the role of weight is demonstrated. For the material, I don't know."*—"Take these steel ones and these copper ones."— *"I think I have to take two rods with the same form. Then to demonstrate the role of the metal I compare these two* [steel and brass, square, 50 cm. long and 16 mm.^{2} cross section with 300 grams on each] *or these two here* [steel and brass, round, 50 and 22 cm. by 16 mm.^{2}]: *for length I shorten that one* [50 cm. brought down to 22]. *To demonstrate the role of the form, I can compare these two"* [round brass and square brass, 50 cm. and 16 mm.^{2}

for each.]—"Can the same thing be proved with these two?" [brass, round and square, 50 cm. long and 16 and 7 mm.^{2} cross section].— *"No, because that one* [7 mm.^{2}] *is much narrower."*—"And the width?" —*"I can compare these two"* [round, brass, 50 cm. long with 16 and 7 mm.^{2} cross section] [Inhelder and Piaget, 1958: 60].

The elegance of reasoning demonstrated here is based on the systematic verification of one variable at a time with "all other things being equal." And if one were to give substage III-B a theoretical name it ought to contain this "all other things being equal" quality.

A second set of formal groupings which appears in the propositional logic of the adolescent is made up of four transformations, referred to as the INCR group. Each of these letters stands for one of the logical transformations that can be performed on a propositional operation, changing it into a different operation. The acquisition of the INCR group is an important step in the development of logical thought in adolescence. An understanding of these four transformations is necessary in order to solve problems of proportionality and equilibrium.

1. *Identity or identity transformation "I."* This transformation is also referred to as the null transformation, since it results in no basic change; the original proposition retains its identity. A common-sense example of a typical proposition, which will be used to illustrate all four transformations, would be: "You can go to the dance or you can go to the theater." Transforming this statement using only "I" would result in no change of the original proposition. One of Piaget's experiments may provide another illustration. In a balance type weighing scale different size weights can be attached at other points on the crossbar. The problem is to develop an understanding of the concept of equilibrium, which is based on an awareness of proportionality. In an "I" transformation, the subject may increase simultaneously the weight and the distance in such a way that the balance remains unaffected. Any change would be of such a nature that the basic relationship between the elements —the equilibrium of the scale—retains its identity.

2. *Negation or inversion "N."* In an "N" transformation, everything in a given proposition is changed into the opposite of the original proposition. "All assertions become negations, and vice versa, and all conjunctions become disjunctions, and vice versa"

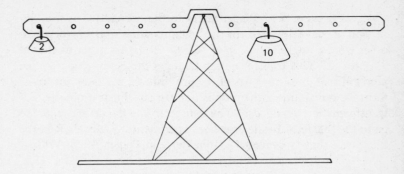

FIGURE 12. The balance scale used to assess children's concepts of proportionality. Different weights can be hung at different points on the crossbar.

Adapted from Inhelder and Piaget (1958).

(Flavell, 1963a: 216). The inverse to "all vertebrates" is "all non-vertebrates." Inversion or negation cancels out an operation and consequently constitutes a form of reversibility. If we apply an "N" transformation to the previous common-sense proposition it would become: "You cannot go to the dance and you cannot go to the theater." In the crossbar scale experiment, an "N" transformation would be to "reduce the distance while increasing the weight, or diminish the weight while increasing the distance or diminish both" (Inhelder and Piaget, 1958: 178).

3. *Reciprocal or reciprocity "R."* The reciprocal of a proposition transforms the proposition without changing the conjunction or disjunction that joins the parts of the proposition. "A is twice as large as B" becomes "B is twice as large as A." Reciprocity does not cancel a factor in the sense that negation or reversal does, but neutralizes one factor, which makes it possible to vary the other. It allows for systematic testing of hypotheses and makes experimental manipulation of variables possible. Application of an "R" transformation to our previous illustration would result in: "Either you cannot go to the dance or you cannot go to the theater." In the crossbar scale experiment "R compensates I by increasing both weight and distance on the other arm of the balance" (Inhelder and Piaget, 1958: 178).

4. *Correlative "C."* Piaget refers to the correlative as the "inversion of the reciprocal," or the "reciprocation of the inverse"; in other words, the relationship of "C" to "R" is the same as that of "N" to "I." This transformation changes the conjunction or disjunction that joins the parts of the proposition, but does not transform the remainder of the proposition. In our illustration, the "C" transformation would be: "You can go to the dance and you can go to the theater." In the crossbar experiment "C cancels R in the same way that N cancels I" (Inhelder and Piaget, 1958: 178).

The appearance of propositional logic and the transformation of propositions is one aspect of formal thought. Another dimension —closely interrelated with propositional operations—is the appearance of combinatorial operations. In an experiment conducted to illustrate the close relationship between propositional logic and combinatorial systems, the subject is exposed to four bottles of colorless, odorless liquids:

1. Diluted sulfuric acid
2. Water
3. Oxygenated water
4. Thiosulfate, and
5. A bottle with dropper, containing potassium iodide, called "g."

The bottles are labeled 1, 2, 3, 4, and g. The subject does not know the chemical elements in each flask. The mixture $1 + 3 + g$ produces a yellow liquid. Adding 4 to this mixture bleaches the color. The experimenter in addition has two flasks, one containing $1 + 3$ and the second containing 2. While the subject is watching, he adds a few drops of g to both bottles, pointing to the different reactions. The subject's problem now is to reproduce the yellow color using any combination of the bottles 1, 2, 3, 4, and g.

The approaches of the concrete operational child are characterized by two forms of behavior: first, he systematically adds g to all combinations, since this is what he saw the experimenter do; second, he appears to think that color is attributed to only one of the elements and thus he reveals the basic difference between a noncombinatorial and a combinatorial structure of intelligence.

Gay (7; 6) also limits himself to 4 × g, 1 × g, 3 × g, and 2 × g, and discovers nothing else. "Could you try with two bottles together?"— [Silence.]—"Try."—[4 × 1 × g] *"It doesn't work."*—"Try something else."—[3 × 1 × g] *"There it is!"*—"And that one [2], do you think that it will be as yellow?"—[No trial.]—"What do you think makes the color, the three together or only two?" *"Here"* [3].—"And that one?" [1].— *"There isn't any color."*—"And that one?" [g].— *"Yes, it's there inside."*—"Then what good are 1 and 3?"— *"There isn't any color"* [Inhelder and Piaget, 1958; 111].

Gay follows the pattern of the early operational child. He adds g to all combinations and ascribes the quality of color to one particular liquid, first to 3 and then to g.

In substage III-A, systematic n-by-n combinations become possible. In addition, even when III-A finds the correct solution, 1 + 3 + g, he is not satisfied and tries other combinations. His interest reaches beyond a solution of the problem to an understanding of the total structure and the total number of combinations.

Sar (12; 3): "Make me some more yellow."— *"Do you take the liquid from the yellow glass with all four?"*—"I won't tell you."—[He tries first with 4 × 2 × g, then 2 × g × 4 × g] *"Not yet.* [He tries to smell the odor of the liquids, then tries 4 × 1 × g] *No yellow yet. Quite a big mystery!* [He tries the four, then each one independently with g; then he spontaneously proceeds to various two-by-two combinations but has the feeling that he forgot some of them.] *I'd better write it down to remind myself:* 1 × 4 *is done;* 4 × 3 *is done; and* 2 × 3. *Several more that I haven't done* [he finds all six, then adds the drops and finds the yellow for 1 × 3 × g]. *Ah! it's turning yellow. You need* 1, 3, *and the drops."*—"Where is the yellow?"— . . . —"In there?" [g]— *"No, they go together."*—"And 2?"— *"I don't think it has any effect, it's water."* —"And 4?"— *"It doesn't do anything either, it's water too. But I want to try again; you can't ever be too sure* [he tries 2 × 4 × g]. *Give me a glass of water* [he takes it from the faucet and mixes 3 × 1 × water × g—i.e., the combination which gave him the color, plus water from the faucet, knowing that 1 × 2 × 3 × 4 × g produce nothing]. *No, it isn't water. Maybe it's a substance that keeps it from coloring* [he puts together 1 × 3 × 2 × g, then 1 × 3 × 4 × g] *Ah! There it is! That one* [4] *keeps it from coloring."*—"And that?" [2].— *"It's water"* [Inhelder and Piaget, 1958: 116–117].

Substage III-B, while not basically different from III-A, manipulates these materials more systematically, more quickly, and with an eye toward proof. Piaget describes this method "as a generalization of substitution and addition."

Eng (14; 6) begins with $2 \times g$; $1 \times g$; $3 \times g$; and $4 \times g$: *"No, it doesn't turn yellow. So you have to mix them."* He goes on to the six two-by-two combinations and at last hits $1 \times 3 \times g$: *"This time I think it works."* —"Why?"— *"It's 1 and 3 and some water."*—"You think it's water?" — *"Yes, no difference in odor. I think that it's water."*—"Can you show me?"—He replaces g with some water: $1 \times 3 \times$ water. *"No, it's not water. It's a chemical product: it combines with 1 and 3 and then it turns into a yellow liquid* [he goes on to three-by-three combinations beginning with the replacement of g by 2 and by 4—*i.e.*, $1 \times 3 \times 2$ and $1 \times 3 \times 4$]. *No, these two products aren't the same as the drops: they can't produce color with 1 and 3* [then he tries $1 \times 3 \times g \times 2$]. *It stays the same with 2. I can try right away with 4* [$1 \times 3 \times g \times 4$]. *It turns white again: 4 is the opposite of g because 4 makes the color go away while g makes it appear."*—"Do you think that there is water in [any of the] bottles?"— *"I'll try* [he systematically replaces 1 and 3 by water, trying $1 \times g \times$ water and $3 \times g \times$ water, having already tried $1 \times 3 \times$ water]. *No, that means 3 isn't water and 1 isn't water."* He notices that the glass $1 \times 3 \times g \times 2$ has stayed clearer than $1 \times 3 \times g$. *"I think 2 must be water. Perhaps 4 also?* [He tries $1 \times 3 \times g \times 4$ again] *So it's not water: I had forgotten that it turned white; 4 is a product that makes the white return"* [Inhelder and Piaget, 1958: 120–121].

Another illustration of the same principle of combinatorial operations is suggested by Hunt. His example is particularly relevant, since it demarks the preadolescent thought processes from those found in adolescence. He begins with the assumption that animals are classified into two basic classes:

1. Vertebrates (V) and its inverse, invertebrate (I), and
2. Those animals that live on land, terrestrial (T), and those that live in water, aquatic (A).

Hunt (1961) hypothesizes what would happen if the subjects were asked to describe all possible combinations of animal life on a newly discovered planet. The concrete operational child in all probability would respond with four classes of animal life:

1. (VT) vertebrates terrestrial
2. (VA) vertebrates aquatic
3. (IT) invertebrates terrestrial
4. (IA) invertebrates aquatic.

The adolescent who possesses formal operations and can bring combinatorial analysis to bear on the problem might be able to conceive of sixteen forms of animal life. Thus, his thought would correspond to the sixteen possible relations that are considered to be the inevitable outcome of combining two such propositions by modern logic.

1. No animals at all
2. Only (VT)
3. Only (VA)
4. Only (IT)
5. Only (IA)
6. (VT) and (VA), but not (IT) or (IA)
7. (VT) and (IT), but not (VA) or (IA)
8. (VT) and (IA), but not (VA) or (IT)
9. (VA) and (IT), but not (VT) or (IA)
10. (VA) and (IA), but not (VT) or (IT)
11. (IT) and (IA), but not (VA) or (VT)
12. (VT), (VA), and (IT) but not (IA)
13. (VT), (VA), and (IA) but not (IT)
14. (VT), (IT), and (IA) but not (VA)
15. (VA), (IT), and (IA) but not (VT)
16. All four classes (Hunt, 1961: 232).

The concrete grouping structure of the concrete operational child does not possess the combinatorial system necessary to select the total number of possible combinations that produce the "structured whole." Concrete operations identify the four multiplicative classes VT, VA, IT, IA; but to reason beyond these four concrete combinations requires an understanding of the structured whole and a combinatorial method that sees the relationship between the classes vertebrates and terrestrial as more than multiplicative classes, but sees these four classes as the factors that taken n-by-n produce the sixteen possible combinations.

Educational Implications

In his interaction with children in various experimental situations, Piaget observes that children show resistance to learning from instruction. Apparently, the existing cognitive structure of the subject determines the degree of understanding that the child can bring to the solution of the problem. Piaget so skillfully challenges the subject to the limit of his understanding that the child is seemingly unable to be guided beyond these limits. And even if correct explanations are provided by way of instruction, the child appears to return to his own level of cognitive understanding as indicated by his earlier responses, rather than to produce any generalized cognitive growth that would transcend these earlier established limits.

The protocol of such an interaction between a child and the experimenter may serve to illustrate such a situation. The child is presented with an open box that contains twenty wooden beads; eighteen of these beads are brown, two are white. The child is asked which are there more of, brown beads or wooden beads. The preoperational child cannot distinguish brownness as a subclass to woodenness and consequently would answer "There are more brown beads, because there are only two white ones."

> So you say: "Listen, this is not what I am asking. I don't want to know whether there are more brown or more white beads, I want to know whether there are more brown beads or more wooden beads." And, in order to make it easier, I take an empty box and place it next to the one with the beads and I ask: "If I were to put the wooden beads into that box would any remain in this one?" The child answers "No, none would be left because they are all wooden." Then I say: "If I were to take the brown beads and put them into that box, would any be left in this one?" The child replies: "Of course, two or three white ones would remain." Apparently he has now understood the situation, the fact that all the beads are wooden and that some are not brown. So I ask him once more: "Are there more brown beads or more wooden beads?" Now it is evident that the child begins to understand the problem, sees that there is indeed a problem, that matters are not as simple as they seemed at first. As we watch him, we observe that he is thinking very hard. Finally he concludes: "But there are still more brown beads; if you take the brown ones away, only two or three white beads remain!" [Piaget, 1963: 290.]

Development is seen as an increase in complexity, mobility, and systematization of schemata and logical structures, which result from the equilibrium-equilibration process, but which cannot be substantially accelerated by instruction. Obviously, in the assimilation-accommodation process education plays a significant role, but the assimilation-accommodation process moves in very minute steps; if the gaps in this process are too large, as they apparently are in the incident cited previously, the individual cannot accommodate. The teacher has to be skillful in maintaining the proper level of tension between assimilation and accommodation to foster conceptual growth. On this particular issue, Piaget appears very close to a maturational, or readiness, interpretation of development and reveals a somewhat pessimistic outlook on education.

Interestingly enough, it is on this issue that some of Piaget's close associates and followers seem to depart most strongly from his interpretation. Bruner, who apparently is greatly influenced by Piaget's theorizing seems to take a diametrically opposed point of view. Bruner's now famous postulate: "We begin with the hypothesis that any subject can be taught effectively in some intellectually honest form to any child at any stage of development" (Bruner, 1960: 33), is a statement with which Piaget disagrees rather strongly. On the other hand, Bruner quotes and appears to agree with Inhelder's statement that it may be worthwhile to devote two years of schooling "to a series of exercises in manipulating, classifying, and ordering objects in ways that highlight basic operations of logical addition, multiplication, inclusion, serial ordering and the like" (Bruner, 1960: 46). This would constitute a rather direct employment of Piagetian concepts on the school curriculum.

Research gives evidence that Piagetian problems can be taught and that teaching such concepts accelerates cognitive growth. Ojemann (1963) has shown that guided learning experiences, such as teaching preadolescents the reasons why objects sink or float, significantly affects the child's thought structure. Aebli (1963), a former associate of Piaget, has expanded his teacher's theory of development and modified it toward an educational theory. Aebli uses in one of his experiments the arrangement in which the subject looks at three mountains and is asked to identify what the scenery would look like from different angles. He demonstrated that the method of presentation and the number and nature of significant cues are as important as the child's cognitive structure. He varies the complexity of the problem by providing the subject with: (1) the contours of the mountains only; (2) contours and surface structure of the mountains; and (3) contours, surface structure, and color of the mountains. The findings indicate that the child's ability to perceive the perspective correctly is as much a function of these educational variables as of the child's operational structure.

Aebli and Bruner do not maintain that the child's logical structure can be substantially accelerated by educational procedures. They are, however, somewhat more optimistic than Piaget in attributing a greater importance to the curriculum planner, since they feel that complex concepts can be reduced to fit the logical structure of the child. The task of the educator then becomes that of the "translator" who has to present the curriculum content on such a level and in such a way that it corresponds to the cognitive structure of the child. The curriculum is systematically correlated to the child's capacity to assimilate and accommodate the material. Such translation implies that any learning problem for the preoperational child has to be presented in the form of direct sensory experiences, whereas the preadolescent would have to work with concrete problems, and the adolescent would be able to work with abstract ideas and verbal propositions. More specifically, the formal operations found in the adolescent become the psychological prerequisite for effectively teaching geometry, proportionality, proposition, and probabilistic reasoning. Such an approach would make it mandatory for the educator to assess the operational structure of the child. Efforts are being made both in Geneva and in the United States to construct tests made up of Piagetian test items that will serve this purpose.

The age norms in Piaget's books, however, are only approximations or, at best, generalizations, and not statistical averages. His theory does not provide for variability of behavior or individual differences, an omission that is especially appalling to the educator. Nor is Piaget concerned with variables, such as sex, socioeconomic class, IQ, and reading level. However, knowledge of Piaget's theory gives the educator new insights into the limitations and abilities of children at various stages in cognitive development. Did it occur to anyone that children might think—assuming equality exists—that there is more milk in a thin, tall glass than in a wide, low glass before Piaget's experiments became known?

Finally, it is not only the content of Piaget's theory and the substance of his findings that are relevant to the educator—but his methods as well. The method by which he collects data is frequently referred to as the "clinical method," which means that the child actively searches for the solution of the problem. The examiner stimulates and challenges the child to reflect on his own answers and to use this discourse as a means to clarify his own thought. Piaget (1947a) wholeheartedly believes in the child's autonomy and his active participation in his own cognitive growth. "There are two basic and correlated principles from which an educator inspired by psychology can never depart:

1. That the only real truths are those that one builds freely one's self, and are not those received from without;
2. That moral good is essentially autonomous and cannot be prescribed."

Through his method, he skillfully questions the child and provides for learning, pushing him to the limit of his operational structure without giving him ready-made answers.

Applying Piaget's findings about children's cognitive growth to teaching could have a revolutionary impact on the planning of the curriculum. The content itself would be influenced or, more important, the logical processes by which we think and by which we attempt to solve problems could become a major area of focus in any educational endeavor. Thus, there would be a more systematic emphasis on systems of classification, on reversibility, on logical transformations, and on the process of logic in general.

12

Lawrence Kohlberg's Cognitive-Developmental Approach to Adolescent Morality*

Piaget's Contribution to an Understanding of Children's Moral Judgment

Piaget, in *The Moral Judgment of the Child* (1932), postulated that the development of children's moral judgment follows the same basic patterns as those of cognitive development in general (discussed in the previous chapter), since moral schemata are based on the child's cognitive structures. Moral development is dependent on such cognitive skills as the perception of reality, the organization and evaluation of experiences, the making of fine discriminations and generalizations, and later, during adolescence, the ability to reason abstractly. Piaget's interest was primarily in moral judgment rather than in moral behavior. The distinction between moral judgment and moral behavior is an important one. Moral judgment refers to the evaluation of the "goodness" or "rightness" of a course of action in a hypothetical dilemma situation. Moral behavior refers to the individual's ability not to steal, to lie, to cheat, and so on, in an actual situation in which these temptations offer themselves. Piaget and Kohlberg have assumed that the structures underlying verbal moral judgment and nonverbal moral behavior are related but not identical. Various research studies have demonstrated that the relationship between moral judgment and moral

*Chapter 12 has been published as "Kohlberg's Cognitive-Developmental Approach to Adolescent Morality," *Adolescence,* 1974, (in press).

behavior is not very high (Hartshorne and May, 1928–1930), although some positive relationships have been observed (Rubin and Schneider, 1973). The fact that a person knows the right behavior is no assurance that he will actually behave that way.

Piaget found that a basic shift in the quality of the child's moral judgment takes place when he progresses from preoperational thought processes to operational thought processes at about the age of seven and again at twelve when concrete operational thought gives way to formal or abstract thought processes. The morality of the preoperational child is identified as "morality of constraint" or "moral realism" and is described as showing "blind obedience" to authority. Justice is seen as resting in the person who has authority. The child's moral concepts have developed from his parents' teaching of what is right and what is wrong; he does not yet have the intellectual structure to consider other alternatives nor the emotional capacity to empathize with others. The preoperational child is not yet able to decenter—that is, to shift from one point of view to another or to take the view of another person into account. As the child's capacity to decenter increases, he becomes more altruistic in orientation and behavior (Rubin and Schneider, 1973). The preoperational child approaches moral dilemmas from an "objective" viewpoint—that is, he is primarily concerned with the objective amount of physical damage caused by an act rather than the intent or motivation behind the behavior. As the child begins to develop operational thought processes, his moral judgment is identified as "morality of cooperation" and begins to reflect a "subjective" morality—that is, his primary concern is no longer with the objective amount of damage caused, but with the subjective intention or motivation of the act. The child begins to take the viewpoint of others into consideration and understands reciprocal relationships. In one of Piaget's stories, the question is who is naughtier: John who opens a door and accidentally breaks fifteen cups that were behind the door and that he did not see, or Henry, who tries to get some cookies, climbs on a chair, and, in the process, breaks one cup. The preoperational child feels that John is naughtier since the primary concern is with the objective damage. The operational child judges Henry to be the naughtier, since now subjective intention is given more weight than objective material damage.

The preoperational child's moral judgments have two essential characteristics: moral realism and immanent justice. Moral realism means that moral rules have an existence of their own and cannot be changed. Any suggested change in the rules strikes the child as a transgression (Piaget, 1932: 18). Immanent justice refers to the child's belief that his misbehavior inevitably brings on pain or punishment as a natural consequence of his transgression of rules. For example, the child who steals and later, on his way home, falls and hurts himself becomes convinced that the fall was the punishment for his stealing. The shift from moral realism to "moral relativism" reflects that the child no longer blindly follows orders but considers the intent of the act rather than the letter of the law. And the law—or the rules that govern his behavior—can be changed. Most of Piaget's early work on the development of moral judgments was concerned with children rather than with adolescents.

The highest stage of moral development, characteristic of adolescence, is dependent on the attainment of formal reasoning or abstract operations, and is referred to as moral autonomy. The development of this orientation begins at the age of eleven or twelve. In a game situation the adolescent is not only interested in the rules of the game, but in anticipating all possible cases to which these rules apply. Now that abstract thought is possible, the adolescent develops a sense of ethical and moral responsibility that is based on abstract principles of what is right and what is wrong.

> The same is true of the concept of social justice and of rational, aesthetic, or social ideals. As a result of the acquisition of such values, decisions, whether in opposition to or in agreement with the adult, have an altogether different significance than they do in the small social groups of younger children. . . . The possibilities opened up by these new values are obvious in the adolescent, who differs from the child in that he is not only capable of forming theories but is also concerned with choosing a career that will permit him to satisfy his need for social reform and for new ideas [Piaget and Inhelder, 1969: 151].

Levels of Moral Development

Kohlberg, inspired by Piaget's cognitive-developmental approach to moral development, expands the structural cognitive approach through more systematic longitudinal, cross-cultural, social class, and educational research (Blatt, 1959; Kohlberg, 1963, 1969; Kohlberg and Blatt, 1972; Kohlberg and Kramer, 1969; and Turiel, 1966, 1969). Kohlberg distinguishes three basic levels of moral development: the preconventional or premoral level; the conventional level; and the postconventional or autonomous level. Morality is an idea of justice that is primitive, undifferentiated, and egocentric in young children, but that becomes more sophisticated and social as the adolescent moves through specific stages of moral thinking; it may reach, in some individuals, an awareness of universal values and ethical principles.

The preconventional level of moral thinking is prevalent during childhood and includes approximately the ages four to ten. The child is responsive to the definitions of what is good and bad provided by his social reference group, and he is often well behaved. However, the reasons for his moral judgments are different from those of adults, since his moral structure is still less differentiated. Moral decisions are primarily egocentric, based on his own self-interest and material considerations. He interprets acts as good and bad in terms of the physical consequences: that is, he operates in terms of what Piaget calls "objective judgments."

The second level is the conventional or moral level, which is less egocentric and more sociocentric in basic orientation. Kohlberg describes it as conformity to social conventions, expressed by a strong desire to maintain, support, and justify the existing social structure. In general, most adolescents and even the majority of adults operate on the conventional level. As an individual progresses into adolescence, it becomes increasingly more difficult—in contrast to Freud's, Erikson's, and Gesell's theories, and even Piaget's cognitive stages of development—to associate any one chronological age, or even a developmental period such as adolescence, with any one level of thinking. Many adults continue to function at the conventional level, while some mature adolescents operate at the postconventional level.

The third level is the postconventional or autonomous level. The approach to moral issues is no longer based on egocentric needs, nor on conformity to the existing social order, but on autonomous, universal principles of justice that have validity even beyond existing laws, social conventions, or one's group of social peers. At the highest level of moral development, moral judgment and moral behavior are more closely related than at the two earlier levels.

Kohlberg further subdivides each of his three levels into two stages and thus creates a more differentiated and elaborate theory of six stages of moral development, or, since it does refer to adults as well, a typology of moral orientation that has been applied to conservative, liberal, and radical political orientations (Hampden-Turner and Whitten, 1971). Each stage of moral development represents a distinct moral philosophy that has implications for social and political organization. The classification of individuals into these moral stages is based on their resolution of verbal moral dilemmas that Kohlberg presents to his subjects. The following story illustrates one of Kohlberg's philosophical dilemmas. A woman is dying of cancer. A new drug that could save her life has been discovered by the local druggist. The druggist, who has not invested much in the drug, sells it for $2,000—about ten times what it cost him to make the drug. The sick woman's husband tries to borrow money from friends, but he can only raise $1,000. He approaches the druggist, asking him to sell the drug for half the price or let him, the husband, repay the rest at a later time. The druggist refuses. The husband, in desperation, breaks into the store and steals the drug. Should he have done so? Why? The subject, if necessary, is questioned as to the rightness or wrongness of his decision, the rights of the druggist, the duties of the husband, the appropriate punishment for the husband, and the obligations an individual has toward relatives and nonrelatives. Classification of responses is not so much based on what an adolescent decides to do in such a dilemma, but on the moral reasoning that leads to the proposed answer or the moral structure behind the response. This means that all classifications are based on moral verbal behavior that may not be directly related to nonverbal moral behavior.

Stages in Moral Development

Stage One: Obedience and Punishment Orientation. The main motive given for obeying a rule at this stage is to avoid punishment and achieve gratification. The child's conscience is based on an irrational, egocentric fear of punishment. He manifests an unquestioning submission to superior power and an effort to avoid trouble. He is still confused concerning the value of human meaning and human life, and people are valued according to the benefits they can bring him. The physical damage rather than the human intent of an act is considered in evaluating its goodness or badness. This confusion of the physical with the social-moral world is what Piaget calls "moral realism." In the previously described dilemma, the subject may fear that God will punish him if he lets his wife die.

Stage Two: Instrumental Relativist Orientation. The child can now distinguish between the physical and the social-moral world, but he confuses individual needs and what he thinks is right and wrong. At this stage, morally right behavior is based on what satisfies one's own needs, reflecting a basic hedonistic orientation. And the major motivation is to manipulate others in order to obtain rewards. The notion of reciprocity is beginning to emerge, and, consequently, under certain circumstances the needs of others are taken into consideration. However, interpersonal relationships are viewed as analogous to the economic marketplace. That is, reciprocity is based on an exchange of powers and favors rather than on considerations of loyalty and justice. A philosophy of "you scratch my back and I'll scratch your back" prevails. Fairness, reciprocity, and sharing do exist, but they are viewed in pragmatic, physical, personal, utilitarian ways. Tom Sawyer's episode of the whitewashing of the fence is characteristic of this level of moral development. The criterion for making a moral judgment is based on selfish needs as in the case of the child who believed the man should steal the lifesaving drug for his ill wife because if she dies, nobody will look after his interests and needs. The stage two subject cannot yet decenter his thinking to take the position of another individual in an objective manner. Stages one and two are typical of preadolescents and delinquents and are basically premoral, since self-interest and material considerations determine moral decisions.

Stage Three: Interpersonal Concordance Orientation. Kohlberg refers to this first stage of the conventional level as the "good-boy"— "good-girl," approval-seeking orientation in moral development.

Need and morality can be distinguished, but the confusion now is between social approval and right or wrong. Good behavior is now defined as behavior that pleases or helps others, and the child will try to behave well in order to win the approval of others. Morality is now defined by the ties that the individual has to his social group. The child seeks to win the approval of his immediate social group through virtuous behavior and to live up to the expectations he thinks others have. There is conformity to what is believed to be majority opinion on "natural behavior." In an Ash-type experiment seventh grade adolescents in stage three were more conforming than their age-mates who had attained higher or lower social judgment levels (Saltzstein, Diamond, and Belenky, 1972). Behavior is judged by intention, as in Piaget's subjective stage, frequently expressed in the child's concern with "he means well." Often this argument is overused, as with the cartoon character Charlie Brown in *Peanuts.* Stage three also describes the Mary Poppins type of moral philosophy. A stage three subject, as a husband, will do what any responsible husband is supposed to do—protect his wife.

Stage Four: Orientation Toward Authority, Law, and Duty. Morality at stage four is characterized by a strong belief in "law and order," which becomes a primary value. Moral rules are separated from feelings of approval, but the rules are concrete, "thou shalt not . . . ," rather than abstract principles of justice. One obeys and respects the law in order to avoid the penalty that legitimate authority can impose. Breaking the law results in guilt feelings. Therefore, moral behavior is motivated by guilt and fear of legitimate censors. The basic orientation is a faith in existing authority, fixed rules, and the maintenance of social order at any price. The emphasis is on doing one's duty—exemplified, for instance, by Colonel Saito in the *Bridge over the River Kwai,* who rigidly maintained his lifelong orientation toward duty, authority, and a fixed social order. Moral behavior is obeying the law, doing one's duty, showing respect for authority, and maintaining the social order. "Life is conceived as sacred in terms of its place in categorical moral and religious order of rights and duties" (Kohlberg, 1970: 184). Since marriage is an institution essential to society and based on law, the stage four subject, as the husband in the earlier example, may consider it his lawful duty to steal the drug.

Stages three and four are the conventional group- and law-oriented levels of moral development in which most adolescents and even the majority of adults function. However, Kohlberg (1964) has argued that in late adolescence the continued endorsement of conventional morality reflects a deficiency in moral development.

Stage Five: Social Contract Orientation. Moral judgment at this postconventional level of moral development is defined in terms of general principles such as individual rights, human dignity, equality, contractual agreement, and mutual obligations. Consequently, this stage is referred to as the principled stage. Moral principles have been examined and are agreed upon by the society as a whole. Moral behavior is motivated by a concern for the welfare of the larger community and a desire for community respect. The purpose of the law is to preserve human rights. Therefore, unfair or unjust laws must be changed. In contrast to the person in stage four, the individual in stage five is much more willing to view the law as flexible and changing, as long as these changes follow rational deliberations and considerations of social utility and are based on consensus. This is the official morality of the American Constitution and government. However, although the American democracy is philosophically based on the moral judgment represented by stage five, Kohlberg reports that only one out of three adult Americans has actually reached this level of moral development. The husband who is a stage five subject may decide to steal the drug in order to save his wife. The husband and wife promised to love each other regardless of the circumstances, and their moral commitment to each other is sanctioned by society.

Stage Six: Universal Ethical Principles Orientation. Morality at the highest principled stage of moral development is viewed as a decision of conscience that is based on self-chosen ethical principles that place the highest value on human life, equality, and dignity. The concept of justice goes beyond any particular existing social order that emerges. These ethical principles are characterized by consistency, logical comprehensiveness, and universality. They are abstract, such as the golden rule or Immanuel Kant's categorical imperative, rather than specific moral rules such as the Ten Commandments. One cannot be at the individual principled level without having been first at the social contract level and without having understood the basic contractual nature of the existing social order. The individual governed by universal ethical principles may practice civil disobedience, not out of disrespect for the law, but out of respect for a higher morality than the existing law. Unjust laws may be broken, because morality is grounded not in legality, but in ethical principles of justice and in respect for the rights of the individual. In practicing civil disobedience, the individual accepts the penalty in order to demonstrate the principles of justice, human rights, and the dignity of human beings to society at large. The stage six individual feels that no law, no contract, no moral obligation, and no fear of punishment can interfere with his desire to save those he loves. As the husband in the story, he will steal the drug first of all to save the life of his wife; secondly, he will steal the drug and accept the penalty to demonstrate to society that the right to live is so fundamental that it must and should take precedent over the right to make a profit. The visionaries and moral leaders of society—Joan of Arc, Abraham Lincoln, Henry David Thoreau, Martin Luther King, Jr., and Claus Schenk von Stauffenberg, for example—seem to have been governed by universal ethical principles that challenged the existing morality of their society and times.

The thinking of a man oriented toward universal moral principles can best be expressed by a brief quote from Martin Luther King's letter from a Birmingham jail:

> I do not advocate evading or defying the law, as would the rabid segregationist. That would lead to anarchy. One who breaks an unjust law must do so openly, lovingly, and with a willingness to accept the penalty. An individual who breaks a law that conscience tells him is unjust, and who willingly accepts the penalty of imprisonment in order to arouse the conscience of the community over its injustice, is in reality expressing the highest respect for the law [King, 1964: 86].

The Invariant Developmental Sequence in Moral Thinking

Kohlberg (1970) proposed that these six stages of moral development represent an invariant developmental sequence—they are universal and the thinking of any one stage is consistently applied to a variety of situations. Development moves from the lower to the higher stages in an invariant sequence, which means that the child moves step by step through each of the stages. The sequence of these stages is constant, and a child cannot skip a stage, but the age at which a person reaches a certain stage differs from individual to individual and from culture to culture. An adolescent cannot function at stage five without having previously moved through stages three and four. A child may remain fixated at any one stage and not move on, but if he eventually does move on, it is in a stepwise progression. Children and adolescents do move through these stages with varying speeds so that the relationship between chronological age and stage of moral judgment becomes less precise as one grows older. To give age approximations is no longer appropriate after the child has left stages one and two, which are generally associated with childhood. The moral thinking of stages three to six can be found in adolescents as well as adults, and some adults never reach stage five or six. Thinking at stages five and six is most commonly found in college-educated middle-class youth, and even they may regress to earlier stages of moral development after their college education has been completed. Only about 10 percent of American adults reach stage six, and many adults continue to function on the "law-and-order" level of moral development, giving this issue potency in election campaigns. Stages five and six, based on principled morality, do have as a prerequisite the attainment of abstract formal operations in mental development. Consequently, one cannot simply associate any one stage of moral development with adolescence. But since adolescence is a period of progression through several of these stages, all of Kohlberg's stages are relevant to a discussion of theories of adolescence. Much of Kohlberg's research deals with subjects in the age range from ten to sixteen and a follow-up in their twenties. Adolescents may be found at any one of Kohlberg's stages of moral development, though most have passed through stages one and two, excluding individuals whose concept of justice develops late or who are delinquent in their moral orientation. A few morally precocious adolescents may already have reached stage five, or in an exceptional case, stage six. However, adolescence is characterized by progression through at least some of these stages of moral thinking.

When Kohlberg maintains that these stages are universal, he believes that the moral structure reflected in the moral decisions in his dilemma situations is not just a matter of learning cultural values, but that the sequential patterning of these stages occurs under varying cultural conditions and that the principles of justice reflected in stages five and six are free from culturally defined content.

Consistency does not imply "moral character" or moral trait. There is, however, a high degree of consistency from one moral stage to another, and within a moral stage. The thinking of about 50 percent of the individuals tested was within a single stage, even though the subjects responded to a variety of moral dilemma situations. Some, who apparently were progressing from one stage to another, were responding partly in stage three, partly in stage four, but rarely in stages two or five.

Cross-Cultural, Socioeconomic, and Political Differences in Moral Thinking

In support for the claim of cultural universality, Kohlberg (1964) has conducted research in the development of moral thinking of adolescents not only in the United States, but he has also presented cross-cultural evidence from Great Britain, Canada, Taiwan, Mexico, and Turkey. The data presented in Figures 13 and 14 support his claim of the universality of his developmental stages, although his sample includes few primitive societies. In all societies studied, he finds that stages one and two decline sharply as a function of age, especially between ages ten and thirteen. The thinking representative of stages three and four increases until middle adolescence, and in primitive societies until late adolescence, and then begins to decline or levels off. Moral judgments representative of stages five and six show a very slow but steady increase during adolescence in all societies, although the total percentage of even late adolescents reaching these advanced stages remains very small —a fact that appears to be more pronounced in educationally and technologically underdeveloped societies (Kohlberg, 1970). These patterns of changes in moral thinking in adolescents apparently remain the same in all cultures studied. Kohlberg reports that anthropologists had warned him that he would have to throw away his culture-bound stories and stages. In a dilemma situation in which the wife is starving to death and the husband has no money to buy food and thus must choose between stealing or letting his wife die, Taiwanese adolescents typically gave stage-two responses: he should steal because if he lets her die, he must pay for the funeral. In the Atayl village, where funerals are not so expensive, the typical stage-two response was that the husband should steal because he needed the wife to prepare his food. Thus, while the specific content of responses is influenced by prevalent cultural patterns of living, the underlying moral philosophy is basically the same in both responses.

Kohlberg did find that there are cultural differences in the specific stages when adolescents progress from one moral stage to a more advanced stage. In general, more advanced forms of moral judgment appear later in more primitive societies. For example, in

why?

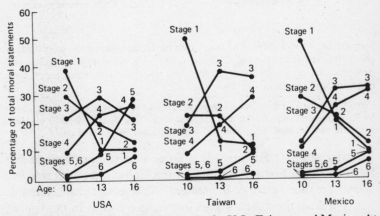

FIGURE 13 Middle-class urban boys in the U.S., Taiwan, and Mexico. At age 10, the stages are used according to difficulty. At age 13, Stage 3 is most used by all three groups. At age 16, U.S. boys have reversed the order of age 10 stages (with the exception of 6). In Taiwan and Mexico, conventional (3–4) stages prevail at age 16, with Stage 5 also little used.

From Lawrence Kohlberg, Moral Development and the Education of Adolescents. In R. F. Purnell, *Adolescents and the American High School.* © 1970 by Holt, Rinehart and Winston, Inc., New York. Reproduced by permission.

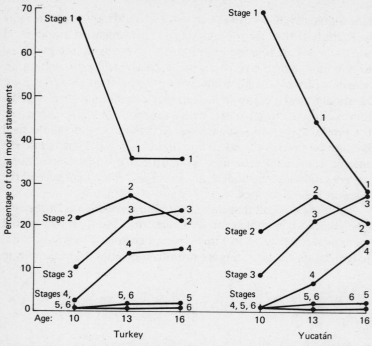

FIGURE 14. Two isolated villages, one in Turkey, the other in Yucatán, show similar patterns in moral thinking. There is no reversal of order, and preconventional (1–2) thought does not gain a clear ascendancy over conventional stages at age 16.

From Lawrence Kohlberg, Moral Development and the Education of Adolescents. In R. F. Purnell, *Adolescents and the American High School.* © 1970 by Holt, Rinehart and Winston, Inc., New York. Reproduced by permission.

Yucatán, more sixteen-year-old children were still in stage one and fewer in stages five and six than in the United States. Stages five and six are rarely attained in preliterate villages or tribal communities. The findings comparing socioeconomic classes in the United States are not too different from the results from cross-cultural comparisons. The basic pattern of moral development of middle- and lower-class youth is the same, but "middle-class children were found to be more advanced in moral judgment than matched lower-class children" (Kohlberg, 1970:154). Kohlberg argues that basic moral values are not specifically related to social class, as frequently used terminology such as "middle-class values" implies, but that middle- and lower-class individuals subscribe to similar basic moral values.

Among young adults, those who are political conservatives and refer to law and order and the maintaining of the political system tend to make moral judgments characteristic of stage four. Adults in stage three emphasize "conformity to stereotyped roles" and think in terms of cultural stereotypes, such as Miss America, the drug addicts, our boys, red-blooded Americans, and so on. Liberals and moderates try to make stage five moral judgments, whereas radicals and revolutionaries are strangely divided between idealistic stage-six and egoistic stage-two reponses (Hampden-Turner and Whitten, 1971). Individuals in stage six and less so in stage five provide for innovation, experimentation, and change in a society. Individuals in stages three and four represent the conventional and conservative elements in society.

Relationship of Kohlberg's Stages of Moral Judgment to Other Stage Theories

According to Kohlberg, there is a point-to-point relationship between his stages of moral judgment and Piaget's stages of cognitive development. Piaget's concrete operations correspond to the preoperational level of moral development. The earlier concern of the operational child with categorical classifications is related to the punishment-obedience orientation of stage one in moral thinking. The concrete reversibility of thought patterns, still part of Piaget's operational stage in logical thinking, has its analogue in Kohlberg's stage two of an instrumental relativistic moral orientation. The basic shift from childhood to adolescence is reflected in a dramatic shift from concrete to formal or abstract thought processes, just as the shift from preconventional to conventional morality constitutes the basic difference between child and adolescent moral structure. Piaget's earlier substage of formal operations concerned with relationships involving the inverse of reversibility corresponds to Kohlberg's interpersonal concordance orientation (stage three). Piaget's more advanced substage III-B of formal abstract operations encompasses Kohlberg's stage four orientation toward authority, law and order, and makes the more advanced postconventional principled stages five and six possible. Sixty percent of a group of sixteen-year-old adolescents had attained formal operational thinking, but only 10 percent had reached the postconventional levels of moral thinking. But all 10 percent who had reached the postconventional level of principled morality were able to think in terms of logical, abstract, formal operations. The relationship between Piaget's logical stages and Kohlberg's moral stages is such that the attainment of logical thought is a necessary precondition for the attainment of the corresponding level of moral thought. However, having attained a certain stage in logical thought, it does not follow that an individual has necessarily attained the same level in moral judgment. It may be, and frequently is, lower but never higher.

Kohlberg's stages of moral development have also been related to Erikson's stages of ego-identity. The research is based on Marcia's (1966) methodology and was conducted by Podd (1972). Podd classified college students into Marcia's four identity statuses: identity achievement, moratorium, foreclosure, and identity diffusion (see pages 69–80 for definition of these statuses and discussion of Marcia's work). Podd also independently classified the same individuals into four groups of moral development based on Kohlberg's moral stages: the preconventional level (stages one and two), the conventional level (stages three and four), the principled level (stages five and six), and a transitional group that he added. While the results do not provide simple clear-cut relationships, interesting patterns between moral development and identity development emerge and, in general, support the theoretical links between identity status and moral thinking. Podd had hypothesized that the most mature level of reasoning would be found in the identity achieved subjects. About two-thirds of the morally principled subjects on Kohlberg's test were identified as having achieved a mature identity. None of the subjects who were transitional in their moral thinking had achieved a mature identity, but approximately two-thirds were identity diffused. Forty percent of the subjects subscribing to a conventional level of morality had also achieved a mature identity, and 30 percent of conventional subjects were foreclosures. Foreclosure subjects showed, as hypothesized, a strong tendency to use a conventional mode of moral thinking.

Those subjects who tended to be transitional in their moral orientation were also transitional in respect to their identity status. "People undergoing an identity crisis were found to be unstable and inconsistent in their moral reasoning" (Podd, 1972: 497). Therefore, before an individual can effectively question the conventional morality of his society, he must first have questioned his own identity—that is, he must first have completed the moratorium stage.

Kohlberg's Moral Judgment Scale was administered to a large group of students at the University of Berkeley at a time when students decided to take over the administration building in support of the Free Speech Movement (Haan, Smith, and Block, 1968). Of approximately 200 students arrested, the following patterns of moral thinking were observed. Stage six subjects verbally indicated that protest was a reflection of their principled morality and that they were more concerned with civil rights and civil liberties and the relationship between students as a group and the university as a community. Eighty percent of the stage six subjects had been arrested. For stage five subjects the issue was less clear-cut, and only 50 percent were arrested. For students in stages three and four subscribing to a conventional morality, the issue was again clear-cut against the protest, and only 10 percent participated in the sit-in leading to arrest. However, students at stage two were almost as likely to be arrested due to their participation in the protest as students at stage six. Sixty percent of stage two subjects were arrested; however, their protest was motivated by egoistic relativism and revenge, rather than by autonomous morality. They were more concerned with their own personal rights than with human rights. College students who still responded with stage two solutions to the moral dilemmas tended to use the protest movement to fight their own personal battle with society. The study illustrates that moral structure is not identical with moral behavior and that not all political civil disobedience is based on principled morality. College activists are comprised of individuals in the highest, as well as the lowest level of moral development. While protesting may be a sign of mature and advanced morality, it can also be a sign of immature and selfish stage two morality. "Protest activities, like other acts, are neither virtuous nor vicious; it is only the knowledge of the good which lies behind them that gives them virtue" (Kohlberg, 1970: 159).

Kohlberg suggests that even though only a small majority of adolescents have actually reached a postconventional level of moral reasoning, some adolescents, particularly hippies and street people, live in what superficially appears to be a postconventional subculture, in that it challenges, questions, and criticizes the conventional morality of society on what may sometimes appear to be principles. Moreover, the moral philosophy of the individual hippie is largely based on "do your own thing" (stage two) morality and "be loving and nice" (stage three). The most frequent challenges to conventional morality are based on reasons that must be classified as stage three, as "laws being too harsh and mean," or on a more egoistic stage two rationale, as "why shouldn't I have fun?" rather than on more universal principles of morality. Hippies seem to have "adopted the style of the revolution without the awareness of the revolutionary" (Hampden-Turner and Whitten, 1971: 76). In other words, the morality of hippies, even though it may appear postconventional, is characterized by a high degree of relativism and fluidity, rather than by principles.

Educational Implications

The issue of teaching moral values and moral behavior in the public schools is a controversial one, and little time and effort is provided for "character education" in the curriculum of today. There is the fear among parents that arbitrary values may be imposed upon unsuspecting children. Consequently, the teaching of moral issues has been disguised in such "value-neutral" approaches as mental health, life adjustment, and personality development. Parents, partly because of their own confusion as to what is right and partly because of their inability to teach effectively those moral virtues that they do believe in, increasingly demand that values and moral behavior be taught in school. However, there is little consensus as to what those values are and how they should be taught. Teachers and schools have been reluctant to teach moral values, partly because the teaching of middle-class values might offend and confuse the child who is exposed to lower-class values at home (and school critics such as Paul Goodman and Edgar Friedenberg feel that the teaching of middle-class values interferes with the learning process of lower-class children), and partly because of the wide endorsement of a relativistic moral philosophy, not only among adolescents, but even among theologians. A teacher might say: "I will expose them to my moral philosophy, but I will not impose it upon them; who am I to say that I am right and they are wrong?"

The relativistic philosophy of "doing your own thing," which prevails today, questions the schools' right and obligation to teach morality. Thus American schools have progressed from the formal teaching of Christian moral values in the strict Puritan tradition of the seventeenth century to the much more subtle and indirect approach of moral fables in which misbehavior inevitably results in painful consequences. This is the approach of the McGuffey readers and was quite prevalent in the public schools in the middle and latter part of the nineteenth century. During the earlier part of the twentieth century emphasis fell again on the teaching of virtues such as honesty, service, and self-control, an approach that Kohlberg identifies as the "bag of virtues" approach to teaching morality. More recently schools and teachers have denied that it is their role to teach virtues and moral values, especially when values were defined narrowly in terms of "white middle-class values." Consequently some teachers have abandoned the teaching of moral values in favor of teaching reading, writing, and arithmetic. Even among professionals the Supreme Court interpretation of the First Amendment concerning school prayer has been construed to eliminate any form of moral and ethical education from public schools, not only religious ones (Ball, 1967). Kohlberg (1967), in contrast, feels that the school can no more be committed to value neutrality than is the law, the Constitution, or the government. Two people obviously have the right to hold different values, but this does not mean therefore that both sets of values are equally valid. It is a fallacy to believe that because a person has a sincere commitment to a set of values that these values are therefore necessarily valid, sound, mature, or beneficial. Public schools have a commitment to the development of the idea of justice in their pupils, and Kohlberg attempts to make this commitment explicit. Schools frequently do have what Kohlberg calls "a hidden moral curriculum"—be obedient, stay in your seat, make no noise—that becomes most obvious in the kind of behavior that teachers reward and punish. The underlying moral assumptions and values may actually be unconscious on the teacher's part and may be quite different from what a teacher would consciously define as his system of moral values.

The earlier version of moral education consisted of teaching a "bag of virtues." The bag of virtues included honesty, service, self-control, friendliness, and moral virtues. Aristotle already had proposed a similar bag of virtues including temperance, liberality, pride, good temper, truthfulness, and justice. The boy scout bag adds that a scout should be honest, reverent, clean, and brave.

Traditionally, children were encouraged to practice virtuous behavior—they were told about the advantages of good behavior and were warned of the harm that could befall them if they were not virtuous. Reward and punishment were used as well. To illustrate the point, teachers used didactic stories in which good little boys and girls were rewarded materially and bad boys and girls were punished. According to Kohlberg and Piaget, (this amounts to training for an immature stage of moral development, since in mature moral development the abstract principle is more important than the material reward.) The problem with the bag-of-virtues approach to moral education is that there are no such psychological traits; virtues such as honesty are evaluative labels that are not reflected in consistent behavior. The Hartshorne and May (1928–1930) studies pointed out that participation in the character-education program as provided in schools, Sunday schools, and Boy Scouts does not contribute to improved moral behavior as measured by a test involving honesty, self-control, and service. Virtually all children cheated no matter what their moral education had been. Cheating was not a consistent trait but dependent upon the situation; some children cheated in one situation, but this did not predict their behavior in other situations. More recent follow-up studies have supported these earlier findings, and moral knowledge and moral behavior showed only low correlations. Children who did cheat were just as likely to say that cheating was wrong as those who did not cheat. Kohlberg, when asked "how can one teach morality?" answers as Socrates might have answered when asked the same question: "You must think I am very fortunate to know how virtue is acquired. The fact is that far from knowing whether it can be taught, I have no idea what virtue really is" (Kohlberg, 1970: 144).

Kohlberg is convinced that moral thinking can be enhanced through educational procedures that have been tried experimentally. The goal of his approach is to aid and encourage the child in his natural developmental tendencies through educational intervention, to take the next step in a direction to greater moral maturity toward which the child is already predisposed. Kohlberg does have specific suggestions for the teacher wanting to teach moral values. His suggestions are radically different from teaching a bag of virtues by preaching, rewarding, punishing, cajoling, and demanding. Morality is not viewed by Kohlberg as a bag of virtues but as an understanding of justice; consequently, he wants schools to become concerned again with moral development, moral thinking, and an understanding of justice. *Summerhill*

Progress from one stage to the next results—like development in Piaget's theory in general—from adaptation to cognitive disequilibrium. Kohlberg assumes that the advance from one moral stage to the next higher one is not simply an addition of more or better understanding, but a reorganization and restructuring of earlier moral thinking modes. Cognitive disequilibrium can be brought about by challenges, interactions, and debate with one's peers. Consequently, social interaction with one's peers and with the moral ideas and ideals slightly ahead of one's own conceptual development are hypothesized to stimulate cognitive and moral development. Also moral development was described by Kohlberg (1969) as a function of role-taking ability through which a person learns to restructure his own moral schemata and incorporate those of others. Consequently, role-taking opportunities and interaction with one's peers should facilitate moral development. Keasey (1971) investigated these hypotheses and found that the stages of moral development of early adolescents were positively related to the degree to which an individual was rated by himself, his peers, and his teacher as high in social participation and social interaction. Adolescents with a significant amount of peer group involvement, role-taking opportunities, and social interaction advanced more rapidly through the moral stages than children who were socially withdrawn or lacking in social participation opportunities. Selman (1971), too, found that "the ability to understand reciprocal social perspectives"—that is, role-taking skills—was positively related to higher levels of moral thoughts and was viewed as one precondition for progression in moral development.

Kohlberg's (1970) approach to teaching moral values involves several steps. First of all, it is essential to create in the student a feeling of dissatisfaction about his concept of good and bad, right and wrong. This moral disequilibrium is brought about by exposing the adolescent to choice situations involving a moral conflict or a moral dilemma for which the subject has no easy, readily available solution. The second step is to engage him in a discussion with his peers, a discussion in which different interpretations, disagreements, and conflicts are freely expressed, thereby inviting role taking. Ideally, the moral arguments should be those one stage beyond the subject's moral development, since arguments two or three stages ahead of a person cannot easily be assimilated. Children and adolescents can understand the moral argument of all stages preceding their own, but they can rarely comprehend an argument that is more than one step advanced beyond their own (Turiel, 1966, 1969). By creating a cognitive dissonance and listening to the arguments of others, the adolescent will see aspects of the moral dilemma that were inaccessible to him before. As he thinks about the problem, he will incorporate into his thinking suggestions made by others. The advance from one moral stage to the next higher one is brought about by cognitive conflict, since resolution of conflict leads to a reorganization of structure—an idea not unlike Piaget's progression in cognitive development from equilibrium through disequilibrium to a higher level of equilibrium (Turiel, 1966, 1969).

Research studies (Blatt, 1959; Kohlberg and Blatt, 1972) in which this technique has been utilized have shown that 50 percent of the preadolescent experimental subjects moved up one stage and an additional 10 percent moved up two stages. In a control group not exposed to the teaching of moral thinking, only 10 percent moved up one stage in the same period of time. Follow-up data suggest that the gain in moral structure was not temporary, but permanent. In an experiment (Hickey, 1972) involving juvenile delinquents—who were originally in stages one or two and who espoused an "If I'm not getting nothing, I'm not giving nothing" philosophy—most had moved to a stage four law-and-order morality after an exposure to Kohlberg's method of creating cognitive dissonance.

Kohlberg is concerned that schools themselves are not very highly developed institutions in terms of the moral philosophy that underlies their day-to-day operation. The school management seems to blend a fear of punishment (stage one) with an ever-present concern with law and order (stage four).

13

The Implications of Social Learning Theory for an Understanding of Adolescent Development*

Social learning theory, especially with its unique implications for child and adolescent development, has emerged fairly recently. Baldwin (1967) describes it as "a theory in the making," partly because its formalizations are not as rigidly stated as those of behavioristic learning theories or psychoanalytic theory and partly because, from its inception, social learning theorists have been firmly committed to verification of hypothetical relationships by way of empirical research. Since social learning theorists have objected to the use of theoretical constructs without empirical support by advocates of other developmental theories, they have been thoroughly committed to a position in which theory and empirical research findings are viewed as closely interrelated and interdependent. However, since research findings in relatively complex forms of social behavior frequently do not systematically and unequivocally support theoretical hypotheses, continuous revisions of and additions to theoretical postulates have been an essential characteristic of social learning theory.

Social learning theory is eclectic in that it draws on concepts, hypotheses, and methodology from a variety of different psychological sources. Some research hypotheses are influenced by psychoanalytic constructs such as identification, frustration, aggression, regression, repression, rejection, dependency, ego

*Chapter 13 has been published as "The Implications of Social Learning Theory for an Understanding of Adolescent Development," *Adolescence,* 1974, (in press).

strength, and transference, but they are investigated within the methodological approach of the experimentalist rather than the clinician. While social learning theory develops its own theoretical constructs, of which modeling and imitation are the most important for this discussion, it freely draws on constructs of behavioristic learning theory, especially reinforcement. But even Skinner's concept of direct reinforcement is expanded to include social dimensions: vicarious reinforcement and self-reinforcement. Consequently, the nature of problems and concerns of social learning theorists go far beyond those of the narrow connection between a stimulus and a response and include the contribution of the mother-child relationship to personality development, the importance of models and the imitation of models (that is, modeling) in the learning process. In addition, social learning theory has drawn freely on the findings of cultural anthropology. In short, the realm of investigation for the social learning theorist is the whole spectrum of the socialization process by which children learn, often through indirect teaching, to conform to the cultural expectations of acceptable behavior. The significance of the socializing agents as "a source of patterns of behavior" has been neglected in other theories, even though observational and empirical evidence indicates that this social aspect of the learning process is fundamental to socialization and personality development. Because of its eclectic orientation, social learning theory has contributed as much to an understanding of learning as to development and personality theory.

The advent of social learning theory cannot easily be credited to a single individual, since it constitutes a merger of thought that came not only from Clark Hull's drive reduction theory and from Skinner's reinforcement theory, but also from Freud's psychoanalytic theory. Social learning theory has been described as the translation of psychoanalytic constructs into behavioristic terminology. Men such as Miller and Dollard, as well as Mowrer, who long since have been concerned with the relationship between psychoanalytic theory and behavioristic theory and who have attempted to bridge the gap between these diverse points of view, seemed to give an early impetus to an approach to basic human, social, and developmental problems that developed into social learning theory. The concern with social aspects of learning is not new but the systematic development of a theory of social learning begins with the publication of Miller and Dollard's *Social Learning and Imitation* (1941) and has been continued in the works of Mowrer and Sears. Miller and Dollard systematically integrated the concept of imitation—which will be discussed later—into behavior theory. They referred to subjects imitating the behavior of their leader as "matched dependent behavior," because the subjects depended on their leader for cues in order to produce matching responses; but imitation was still viewed as only a special case of instrumental conditioning.

However, within social learning theory, especially the more recent developments, there is diversity rather than unanimity in point of view, in emphasis, and in some rather basic conceptualizations. Some theorists tend to be closer to S-R (stimulus-response) explanations, whereas others are more oriented toward psychoanalytic constructs, and it is this cross-fertilization and open-mindedness that give social learning theory its vitality. Common to all appears to be the application of behavioristic constructs to basic social and developmental problems and a belief that environmental, situational, and social, rather than biological and maturational factors are primarily responsible for learning and development. They believe that the rewarding of imitative responses is the psychological explanation of the socialization process. Rotter and Crandall have placed particular emphasis on the efforts expanded in obtaining goal satisfaction, the value of the goal, and the expectancy of obtaining it. For them the individual's subjective expectation is the central construct of social learning theory. Sears selected the parent-child relationship and especially the mother-child relationship as the focus of his research and theory. He suggested the study of dyadic units, rather than the monadic units of the stimulus-response type learning of an individual without social interaction, as in a Skinnerian program. The study of dyadic units illustrates his social emphasis and includes the combined actions and interactions of two or more people.

"Individual and group behavior are so inextricably intertwined both as to cause and effect, that an adequate behavior theory must combine both in a single internally congruent system" (Sears, 1951: 476). Sears has concentrated his efforts upon the study of both the antecedents and the consequences of early child development, and while initially the parents' behavior is seen as the antecedent and the child's behavior as the consequent, both behaviors later become a matter of interaction. Antecedent-consequent statements are characteristic of social learning theory, since it is the relationship between social and environmental antecedents and their behavioral consequences that is the focus of investigations and theorizing. A well-known statement in this regard is Miller and Dollard's (1939) hypothesis that frustration is the inevitable antecedent of aggressive behavior.

While Sears has contributed a considerable amount of information about patterns of child rearing (1957), the focus of his work has been on childhood rather than adolescence. It is primarily through the work of Bandura (1925–   ) and Walters (1918–1967) that a number of studies emerge that express an explicit concern with the application of social learning theory, or, as they refer to it, a sociobehavioristic approach to adolescence. Bandura, a student of Sears, has remained closer to Sears, while Walters was closer to Skinner. Their major works relevant to theories of adolescence are *Adolescent Aggression* (1959) and concentrating more specifically on child behavior *Social Learning and Personality Development* (1963), as well as innumerable research studies. Since Bandura and Walters are more concerned than other social learning theorists with the period of adolescence, the major emphasis in this chapter will be on the work of these two men and their collaborators. However, it would be incorrect to identify Bandura and Walters' contribution as a "theory of adolescence," since they do not view adolescence as a separate stage, qualitatively different from either childhood or young adulthood, but are convinced of the continuity of human development from infancy to adulthood. Indeed, the contribution of social learning theory to an understanding of adolescence consists of seriously questioning the widely held assumption that adolescence is a distinct stage in human development that has its own unique characteristics and requires its own set of theoretical explanations. A sociobehavioristic approach to adolescence implies that the principles of learning that help explain child development (Sears, 1951, 1957) are equally applicable to adolescent development, since no fundamental qualitative differences exist among childhood, adolescence, and adulthood. What may differ at different age levels are sociocultural expectations, and adolescents frequently select different models than do children. On many important social learning theory concepts, such as imitation, the frustration aggression hypothesis, and the nature of adolescence,* Bandura and Walters are almost as critical of Miller and Dollard's earlier writing as they are of Freudian and Skinnerian theory.

Modeling, Imitation, and Identification

Bandura and his collaborators have shown that children watching the behavior of a model are quick in imitating the specific responses as well as the generalized response patterns of the model. This phenomenon of modeling has been observed repeatedly in a variety of experimental situations. Furthermore, personal observation of children and adolescents imitating mannerisms, language idiosyncrasies, and habits of their parents and teachers, often to the embarrassment of the model, are commonplace. Bandura, Ross, and Ross (1963b) demonstrated that watching unusual aggressive behavior heightened children's aggressive responses significantly when compared to controls who had observed a nonaggressive model. The first experimental group watched a real-life aggressive model; the second group saw the same model portraying aggressive behavior on film; the third group observed an aggressive cartoon character depicting the same behavior. Many of the children's responses in the test situation were rather accurate imitations of the unusual aggressive acts of the model, especially of the real-life and the film model. The overall increase in aggressive behavior was highly significant and about the same for all three experimental situations, but the cartoon aggressive model elicited less precise imitation. Walters and his associates have shown that the increase in aggressive behavior as a result of watching an aggressive model is not limited to children; they produced similar findings with high school students, young women, and male hospital attendants. These social learning theory studies on imitation of aggressive behavior have been influential in awakening social concern about the potential

*Early learning theory in sharp contrast to Bandura and Walters maintained "Adolescence is known in our society as a period of increased aggressiveness and irritability . . ." (Dollard, Miller, Doob, Mowrer, and Sears, 1939: 72).

danger of children and adolescents repeatedly watching aggressive behavior on the television screen, since "exposure to filmed aggression heightens aggressive reactions in children" (Bandura, Ross, and Ross, 1963b: 9).

The potency of watching and imitating a model in altering response patterns has been demonstrated in such divergent areas as moral judgment (Bandura and McDonald, 1963); self-imposed delay of reward pattern exhibited by the model (Bandura and Mischel, 1965); and self-reinforcement patterns closely following those of the model (Bandura and Kupers, 1964). And in contrast to popular belief, Bandura and Walters' (1959) findings suggest that adolescent boys may be more likely to engage in sexual intercourse when double and multiple dating, thereby imitating the sexual advances of each other. When behavior patterns are inhibited in the subject, observing a model perform that behavior seems to remove personal inhibitions. The factor that predicts drug use in an adolescent most accurately is whether or not his friends use drugs. Apparently, an "if he can do it, I can do it" viewpoint prevails. According to Bandura, a great variety of social learning phenomena are acquired because a learner observes a model's behavior and imitates the behavior observed.

As children grow older they tend to imitate different models from their social environment. The young child usually identifies with his parents and attempts to imitate their behavior, including language, gesture, and mannerism as well as more basic attitudes and values. Identification with his teacher is not uncommon for the child entering school or for the preadolescent. The child does imitate speech patterns and mannerisms that he has observed in his teacher. Ideas about social or community issues that the child expresses in dinner conversations and that are new to the family are often those of his teacher. With the onset of adolescence parents and teachers frequently decline as important models, at least in regard to issues and choices that are of immediate consequences. During adolescence it is the peer group and selected entertainment heroes who become increasingly important as models, especially if communication between parents and adolescent breaks down. The adolescent peer group is particularly influential as a model in the use of verbal expressions, hair style, clothing, food, music, and entertainment preferences, as well as in regard to decisions related to rapidly changing social values (Brittain, 1963). Some of the problems that arise during adolescence may be the result of an individual modeling the behavior of his peers, who may be no more knowledgeable, intelligent, mature, and wise than he himself.

Related to modeling and important in Bandura's social learning theory are the concepts of identification and imitation. In his earlier writing Bandura uses the concept of identification frequently, but later he rejects it as lacking specific content. Different definitions have been advanced for the concepts "identification" and "imitation." Although there is no complete agreement about the specific meaning of these concepts, identification is viewed as a more general way of modeling the behavior of another person even without his presence. Identification includes the incorporation of the model's values, beliefs, roles, and attitudes. Imitation, on the other hand, refers to the rather specific reproduction or matching of behavior sequences almost in the nature of mimicking behavior while the person whose behavior is imitated is or was personally present. Experimental psychologists speak of "imitation" whereas personality theorists speak of "identification." Bandura and Walters (1963) discuss the difference in existing definitions but prefer to use "imitation," which they define as referring to "the occurrence of matching responses."

The role of imitation has been recognized since antiquity as an important method for learning, and it is indeed surprising that behavioristic learning theory has shown so little concern for imitating and modeling. Imitation is particularly relevant for learning complex social behavior, such as language, self-control, altruism, aggression, sexual behavior, and so on. Imitation also plays an essential role in the learning of basic perceptual-motor skills such as handwriting, and much of the learning in the gymnasium and on the sports field is the result of observing and imitating a model who shows how to play correctly. In many languages the term "to teach" is synonymous with "to show," or, as in Hebrew, has the same root, revealing that modeling, or showing, is the basic method of teaching when the emphasis is on skills that can be acquired through observational learning (Bandura and Walters, 1963). The adolescent who wants to learn to drive a car does so first of all by observation and imitation. A youth totally naïve in the use of cars would endanger his own life and that of others if he were to attempt driving solely on the basis of trial and error or reinforcement. Bandura (1962) reports that natives in a Guatemalan subculture learn to operate a cotton textile machine by observing the correct operation of the machine for a number of days. During this training period the youthful trainee asks no questions and is given neither verbal instruction nor reinforcement. Yet, when she feels confident that she can master the process herself, she takes over the operation of the machine and usually succeeds on the very first trial in operating the machine without any difficulties and without further instruction. This kind of learning is based only on the apprentice observing an appropriate social model and imitating the behavior of the model.

Social Learning Theory Contrasted with Stage and Trait Theories

Stage theorists of development, such as Gesell, Freud, Erikson, and even Piaget, have postulated fairly specific age-related behavior dispositions that follow an invariant developmental sequence, possess cross-situational consistency, and are more or less universal and predetermined. Social learning theory, in contrast, assumes that behavior is primarily determined within a social situational context. Consequently, social learning theory focuses on the interrelationship between environmental and social changes as antecedents and the behavioral changes that occur in a given individual as consequences rather than as a function of age. Descriptions and statements about adolescence are not of such a general, all-encompassing nature, as is Erikson's theory, for example, which predicts that an adolescent will inevitably experience an identity crisis, or Piaget's prediction that adolescent thought processes will begin to follow formal logic and become increasingly more abstract. Rather social learning theory statements are predictions of relationships between external factors and behavior. The strong emphasis in the sociobehavioristic approach on the influence of social conditions and cultural expectations, even on adolescent sexual behavior, becomes obvious in a statement such as: "In North American society, the marked increase in heterosexual behavior in middle and late adolescence is certainly due less to hormonal changes than to cultural expectations" (Bandura and Walters, 1963: 150). It appears as if Bandura overstated his case, for hormonal changes during adolescence are related to sexual drive. Even Margaret Mead—who is certainly not an advocate of biological determination in adolescent development—recognizes that "the development of heterosexual interest and activity at puberty does serve to distinguish this period from the period preceding it and from maturity" (Mead, 1952: 537). The word "puberty" carries distinct connotations of physiological and hormonal changes. While Bandura admits that such changes in behavior do occur, he explains the phenomenon differently. In general, pronounced changes in behavior may occur during adolescence, not because of internal maturational forces but because of sudden changes in the social training situation, family structure, peer group expectation, or other environmental factors; and, according to Bandura, such changes are less common than much of the literature on the so-called rebirth or storm and stress of adolescence leads one to believe.

Bandura, in an article, "The Stormy Decade: Fact or Fiction," has seriously questioned the stage theory assumption that adolescence is a turbulent decade inevitably characterized by "storm and stress, tension, rebellion, dependency conflicts, peer-group conformity, black leather jackets and the like" (Bandura, 1964: 224). While he does not deny that some of these kinds of behavior occur in some individuals, such behaviors are viewed as being due to cultural conditioning and social expectation rather than as inevitable developmental phenomena characteristic of the period of adolescence per se. (Aggressive behavior in adolescence—when it does occur— is viewed as the consequence of specific antecedent conditions in the childrearing pattern and the parent-child relationship such as dependency training, socialization pressure, imitation and modeling, rather than as the result of adolescent adjustment problems.) Whenever such behaviors occur, they are viewed as being lawfully related to existing situations or to the preadolescent social situation —that is, the antecedent environmental conditions. The prototypical adolescent with his turmoils and anxieties,* sexual tensions, compulsive conformity, and acute identity crisis so commonly de-

---

*Cattell and Scheir (1961) do find—in contrast to Bandura's claim—that during adolescence a noticeable increase in anxiety distinguishes that period from childhood and adulthood. "In the normal person, free anxiety is very high in adolescence, drops sharply as adulthood is reached ..."

scribed in the literature, according to Bandura (1964), fits only the actual behavior of perhaps "the deviant ten percent of the adolescent population." The "myth" that such behavior is believed to be a normal aspect of adolescent development is due more to cultural expectations and the representation of teen-agers in movies, literature, and the mass media than based on actual facts. Bandura (1964) does find, as does Offer (1969) in *The Psychological World of the Teenager,* that responsible, happy, well-adjusted, parent-respecting youth are more common than had been assumed. Such positive findings are also interpreted not as characteristics of adolescence per se but in the light of antecedent home conditions such as having experienced a warm, supportive preadolescence in which firmness and socialization pressure in childhood slowly gave way to increasingly more freedom during adolescence. As a general law of social and personal development, social learning theory assumes that there is continuity in human growth patterns and in the learning process and that no basic changes or clear-cut new stages in the mode of thinking appear at any age level. Bandura and McDonald (1963) tested Piaget's (1932) theory that objective moral judgment, which considers the material damage in an act, gives way at about the age of seven to subjective moral judgment, which considers the intent of the wrongdoers rather than the amount of damage. They did not find a distinct or abrupt change in the moral responses of their subjects, but there was a pronounced increase in subjective moral judgment and a decrease in objective moral judgment as a function of age. Bandura and McDonald consider changes in moral judgment to be primarily the result of changes in reinforcement contingencies in combination with the effects of modeling, rather than a function of maturation or a change from the preoperational to the operational stage in logical thinking. Bandura and McDonald (1963) demonstrated further that age specific social responses such as moral judgment can be modified through the utilization of appropriate models and the application of social learning principles. Since the age specific behavior postulated by Piaget's theory of two distinct stages of moral judgment can be modified through modeling and social reinforcement, some doubt is cast on the validity of the stage concept. It appears as if external social experiences have greater impact on behavior changes than the internal maturational forces postulated by stage theorists. Bandura and Mischel (1965) also show that delay of reward behavior can be modified through modeling techniques.

In contrast to stage theories, social learning theory is concerned with *interindividual* rather than with *intraindividual* differences. Some of the environmental variables that are utilized in explaining interindividual variations in behavior are intelligence, sex, age, race, socioeconomic status, culture, home atmosphere, exposure to models, and different reinforcement schedules. "To the extent that children representing such diverse backgrounds experience differential contingencies and schedules of reinforcement, as well as exposure to social models who differ widely in the behavior they exhibit, considerable interindividual behavior variability would be expected" (Bandura and McDonald, 1963: 274).

Trait theorists, such as Raymond Cattell (1961), have measured the basic components or traits of personality and postulated cross-situational consistency and developmental stability of behavior patterns, since they assumed that it was not so much the external situation but the internal trait or disposition that determined behavior. Since the primary cause of behavior is located within man, trait theorists have searched for consistency in man's behavior across situational changes and ascribe consistency in behavior to such traits as ego strength, reality orientation, self-control, self-concept, maturity, and energy-binding ideation. Social learning theorists, in contrast, see situational changes in a lawful way related to behavior changes and, consequently, investigate the observable external causes of behavior. An adolescent may be rebellious, disobedient, insensitive, nonconforming, and tough, and yet the same person may also be obedient, sensitive, conforming, and considerate. Social learning theory would not look at some of these traits as real and at the other group as defenses or compensations; nor would it view these diverse traits as inconsistent, arbitrary, or capricious. Social learning theory would consider all of these behaviors as lawfully related to specific social situations and antecedent factors. In other words, the issues then become when, how, where, and in interaction with whom did what behavior occur? Or what happened to the individual prior to the occurrence of the particular behavior?

Any consistency in behavior that can be observed is the result of similarity in the antecedent external social conditions rather than an internal trait. If antecedent conditions differ markedly or are expected to differ, behavior will differ and may appear quite inconsistent. A widely held assumption, especially among stage theorists, is that a consistent characteristic of middle adolescence is an antagonism toward adult authority. However, to illustrate the importance of antecedent social conditions, one might consider the common observation of an adolescent who has pronounced feelings of antagonism toward his father while, at the same time, expressing a great deal of admiration and respect for other adult authority figures such as his football coach, adult Boy Scout leader, or minister.

Social Learning Theory Contrasted with Behavioristic Learning Theory

Social learning theory also recognizes the very limited applicability of reinforcement theory to a wide variety of especially complex forms of social behavior such as language learning. Bandura (1962) considers the use of operant or instrumental conditioning as "tedious and ineffective" for most human learning. Skinner and others have assumed, without sufficient empirical verification, that reinforcement principles based on the findings of studies in highly structured laboratory situations apply equally to complex social situations. However, for a novel response to be reinforced, at least an approximation of that response must occur. Many complex forms of social learning would not easily emerge if they had to rely on reinforcement or drive reduction alone. A response that has never been made and observed has a zero probability of occurring and can hardly be acquired if there is no reliable eliciting stimulus. Reinforcement theory assumes that learning takes place only after a response has been made and is reinforced. However, reinforcement is not a precondition for the acquisition of a new response; it can only change the probability that an existing response will occur in the future. Bandura (1962) feels that people would not be socialized and many vocational and recreational skills would never be learned if they depended solely on reinforcement. A new behavior repertoire can only be learned from observing a model exhibiting that behavior and matching or imitating the behavior modeled.

Operant conditioning effectively explains how the learned behavior is maintained and strengthened but not how it is initially acquired. The initial acquisition of a response pattern is more effectively explained by imitation, and this kind of observational learning can take place without direct reinforcement. Similarly, trial-and-error learning can be eliminated, or the number of trials reduced, by providing an opportunity to observe the necessary behavior performed by an appropriate model. This process of observing and imitating is referred to as modeling and constitutes the cornerstone of Bandura's sociobehavioristic approach. "What you know and how you behave depends on what you see and hear and not just on what you get" (Mischel, 1971: 71).

Social learning theory makes a clear and important distinction between the acquisition of potential response patterns and actual performance or responding. The acquisition of potential response patterns is a function of observing the behavior of others and depends on social variables, sensory input, and cognitive operations. Acquisition learning does take place before the subject responds, and many response patterns are acquired but not performed. Acquisition learning is particularly obvious in language learning. However, whether the acquired behavior will actually occur and the probability that it will occur are dependent on reinforcement (Mischel, 1971). In social learning theory, reinforcement takes the place of a secondary, supportive role in the learning process. Most complex learning is viewed primarily as social—namely, the imitation of social models, especially in the learning of novel response patterns. The difference between acquisition and performance may be illustrated by the fact that most adolescent boys may know how to use lipstick and cosmetics—the response patterns having been acquired through observation. However, because these responses have never been reinforced, their probability of occurring is very low and may actually be zero. Many response patterns are acquired through observing a model but are not expressed as long as the learned behavior is not functional. However, if the social situations change so that the acquired response patterns become functional, the previously acquired behavior may be performed without further observations, without trial and error, and without reinforcement. When social situations change, for example, children may surprise parents with language patterns or language skills that were acquired earlier but that had never before been used.

Some social behaviors may seem to be much more dependent on the behavior of the model that is observed and imitated rather than upon the reinforcement or punishment. One fairly persistent research finding is that parental punitiveness toward aggressive behavior appears to be associated with more rather than less aggressive behavior in the child.

> Indeed, parental modeling behavior may often counteract the effects of their direct training. When a parent punishes his child physically for having aggressed toward peers, for example, the intended outcome of this training is that the child should refrain from hitting others. The child, however, is also learning from parental demonstration how to aggress physically and this imitative learning may provide the direction for the child's behavior when he is similarly frustrated in subsequent social interactions [Bandura, 1967: 43].

"Do as I say, not as I do" is exactly the reverse of what social learning theory predicts will happen. The imitation of the model, the "as I do" part, apparently is more potent than the reinforcement or the punishment provided by the "as I say" part. And many adolescents complain about their parents' "hypocrisies," since their "model" behavior belies their verbal recommendations and admonitions. Many manuals on discipline emphasize that the modeling of desirable behavior is actually a much more potent influence than any verbalization or reward punishment system. "There is no sure way to guarantee that your child will grow up to be the kind of person you would like him to be. The most likely way is for you to be the kind of person you would like him to be."

In addition to its establishment, the maintenance of response patterns or learning in the behavioristic sense does not depend only on direct external reinforcement as in Skinner's theory. Bandura expands the traditional concept of reinforcement to include *vicarious reinforcement* and also *self-reinforcement.* Vicarious reinforcement depends on the positive or negative consequences that the subject observes in others—that is, in the model. Observing social models that are rewarded for aggressive behavior increases the likelihood of this behavior occurring in the observer, just as aggressive behavior punished in the model inhibits the same behavior in the subject.

Bandura, Ross, and Ross (1963c) showed two films of Rocky the Villain exhibiting almost identical aggressive behavior, except that in one instance his aggressive behavior was rewarded and in another it was punished. Children who watched the movie and saw that the aggressive behavior of Rocky was rewarded were quick in imitating both the physical violence and the verbal abuse that they had observed. Actually, they showed about two times as much aggressive behavior as a control group. However, in the situation in which the children observed that the villain was punished after his aggressive act they showed little imitation of the behavior they had watched. However, even though punishing the villain inhibited the overt learning effects that resulted from observing the "bad" model, it did not suppress the latent tendencies. Children did acquire these response patterns and could describe them with considerable accuracy, but they did not perform them unless such response patterns became functional under either the impact of provocation or the prospect of reward.

Self-reinforcement means that the learner actually rewards himself for work that he considers of good quality. Verbal self-evaluations, which people administer frequently, are part of the self-reinforcing event. Bandura claims that "most human behavior is altered and maintained in the absence of immediate reinforcement" (Bandura, 1971: 248). In a variety of experiments children give themselves candy or tokens for attaining self-selected levels of performance on a miniature bowling game. The standards for their self-reinforcement are adopted from the comparison model (Bandura and Kupers, 1964, and Bandura and Whalen, 1966); if the standards of the model are stringent, self-reinforcement is infrequent, but if the standards of the model are lenient, self-reinforcement is generous. Bandura and Perloff (1967) demonstrated that self-reinforcement and external reinforcement are equally effective, and both are significantly more effective than noncontingent reward or a nonreward condition. Once the performance of a desirable response pattern has acquired a positive value, such as an adolescent shooting baskets, he himself can administer his own reinforcement by producing the desired basket and feeling good about his improving skills. Common observation illustrates that this kind of self-reinforcement can keep the behavior going for several hours on a Saturday afternoon. Adolescents are learning to set their own level of performance, and reaching that level makes them feel good, proud, or satisfied and, therefore, carries its own reward. In other words, as we grow more mature, self-reinforcement patterns stabilize and become less and less dependent on parents, teachers, and bosses giving us our rewards. We increasingly judge the appropriateness and the quality of our own responses and reward them accordingly. Successful socialization requires that our own judgment for a piece of work become a more important reinforcer than some outsider administering praise, candy, money, or other reinforcers. A mature adolescent may be able to make himself feel good about work well done—that is, provide self-reinforcement—even though a critical teacher or an impatient father expresses dissatisfaction. In contrast to Skinner's emphasis on direct reinforcement often contingent upon fairly specific piecemeal types of responses, social learning theorists maintain that the more important reinforcers in terms of mature complex social behavior are self-administered.

The Antecedents of Adolescent Aggression

Bandura (1973b) rejects all hydraulic motivational theories of aggression—such as Freud's aggressive instinct theory, Lorenz's aggressive urge theory, and even Miller and Dollard's reactive drive theory—since they view aggression as the natural response to frustration. Aristotle believed that emotional expression purges the emotions. Similarly, hydraulic models hold that as long as the cause of aggression is within the individual, the aggressive energy must find an outlet. Aggression is assumed to be reduced by aggressive behavior, and therapy provides safe and approved outlets for aggression.

Plato, in contrast, held that the overt expression of emotion arouses rather than reduces emotions. Bandura feels that Plato is the better psychologist. Social learning theory postulates that the causes of aggression are external, social, and environmental and can be found in the dependency training in childhood, imitation of aggressive models, and lack of internalization of social values. Numerous studies (Bandura, Ross, and Ross, 1963b, 1963c) have shown that exposure to aggressive models increases aggressive behavior in the observer. As an alternative to the frustration-aggression hypothesis, Bandura assumes that, rather than frustration leading to aggression, frustration produces

> emotional arousal that can elicit a variety of behaviors depending on the types of reactions people have learned for coping with stressful conditions. When distressed, some people seek help and support; others display achievement behavior; others show withdrawal and resignation; some aggress; others exhibit heightened somatic activity; others anesthetize themselves with drugs or alcohol; and most intensify constructive efforts to overcome their problems [Bandura, 1973b: 204].

Bandura and Walters' interest in the period of adolescence finds its most explicit expression in an extensive study *Adolescent Aggression* (1959). The study is—as the subtitle, "A Study of the Influence of Child Training Practices and Family Interrelationships," suggests—concerned with the antecedent variables in the parent-child relationship that contribute to the development of antisocial aggressive behavior in adolescents. The specific antecedent home conditions investigated were derived from social learning theory hypotheses and involve such variables as dependency training, sex attitudes and behavior, the handling of discipline in the home, identification processes, and the socialization process in general. The socialization process is viewed as "the development of habitual response patterns that are acceptable in the society in which the individual lives. The learning of such habits, or cue-response associations, requires the presence of some kind of drive or motivating process and the occurrence of a reward or reinforcement" (Bandura and Walters, 1959: 23).

The conditions that contribute to effective socialization include the development of a dependency motive, so that the child desires approval and affection from others. In addition, since dependency alone is not sufficient, socialization pressure needs to be exerted by way of demands, restrictions, and limitations—in short, through discipline—so that the child learns to conform to the patterns of society. This socialization process is facilitated by the amount and quality of personal contact parents give their child and by withholding of secondary rewards such as approval and attention, while at the same time keeping the child in a dependent relationship. The socialization process is delayed or disrupted if dependency behavior is punished or discouraged, if parental discipline methods are inconsistent within the home, and if the parents' values are in conflict with the prevalent values of the community and society. One basic assumption of Bandura and Walters' study is that antisocial aggression develops from a disruption in the adolescent's earlier dependency training in relationship to his parents. Dependency needs could be frustrated by lack of affectional nurturance, by parental rejection, or by lack of close dependency ties with one or both of his parents. An impairment in the development of healthy dependency relationships may directly contribute to feelings of hostility and to aggressive behavior. In addition, children without dependency motives experience less guilt and lack the capacity to control aggressive feelings sufficiently when aroused.

Bandura and Walters obtained their data from two groups of carefully selected boys aged fourteen to seventeen. Twenty-six pairs of boys were matched on a one-to-one basis in regard to age, intelligence, father's occupational status, and area of residence. They differed in that the aggressive boys had a history of repetitive antisocial, aggressive patterns of behavior, and many of them were on probation. The nonaggressive control boys were neither markedly aggressive nor withdrawn. Both groups came from intact families, had average or above-average intelligence, did not live in a high-delinquency neighborhood, and were free from withdrawal tendencies, known organic involvement, or other psychiatric problems. Data were collected through extensive personal interviews of both groups of adolescents as well as their parents. In theoretical orientation, in content and in methodology the study may be considered an extension of Sears, Maccoby, and Levin's *Patterns of Child Rearing* (1957).

Sociological approaches relate incidence of delinquency to population density, poverty, broken homes, deteriorated houses and neighborhood, lack of recreational facilities, and social and personal discontent. The investigators, in contrast, looked at the nature of the parent-child relationship and related it to the absence or presence of aggressive behavior in the adolescent subjects, controlling most of the sociological factors by matching procedures.

In contrast to the psychodynamic disease model of deviant behavior, Bandura and Walters assume that both deviant and prosocial behavior are governed by the same learning principles, rather than by hidden, subconscious, internal dynamics or traits. It is the external stimulus condition that controls normal as well as deviant behavior, rather than underlying dispositions.

Furthermore, since social learning theorists believe in the continuity of human development, antisocial aggressive behavior in adolescent boys is seen not as a problem that emerges with puberty or as related to hormonal changes, but as a failure in the socialization process that begins very early in childhood and continues during development.

The first group of hypotheses developed from social learning theory compared the dependency behavior, dependency anxiety, feelings of rejection, and aggressive behavior in the aggressive adolescents with those of the nonaggressive adolescents. In general, there was no significant difference in mothers' warmth and affection with both groups of boys. However, the aggressive boys were, as social learning theory predicted, less dependent on their fathers, felt more rejected by their fathers, and spent less time with their fathers than the control boys.

The fathers of the two groups of boys did not report any difference in the amount of overt aggression directed toward them. Only a few of the mothers of aggressive boys reported physical aggression directed toward them, but they also admitted that they were more tolerant of aggressive behavior. The control mothers had firmer limits in the amount of aggression they would tolerate. In general, the differences in expression of aggression against parents and parents' tolerance of aggressive behavior between these two groups were not very pronounced. However, it became quite obvious that both the fathers and the mothers of the aggressive adolescents actively encouraged their sons to show aggression outside the home, to use their fists, to stand up for their rights; and the fathers seemed to get some vicarious enjoyment from the aggressive acts of their sons. This difference, especially between the fathers of aggressive sons and the control fathers, was most pronounced. In a follow-up study of aggressive and inhibited preadolescent boys, Bandura (1960) found that the parents of the inhibited boys were nonpermissive and nonpunitive toward aggressive behavior, which means that they neither reinforced nor did they model aggressive behavior. The parents of aggressive boys, in contrast, were nonpermissive and punitive when the aggressive behavior was directed toward themselves, but they encouraged aggression toward other children and permitted sibling aggression.

Aggressive boys had more dependency anxiety—that is, they were less willing to express their dependency, seek help, talk about their problems, and show affection, even though they did have dependency needs. The dependency anxiety generalized from parents to peers and school. The control boys sought and appreciated help from their fathers more, and they also showed more help-seeking and approval-seeking behavior in relationship to their peers, while the feeling of being rejected in relationship to school and peers was more pronounced among the aggressive boys.

In relationship to sexual behavior, no difference was found in the handling of sexual behavior in both groups of parents, except that the fathers of the aggressive boys were more permissive concerning sexual behavior. However, it was found that the aggressive boys had had significantly more heterosexual experiences and expressed less anxiety about sex. Apparently, the permissive attitude in the fathers contributed to the greater sexual experience of the aggressive boys.

Several significant relationships were found in respect to the handling of rules, limitations, and the disciplining of these two groups of boys. The control parents used more reasoning as a disciplinary method and had higher achievement expectations for their sons. The control mothers were more consistent in enforcing rules and were more restrictive—that is, they used more socialization pressure, at least in the home. The methods used significantly more in disciplining the aggressive boys were physical and verbal punishment by their fathers, isolation, and more deprivation of privileges, although the latter method was common in both groups. The relationship between punitive parents and aggressive behavior in their children has been reported repeatedly in the literature; apparently, the more children are punished at home for aggressive behavior, the more aggressively they act toward their peers (Eron, Walder, Toigo, and Lefkowitz, 1963; Sears, Maccoby, and Levin, 1957). The mothers of the aggressive boys reported that their sons resisted their demands, and the aggressive boys themselves admitted that they ignored parental requests and refused to do what they were told to do. The parent-child relationship of the aggressive adolescents may best be described as lacking in warmth and affection.

The final and crucial question from a social learning theory point of view relates to the identification of these two groups of boys with their parents and the internalization of controls. While there was no difference in terms of identification with the mother, control boys identified more strongly with their fathers. The control fathers, in turn, were more demanding of masculine behavior in their boys. The aggressive boys experienced more disruption in affectional relationships between their fathers and their mothers and also more of a disruption in the emotional relationship between themselves and their parents, especially their fathers. In terms of internalization of controls, the nonaggressive group experienced more guilt when they transgressed, whereas the aggressive boys did not. The conscience development of the aggressive boys differed from that of the control boys. The behavior of the control boys was governed by guilt, an internal avoidance, when confronted with temptation. The aggressive boys, in a situation involving transgression of rules, were not governed by guilt, but if they were inhibited at all, by fear of punishment. Since identification is not encouraged and rewarded in the aggressive boys, the internalization of values seems to suffer.

In summary, more important than the shortcomings in the dependency training of the aggressive boys—which were theoretically predicted, but actually only weakly supported—was the imitation process. Aggressive boys seem to imitate their aggressive parents, who tend to use more physical punishment as a method of discipline and who encourage and reward the aggressive behavior of their sons, at least outside the home. By reinforcing aggressive behavior outside the home, by inhibiting aggressive behavior inside the home directed toward the parents, and by modeling aggressive behavior through physically punishing the boys, these parents "fostered displacement of aggression toward objects and situations eliciting much weaker inhibitory response" (Bandura, Ross, and Ross, 1961). These findings resulting from the study of aggressive behavior of adolescent boys in their natural environment are quite consistent with the results of laboratory studies of aggressive behavior of young children (Bandura, Ross, and Ross, 1961, 1963b, 1963c), discussed earlier.

Antisocial aggressive behavior in adolescent boys is the consequence of identifiable socialization variables in the parent-child relationship.

Educational Implications

Social learning theory's basic assumption is that children and adolescents learn most complex skills more effectively by imitating the behavior of their parents, teachers, and peers rather than by reinforcement, trial and error, and, in certain situations, even better than by verbal instruction. Verbal instructions and verbal cues, if they represent the modeling behavior symbolically, can facilitate the learning process, at least for behavior already in the subject's response repertoire. An often neglected aspect of the role of the teacher is the effective model role, demonstrating correct response patterns to be imitated. Only secondarily is the teacher a good reinforcer who uses reinforcement to shape and maintain already learned response repertoires. A teacher serves the model function, and some pupils will imitate his behavior regardless of whether or not the teacher consciously chooses for them to do so. A teacher cannot limit his influence on students to academic competencies only, but he must be aware that some pupils will be influenced by his altruism or selfishness, cleanliness or slovenliness, organization or disorganization, and whether or not he is observed participating in political activities, religious activities, and so on.

Evidence indicates that there are at least three types of effects that observing the model's behavior has on the learner (Bandura, 1965; Bandura and Walters, 1963). First, there is the already discussed *modeling effect*. By imitating the model's behavior, children acquire response patterns that they did not have before, and the modeling responses closely match those of the model. Bandura provides strong evidence that modeling as a teaching-learning technique is more economical than the techniques of operant conditioning, at least in learning novel responses. Second, there is the *inhibitory or disinhibitory effect*, which is based on the consequence the model experiences. If the consequences of the model's behavior are pain or punishment, watching the model's reaction to pain or punishment has an inhibitory effect on the observer. On the other hand, if the model is rewarded for his behavior, this has a disinhibitory effect on the observer, and the probability that the observer will imitate that behavior is increased. Vicarious reinforcement contributes to the disinhibitory influence of modeling. Third, there is the *eliciting effect,* meaning that the model's behavior provides specific cues, or serves as an eliciting stimulus that facilitates the release of similar responses in the observer, thus aiding the learning process. In the case of the eliciting effect of the model the behavior that is imitated is not new, nor was it previously inhibited, but at least similar responses are already in the subject's response repertoire. For example, a study by White (1967) was concerned with the effects of instruction and modeling on the altruistic behavior of preadolescent children. It was shown that in eliciting altruistic responses in students, what the teacher *did* was more important than what the teacher *said.* Apparently, altruistic behavior can be elicited more effectively by modeling than by verbal instruction. Bandura and McDonald (1963) demonstrated that modeling procedures, especially when both the model and the observer are reinforced, are very powerful in changing preadolescents' moral judgments. Live and symbolic models have been found to have a significant influence on the learning of self-control (Bandura and Mischel, 1965).

LaFleur and Johnson (1972) were concerned with the application of social learning theory principles in influencing the behavior of adolescents in a counseling situation. The treatment condition consisted of having the subjects watch cartoon stick-figure models, who were similar to themselves in important characteristics, request information about educational and vocational goals. The cartoon characters in the modeling treatment group remained without reward. However, for the second experimental group, the cartoon characters not only served as models, but they were also reinforced for information-seeking behavior, thus providing modeling and vicarious reinforcement for subjects. A control group of adolescents received information about educational and vocational planning, but they were given no model to observe and imitate. Modeling in the first experimental group was as effective as modeling with vicarious reinforcement in the second experimental group;

but both experimental groups were significantly more effective than the control situation, in which information was merely provided. The first two experimental groups imitated the modeled behavior; these adolescents became more interested in seeking information about planning their future, and they actually acquired more knowledge.

Teachers have an indirect but potent influence on children and adolescents in shaping the latter's values and attitudes by what they, the teachers themselves, are and what they do. This is in addition to the influence they exert through the cognitive, instructional curriculum that relates to their subject matter and teaching methods. Teachers can indirectly encourage altruism, moral values, social conscience, and human decency by exhibiting these virtues themselves. Even though adolescents as a group may reject teachers in general as identification models, it is not at all uncommon that an individual student may experience occasional infatuation, crushes, and adoration of an individual teacher. Furthermore, an adolescent may imitate the behavior of a teacher, even though a more general identification with the teacher as a person is lacking. Consequently, it is important to consider the conditions contributing to the imitation-identification process. First, the behavior to be imitated must be within the subject's perceptual and motor capacity. Furthermore, studies have shown that the identification process is facilitated if the model is warm, friendly, and supportive rather than cold and rejecting. However, each of the factors that generally contributes to imitation and learning must be evaluated in relationship to other factors and the overall context. For example, an overindulgent teacher or parent providing too much warmth and giving the child too much nurturance may inhibit rather than facilitate the learning or behavior that demands effort and self-denial.

Learning is more likely to occur if imitative or matching responses are directly rewarded, so that modeling and reinforcement jointly contribute to the acquisition of response patterns. Imitation, or matching of responses, can be further enhanced by vicarious reinforcement—that is, if the model who is being observed is also being rewarded for his behavior.

Social power and the control of rewards make up another variable that influences imitation, and these factors are of importance in the school situation in which teachers do control the rewards and have social power. In an experiment, Bandura, Ross, and Ross (1963a) utilized an adult model who controlled the distribution of highly attractive toys. A second adult model received some of these toys as did the children who served as subjects. Consequently, the children might have viewed the second model as a rival. Bandura observed that the children were much more likely to imitate the behavior of the first model who had the control (social power) over the toys rather than the behavior of the second model. Related to the findings of this study is the common observation that the higher-status model is much more likely to be imitated than the lower-status model, although the social distance between the model and the subject is of importance.

In addition, it has been demonstrated (Bandura, 1962) that the effectiveness of the model in producing matching responses in the observer depends on a variety of factors, such as the model's attractiveness, prestige, competence, and willingness to dispense rewards and praise. If the model has some characteristics in common with the observing subject, the observer is more inclined to imitate the model's behavior. For children, adults often serve as more powerful models than peers, since they have status, prestige, competence, power and are the dispensers of rewards. However, with adolescents, peer group members do serve as models and may actually have a greater influence on imitative behavior than parents and teachers, partly because they share common characteristics, partly because the peer group has control over the rewards that matter to adolescents.

The model's influence on imitative behavior of the subject also depends on the motivation and other characteristics of the subject. The person who has strong dependency needs, who is lacking in self-esteem or competence, and who, in the past, has been reinforced for producing matching responses, is more likely to imitate the model.

It appears crucial that adolescents have teachers with whom they can and want to identify. Since much learning occurs inadvertently due to the fact that the teacher serves as a socializing agent, it becomes more important that teachers be selected in the light of their qualities as models for youths and their potential for identification. The demand of radical groups that black students be taught by black teachers—since black children tend to identify better with black teachers with whom they share a number of common characteristics—seems to receive some implicit support from social learning theory. Bandura (1962) has also pointed out that the sex of the model and the sex of the subject do influence the imitation of behavior. The power of imitating a model is so great that children will imitate the sex-inappropriate play behavior of a same sex model. Boys watching a male model play with a toy stove increase their stove-playing behavior when the model is gone, just as girls increase their truck-playing behavior after having observed a female model play with the truck (Wolf, 1973).

Social learning theory could also provide a potential explanation as to why school integration does work and does produce results —although often only modest results—that are more effective than other compensatory reforms. As lower-class children move into academic settings in which peer models value learning, take school seriously, and aspire for academic success, their own attitudes and behavior will change to the extent that they accept and imitate the academic striving of their peers.

14
Summary

Contemporary Issues

Recent literature—with the exception of Piaget's concern with adolescent logic and Erikson's emphasis on adolescents' search for an identity—deals with specific aspects of adolescent development and has not advanced any new comprehensive theories about it. Theoretical arguments are increasingly submitted to empirical tests or analyzed in the light of clinical observations. Furthermore, adolescence is frequently investigated through one or a limited number of specific constructs, such as "the adolescent society" (Coleman, 1961) "self-cognition" (Nixon, 1961) "self-discovery" (Friedenberg, 1959) "adolescent self-image" (Rosenberg, 1965), and adolescents' attitudes toward school (Buxton, 1973).

Erikson's concept of ego-identity and its various derivatives continue to be of increasing importance in contemporary writing on adolescence. Friedenberg (1959) even defines adolescence as the social process through which a clear and stable self-identification is established. Erikson maintains that the process of identification is only completed if and when the adolescent has "subordinated his childhood identifications to a new kind of identification, achieved in absorbing sociability and in competitive apprenticeship with and among his age-mates" (Erikson, 1959: 110). The young adult reaching maturity must have obtained a sense of psychological and social continuity and sameness with both "what he was as a child and what he is about to become" (Erikson, 1959: 111), and at the same time he has to bring into agreement his own conception of himself and the conception others have of him.

In order to establish a personal identity, the adolescent needs time, experiences, and relationships with others that do not "count." Both Mead and Erikson speak of youth's need for a "psychological moratorium" in which the individual can experiment freely with his own identity, with his relationships with other people, and with ideas without having to commit himself. He "plays the field" not only in relationship to the opposite sex, but exploring his commitments to life in general. However, the social pressure for success, for good grades, for promotion, for another Boy Scout badge, and later for the right college and the right degree make it increasingly more difficult "to play the field." There is no equivalent in American colleges and universities to the European custom of spending the first semester or even the first year enrolling in a variety of courses for exploratory purposes, as well as participating freely in the social activities, without having to produce any work that decides a student's academic future. In American colleges and universities, in contrast, 25 percent of the freshmen drop out during their first year.

There are two contemporary institutions that seem to fit the model of the "psychological moratorium" well: the Peace Corps and youth cultures, such as, the hippies, and the communes. The appeal that these institutions have had not only to adolescents, but to adults as well, seems to reveal a basic need that such experiences outside of the mainstream of society can fulfill, even for those who yearn to but never actually join them.

The commitment to a Peace Corps experience seems to imply a desire for a "psychological moratorium" *par excellence.* It provides youth with an opportunity to leave the Establishment, the family, the school, the college, and the competitive market place in order to find one's self. In contrast to the psychological benefits, the financial rewards are unattractive and the experience does not yield credits, a diploma, or a degree. However, it provides opportunities to explore one's own values and one's relationships with others; it provides opportunities for trying out new skills, exposure to new ideas, provides a new environment, even a new cultural setting. There seems to be an analogy to the preindustrial European journeyman who left his hometown and frequently his country in order to practice his trade and explore the world before returning with new perspectives and settling in a more traditional pattern of life.

A psychological moratorium also seems to be implied in the life of the beatniks, the hippies, and the communes. Adolescents who join these movements temporarily drop out of the mainstream of the affluent, success-, money-, and achievement-oriented middle-class society from which most beatniks and hippies come. Joining such subcultures is frequently a direct expression of their rejection of the values of the computerized, sterilized, automated, industrial, mass society in which the individual becomes an impersonal number. This feeling is best expressed in the slogan, "Do not fold, spindle, or mutilate." Their denial of conventional sex differences is indicated by the similarity of males and females in hair style, clothing, and the adornment of the body with flowers (for example, the flower children). While sex is part of their experimentation, McLuhan claims that "hippies are not hung up on sex." Their sexual activities are frequently aimless and exploratory and without deep emotional commitment; they change partners freely and partners may be of either sex. The difference between the beatniks and the hippies is not only a chronological one—the beat movement came earlier—but in addition beatniks were more expressedly antagonistic and hostile toward the larger society. The hippie movement represents more of a withdrawal from society into an unreal world of love, psychedelic mind expanding, semireligious and mystical experiences. In one instance, the idea "Make Love not War" was carried out when a group of hippies organized a picnic for the children of the police officers who had beaten them. The hippie culture is a direct expression of adolescent rebellion against the germfree, time-conscious, money-conscious, but frequently loveless middle-class world in which they grew up. Their rebellion is expressed by an almost diametrically opposite value system; a disregard for cleanliness, a communal sharing of all material things, and most of all a recurring theme of love, beauty, honesty, and fun. The hippie breaks down the inhibiting limitations of the middle-class values and gives himself freely to a large variety of new and self-expanding experiences: sex, marijuana, LSD, methedrine, yoga, Oriental religion, such as Zen Buddhism, as well as Indian mysticism and American Indian tribal organization and dress.

That the hippie experience serves as a psychological moratorium is further indicated by the fact that—except for a small hardcore group of bohemian artists—the hippie, after a few weeks or months in a hippie culture, returns to the middle-class home and his middle-class values. The so-called plastic hippies join the hippie culture during the evening or on weekends, but maintain their relationship to the middle-class society during the rest of the week and fulfill their school or work obligations.

It has frequently been said that the hippies are the dropouts of society. If one applies the construct psychological moratorium, he sees that such a statement is actually inaccurate, since the great majority of the hippies return to the affluent, success- and achievement-oriented society from which they came. According to Auerbach,* for some the hippie experience is actually a maturing process and may serve a genuine psychological purpose. For others, however, it involves great risk and may constitute a disturbing experience. Pregnancy, venereal disease, a bad "trip," a jail sentence, infectious hepatitis, and psychotic breakdown as a result of sexual and psychedelic experimentation are not uncommon.

It is obvious that the Peace Corps and the hippie culture differ greatly and appeal to quite different personalities. In the Peace Corps volunteer, one can observe ego involvement, commitment, and willingness to give service without seeking personal material gain; there is altruism and idealism. The hippie culture, in contrast to the Peace Corps, constitutes more of a withdrawal from traditional society. This withdrawal is symbolically expressed in the hippie saying, "drop out." Both the Peace Corps volunteer and the hippie leave the established social pattern in order to experiment in the sense that Erikson uses the term "psychological moratorium." Potentially, both experiences could foster psychological maturation and growth in that they provide for the development of ego-identity and a new perspective on life and society.

Most contemporary researchers write about the much broader and more inclusive adolescent society rather than the limited number of youth who actually join the hippie culture. Nevertheless, it is important to recognize that hippie ideology has permeated not only communes but adolescent society, college campuses, and it

*Dr. Alfred Auerbach, "Current Problems in Sex," lecture delivered at the Friday Research Conferences, Psychiatric Institute, University of Maryland School of Medicine, Baltimore, Md., September 15, 1967.

has even left its mark on adult society, as reflected in pop art, poetry, music, slang, humor, and the decoration of department store windows and boutiques.

In *The Adolescent Society* Coleman (1961) hypothesizes that contemporary adolescents attending public and private secondary schools look increasingly to each other for social rewards and social recognition rather than to their parents, teachers, and adult society in general. While Lewin postulated an "in-between stage," a "social no-man's-land," Coleman finds that the transition period between childhood and adulthood becomes a small teen-age subculture with interests and attitudes that are removed from adult responsibility and adult value structure.

To a certain extent, this has always been true. Today, however, the influence of teachers and parents appears to be declining for several reasons. First, due to the rapidity of social change, knowledge, skills, and values that parents learned when they were young are obsolete for the world in which their sons and daughters live. Consequently, there is a mutual lack of understanding and even lack of communication. Adolescents perceive their parents as "old fashioned" and "out of touch with the times," while parents look at their offspring as "radical, rebellious, and too wild" and nag "when we were that age, we were not allowed to do that kind of thing." Second, economic specialization results in the alienation of father and son. The son has little personal relationship to the father's work and must begin his own vocational training independent of his father. He no longer obtains vocational instruction from his father. Third, the adolescent no longer contributes substantially to the family economy, and the family, in turn, no longer teaches any particular skills and knowledge that prepare the young man and woman for their places in the adult community. All of these factors necessitate prolonged educational training, which extends the period of financial dependency and consequently lengthens the period of adolescence.

This trend is reflected in the current enrollment figures of our high schools. More students go to school for a longer period of time, and the number of students aspiring to high school or college diplomas is slowly but constantly increasing. The high school encompasses an increasingly greater portion of school-age youth, which it reaches not only by way of formal, classroom instruction, but through extracurricular activities as well. The school and, through the school, the peer group have obtained increasingly more autonomy.

The influence of the peer group in shaping values, ideals, attitudes, and interests is reflected in the title of Coleman's book *The Adolescent Society.* Cut off from large segments of society, adolescents have found psychological support and social reward within their own group and depend upon each other. Consequently, this adolescent subculture has created its own vernacular and its own value system. Coleman describes the high school as a "cruel jungle of dating and rating" (Coleman, 1961: 51) with its tightly knit, ingrown cliques. This society "maintains only a few threads of connection with the . . . adult society" (Coleman, 1961: 3). Coleman has collected empirical evidence that describes the value system of contemporary adolescent society and clarifies the existing discrepancy between the adolescents' values and their parents'. Among boys, the adolescent society values the athlete, the car owner, and the right family background. These are important assets in being rated popular or in becoming a member of the leading crowd. Among girls, social success, physical beauty, enticing manners, and nice clothes are highly rated assets, all of which are more important in the adolescent society than they are in the adult society. For neither sex is academic success as important as adults would like to think. Particularly in relationship with the opposite sex, cars are more important for boys and nice clothes are more important for girls than good grades. Coleman warns parents who worry about the academic strain on teen-agers that the emotional strain in the social competition of being "in" and the fear of being "out" might be much more severe than they realize.

Nixon (1961), writing from a psychiatric point of view, postulates that during midadolescence a developmental crisis occurs as part of the dynamics of normal growth. He refers to this crisis as the "advent of self-cognition." He finds two major causes for this crisis among the large number of students "characterized by psychiatric normality" who come to see him for brief, psychiatric consultations: attaining independence—that is, emancipation from parents and teachers; and unresolved questions concerning self-discovery. Nixon directs his attention to this second aspect. Resolving the question "Who am I?" is an extremely important

developmental task requiring introspection. Only systematic introspection helps the individual to learn to know himself more completely and thus leads to self-discovery. Nixon is in agreement with
Erikson, who also maintains that "adolescence is not an affliction
but a normative crisis, i.e., a normal phase of increased conflict
characterized by a seeming fluctuation in ego strength, and yet also
by a high growth potential" (Erikson, 1959: 116). Adolescent crises
are not neurotic or psychotic crises, since they are more easily
reversed. Working through such an adolescent crisis may actually
constitute a growth experience and may contribute to the attainment of self-discovery and the formation of ego-identity. Piaget
(1947) considers it a "duty of the modern adolescent . . . to revolt
against all imposed truth and to build up his intellectual and moral
ideas as freely as he can." The importance of adolescent conflict in
the normal developmental process becomes the major thesis in
Friedenberg's (1959) *The Vanishing Adolescent,* to be discussed
later.

Physiological maturity occurs invariably through biological, developmental processes. It is often assumed that emotional and
psychological maturity are also obtained "automatically," through
interaction with society. Nixon takes issue with such a position,
since emotional and psychological maturity cannot be obtained
without self-discovery. The individual while in the developmental
stage of self-cognition must not be pushed precociously into
maturity without having first acquired a strong ego-identity. If he
is pushed too soon, the result may be a pseudomaturity that interferes with further development. Ego-identity as obtained through
self-cognition is the necessary developmental prerequisite to the
full attainment of genital maturity. This idea is implied in several
of the theories discussed earlier. Spranger in particular distinguished between "pure love" and "sexuality" and for him, too,
pure love is the prerequisite for mature sexuality. Erikson sees the
early, intimate love relationship between adolescents not as primarily sexual but as an attempt to find oneself through the eyes of
another person. And only after a person has found himself does
lasting intimacy become a possibility.

Friedenberg, like most other theorists, perceives adolescence as
a distinct stage of development, different from childhood and
adulthood. He agrees with Erikson, Nixon, and others that the

central, developmental issue of this period is self-definition. The young person is learning who he is, what he feels, what he can do, and what he wants to become. He has to differentiate himself from the culture in which he has grown up and from the people in that culture on whom he has depended. He can only accomplish this by setting himself apart from that culture and by breaking the ties of dependency. This process necessarily involves conflict. Friedenberg says, in fact, that adolescence *is* conflict. "Adolescent conflict is the instrument by which an individual learns the complex, subtle, and precious difference between himself and his environment" (Friedenberg, 1959: 13).

If there is no opportunity for conflict, there is no adolescence, since no sense of individuality can develop. Consequently, adolescence is less of a distinct, social phenomenon in lower social classes (this might explain the fact that Spranger, Remplein, and Gesell are mainly concerned with middle-class youth) or in primitive society (as Mead demonstrated in Samoa). There will be no adolescence in a world that resembles George Orwell's *1984*. "In a society in which there is no difference, or in which no difference is permitted, the word 'adolescence' has no meaning" (Friedenberg, 1959: 13). Friedenberg is disturbed that society is moving toward a *1984* with increased emphasis on manipulative techniques. As society increasingly demands conformity, the process of establishing individuality—the self-defining process—breaks down. The socialization process in high school renounces differences, except for marginal ones. To be different is indecent. The peer group may be as vehement about nonconforming behavior in certain areas as the school administration is in others (haircut, sideburns, miniskirts, and tight sweaters). Conflicts are not valued for their growth potential but are feared as disturbances. They have solutions, and the better schools provide professional services for the solution of problems. The school serves as a mediator rather than a clarifier when conflict arises. "*The Merchant of Venice* is omitted from the reading list in favor of something just as good in which all the Jewish characters are pleasant; the aggressive candidate for student council member is quietly barred from office on grounds of emotional immaturity" (Friedenberg, 1959: 45–46).

These conditions make it increasingly more difficult for the adolescent to define himself through conflict with society. Consequently, adolescents often obtain no clear understanding of who they are and what they stand for. This is the context in which Friedenberg advances his major hypothesis: "Adolescence, as a developmental process, is becoming obsolete" (Friedenberg, 1959: 133).

It is interesting to note the difference between Coleman's and Friedenberg's predictions. Coleman postulates that the adolescent society is becoming more clearly differentiated from childhood and adulthood. The language, pattern of life, and value system take on increasingly distinct features, and the gulf between adolescent society and adult society widens. Only a few threads connect them. In a different context, Friedenberg assumes that society is manipulating the adolescent into a pattern of mass conformity by guiding him through conflict and crisis. In the process, it deprives him of the important experience of establishing his own identity and thus minimizes adolescence as a social, developmental phenomenon. Whether adolescence will vanish, as Friedenberg fears, or become a more clearly differentiated subculture, as Coleman believes, will need to be investigated further.

Generalizations on Adolescent Development

There are obvious disagreements about meaning, definition, characteristics, and future patterns of adolescence. However, there is also substantial agreement among different theories, especially when the older and more extreme theoretical positions are discarded. Empirical evidence appears to have disproved some of their earlier claims.

Theories agree about the existence of endocrinological change and the associated growth of the primary and the appearance of secondary sex characteristics as developmental phenomena during the ages of ten to fifteen. Ausubel, Greulich, Remplein, and Zeller give detailed accounts of these changes and their effects. The actual evidence comes from physiology and medicine. Gesell, Freud, Lewin, and Piaget agree that these changes are important aspects of adolescent development. Barker makes the most systematic attempt to relate physical changes to adolescent behavior. Spranger and Mead deemphasize the influence of the physiological changes of pubescence, but neither denies their existence. Internal, physiological changes related to the attainment of sexual maturity are phylogenetic, developmental phenomena defined as pubescence. Social learning theory considers social expectations and antecedent social conditions as more powerful factors than hormonal changes during pubescence.

Closely related to the endocrinological changes is an increase in sex interest and awareness, combined with increased sexual desires that crave gratification. Whether gratification is permitted, as in Samoa, repressed, as in a puritanical environment, or diverted into substitute outlets, as is frequently the case with American college students, depends upon social factors, as does the mode of gratification. Ausubel (1954) seriously challenges the assumption that sex repression must result in tension and emotional disturbance, as Freud in his theory of repression and Miller and Dollard in their frustration-aggression hypothesis suggested. None of the theories denies that behavioral changes are related to increased sexual tension. But they disagree on the extent to which the behavior involved in sex interest, sex awareness, and sex tension is caused by physiological changes or by social determinants.

There is sufficient evidence of sexual interest and activity both among lower-class children in American society and in primitive societies, such as the Dobuans, to disprove Freud's claim of a universal latency period. But the sexual drive does increase significantly with the maturing of the reproductive organs. The pubescent, for the first time since infancy, must learn to regulate a new biological drive. The specific behavior involved in this regulation is influenced by the cultural taboos and expectations. The fact remains that sex interest, awareness, and activity increase markedly and take on a new quality of urgency, which was absent in childhood. The new sex drive tends to be more diffuse in the beginning and to become more specific and goal directed as the individual grows older. The rapid increase of sexual "outlets" during the early adolescent period is empirically demonstrated by the Kinsey report (1948). One might hypothesize that the number of outlets increases in all societies with the onset of physiological pubescence, but that the nature of the outlets shows wide cultural and individual variations.

Changes in physique brought about by the growth of the primary and the appearance of the secondary sex characteristics result in a substantial change of the individual's body image. This is due partly to the fact that the body changes much more quickly during early adolescence than during most other periods of life. The problems related to voice change, acne, menarche, the development of sex-inappropriate sex characteristics, deviation in development, and early and especially late maturation can have traumatic emotional effects on the young adolescent. The severity of this impact and the confusion or pride that result from these body changes naturally depend on the attitudes toward the body in a given society. They also depend on how early or late these changes occur in relation to the peer group. Studies on early and late maturation provide relevant information on this point. Barker's theory gives great weight to the role of body change and its psychological component, namely the change in body image. However, most theories discuss the adolescent's preoccupation with and the readjustment to the new body image.

Sexual maturation causes shifts in attitude toward the masculine and feminine sex roles. The specific manifestations of masculinity and femininity have their roots in childhood training and vary from one society to another. Nevertheless, the adolescent faces the task of incorporating into his self-concept those sex characteristics that are culturally acceptable. Maladjustment in this area is not uncommon, and Freud considered it important that the adolescent not "miss" the opposite sex. New social relationships must be established during adolescence, especially heterosexual relationships, but also new social relationships within one's own sex group. Gesell gives a detailed account of youth's changing attitude toward his own and the opposite sex during the early adolescent years. Havighurst emphasizes the acceptance of one's own body and its specific reproductive processes. Changes in attitude toward masculinity and femininity are even reported by Mead for Samoan youth. Samoans have less difficulty than Americans in making these adjustments, since Samoan society has fewer requirements and contributes to fewer conflicts; nevertheless, the psychological processes are not basically different.

There appears to be little disagreement on the idea that adolescence is a transition period between childhood and adulthood, except that social learning theorists (Bandura, 1964) and Hollingworth (1928) take the position that human development is a continuous process not divided into stages. If adolescence has become a transition period for some individuals in our society, social conditions are responsible, not some intrinsic aspect of human development. However, Lewin's idea of the adolescent as the marginal man finds support from other theories. Coleman even goes so far as to postulate a teen-ager subculture, the adolescent society, which includes a large segment of the population for a fairly long period of time. The transitional period is more noticeable if the child and adult groups are well defined, as they are in America today. This transition requires a reevaluation of one's relationship to the external world, to the social world, and to one's own internal, psychic world. Sherif, Erikson, and Friedenberg consider adolescence the crucial period for the formation of the mature ego. We find support for this idea even in Mead: "In most societies adolescence is a period of reexamination, and possible reorientation" (Mead, 1949: 361). Piaget (1947) sees adolescence as a "decisive turning point . . . at which the individual rejects, or at least revises his estimate of everything that has been inculcated in him, and acquires a personal point of view and a personal place in life." There is agreement (Havighurst, Kroh, Lewin, Remplein, Piaget, and Spranger, as well as from various empirical investigations) that during adolescence the time perspective expands, and past and future assume greater importance and become clearly differentiated. Piaget speaks of the adolescent as building theories and reflecting beyond the present. This corresponds to a more definite planning of vocational activities, preparation for marriage, and the establishment of more specific and lasting life goals, including the need for achieving emotional and economic independence. Similarly, the irreality or fantasy level decreases in importance and is more clearly separated from reality. Childlike play decreases as obligations, responsibility, and social expectations increase. In societies in which time is of little importance and in which fantasy is welcome, these tendencies will be less obvious.

No exact agreement exists among the various stage theories as to the number, characteristics, and psychological meaning of each of the stages. But most theories postulate an important transitional phase of early adolescence between ten and fourteen for girls and eleven and fifteen or sixteen for boys. This developmental phase is described in terms that are not incompatible: Erikson (1950, 1968) —identity versus role diffusion; Freud (1925, 1953)—second oedipal situation, homosexual crushes, and heterosexual attachments; Gesell (1956)—negativism, introversion, and rebelliousness; Hall (1916)—storm and stress and a new birth; Kroh (1944, 1951) and Remplein (1956)—a second period of negativism, followed by ego experimentation and the formation of a new self-concept; Inhelder and Piaget (1958)—the transition from concrete operations to formal thought; Sullivan (1953)—preadolescence and early adolescence; Zeller (1952)—*Gestaltwandel.*

The most widely accepted assumption is that childhood, adolescence, and adulthood are three periods that can be recognized psychologically and sociologically, and even physiologically. It is also accepted that there are individual as well as cultural differences in the length of adolescence and the age at onset and end. The earlier maturing of girls is generally recognized. The physiological changes of pubescence are frequently used to determine the beginning, while sociological criteria—namely, adult status, duties, and privileges as well as marriage, end of education, and economic independence—are most frequently cited for the end of that period. Termination of adolescence depends primarily on the requirements and conditions of the culture. It occurs earlier in primitive cultures and later in more civilized ones.

The extent to which adolescence is experienced as a period of stress and strain and emotional instability depends upon several factors:

1. Social factors influence the severity of emotional crisis and anthropological theory advances the idea that continuity in cultural conditioning will decrease adolescent difficulties while discontinuities will increase them. Lewin emphasizes a different aspect of the same idea. In his theory, similarity between the status of the child and that of the adult decreases adolescent difficulties; dissimilarity increases them. For social learning theorists (Bandura, 1964) it is not the nature of the developmental process per se that causes stress and strain during adolescence. The social pressures, social expectations, and other socioenvironmental conditions may contribute to storm, strain, and crisis in some individuals during that period in the human life cycle, just as such

conditions may cause emotional trauma earlier or later in the life cycle of other individuals.

2. Sherif and Cantril (1947) add the idea that societies in a period of rapid social change create a particularly difficult adolescent period; the adolescent has not only the society's problems to adjust to but his own as well. Keniston (1965), while he maintains that the transition from childhood to adulthood "is never completely continuous," emphasizes that as social conditions change more rapidly and more drastically, the discontinuity between childhood and adulthood becomes more pronounced.

3. Remplein (1956) considers the individual's personality type an important factor that accounts for the degree of the adolescent's disturbances. The youth with a schizothymic personality experiences pubescence with increased emotional disturbances, since adolescence is a schizothymic developmental period. The pyknic-cyclothymic youth will most likely experience few, if any, disturbances and difficulties during adolescence, since personality type and developmental type are in opposition and cancel each other.

4. Spranger (1955) adds the idea that an adolescent can actively direct and form his growth through will power, self-education, self-determination, and goal-directed efforts. He is not at the mercy of environmental or biological factors but contributes actively to his own development. While Piaget does not emphasize conflict, he too sees the individual as actively participating in his own development.

5. Friedenberg (1959) suggests that society increasingly "dampens out" the kind of conflict and rebellion that makes for stress and strain during adolescence. Being deprived of the opportunity to differentiate himself from society, the adolescent does not experience stress and strain, but neither can he establish his own individual identity. This idea suggests that the degree of adolescent stress and strain is dependent upon the extent of social conflict experienced in reaching maturity. Having to meet challenges, overcome the obstacles of crises, and conquer meaningful frustration can provide potential for growth that leads to psychological maturity. The historian Arnold Toynbee, for example, views societies that meet their historical challenges as growing societies.

Since any combination of these factors is conceivable, adolescence can be experienced in a variety of ways, ranging from Hall's description of a rebirth to Hollingworth's description of gradualness. The disposition to emotional and social difficulties during this period is substantially greater than during other developmental periods. Erikson, Nixon, and Friedenberg consider the adolescent crisis as a necessary developmental phenomenon, since only the resolution of the crisis through self-discovery leads to maturity. However, they explicitly distinguish adolescent crisis from neurotic and psychotic crisis. The hypothesis of a universal period of storm and stress is no longer tenable, and in the light of the findings presented by Bandura (1964) and Offer (1969) one can no longer accept the storm-and-stress concept as applicable to even the majority of adolescents in our society.

References

Aebli, H. *Über die geistige Entwicklung des Kindes.* Stuttgart: Ernst Klett Verlag, 1963.

Allport, G. W. *Personality: A psychological interpretation.* New York: Henry Holt, 1937.

Aristotle. Magna moralia. In W. D. Ross, ed., *The works of Aristotle.* (G. Stock, trans.) Vol. 9. Oxford: Clarendon Press, 1925.

————. Ethica Nicomachea. In R. McKeon, ed., *The basic works of Aristotle.* (W. D. Ross, trans.) New York: Random House, 1941(a).

————. Historia animalium. In R. McKeon, ed., *The basic works of Aristotle.* (D. W. Thompson, trans.) New York: Random House, 1941(b).

————. Politica. In R. McKeon, ed., *The basic works of Aristotle.* (B. Jowett, trans.) New York: Random House, 1941(c).

————. Rhetorica. In R. McKeon, ed., *The basic works of Aristotle.* (W. R. Roberts, trans.) New York: Random House, 1941(d).

Arnold, W. Das Problem der "Entwicklung" in der Systematischen Psychologie. *Psychologische Rundschau,* 1954, *5,* 251–259.

Ausubel, D. P. *Theory and problems of adolescent development.* New York: Grune & Stratton, 1954.

————. *Theory and problems of child development.* New York: Grune & Stratton, 1958.

Baldwin, A. L. *Theories of child development.* New York: John Wiley & Sons, 1967.

Ball, W. B. Religion and public education: The Past-Schempp years. In T. R. Sizer, ed., *Religion and public education.* Boston: Houghton Mifflin, 1967.

Bandura, A. Relationship of family patterns to child behavior disorders. *Progress Report,* U.S.P.H. Research Grant M-1734. Stanford, Cal.: Stanford University, 1960.

————. Social learning theory through imitation. In M. R. Jones, ed., *Nebraska Symposium on Motivation.* Lincoln: University of Nebraska Press, 1962.

————. The stormy decade: fact or fiction? *Psychology in the Schools,* 1964, *1,* 224–231.

————. Behavioral modification through modeling procedures. In L. Krasner & L. Ullmann, eds., *Research in behavior modification.* New York: Holt, Rinehart & Winston, 1965.

————. The role of modeling processes in personality development. In W. W. Hartup & N. L. Smothergill, eds., *The young child: reviews of research.* Washington, D.C.: National Association for the Education of Young Children, 1967.

————. *Principles of behavior modification.* New York: Holt, Rinehart & Winston, 1969.

————. Vicarious and self-reinforcement processes. In R. Glaser, ed., *The nature of reinforcement.* New York: Academic Press, 1971.

————. *Aggression, a social learning analysis.* Englewood Cliffs, N.J.: Prentice-Hall, 1973 (a).

————. Social learning theory of aggression. In J. F. Knutson, ed., *The control of aggression: implications from basic research.* Chicago: Aldine Publishing Co., 1973 (b).

Bandura, A., and Kupers, C. J. Transmission of patterns of self-reinforcement through modeling. *Journal of Abnormal and Social Psychology,* 1964, *69,* 1–9.

Bandura, A., and McDonald, F. J. Influence of social reinforcement and the behavior of models in shaping children's moral judgments. *Journal of Abnormal and Social Psychology,* 1963, *67,* 274–281.

Bandura, A., and Mischel, W. Modification of self-imposed delay of reward through exposure to live and symbolic models. *Journal of Personality and Social Psychology,* 1965, *2,* 698–705.

Bandura, A., and Perloff, B. Relative efficacy of self-monitored and externally imposed reinforcement systems. *Journal of Personality and Social Psychology,* 1967, *7,* 111–116.

Bandura, A., Ross, D., and Ross, S. A. Transmission of aggression through imitation of aggressive models. *Journal of Abnormal and Social Psychology,* 1961, *63,* 575–582.

————. A comparative test of the status envy, social power, and secondary reinforcement theories of identificatory learning. *Journal of Abnormal and Social Psychology,* 1963, *67,* 527–534 (a).

————. Imitation of film-mediated aggressive models. *Journal of Abnormal and Social Psychology,* 1963, *66,* 3–11 (b).

_____. Vicarious reinforcement and imitative learning. *Journal of Abnormal and Social Psychology,* 1963, *67,* 601–607 (c).

Bandura, A., and Walters, R. H. *Adolescent aggression.* New York: The Ronald Press, 1959.

_____. *Social learning and personality development.* New York: Holt, Rinehart & Winston, 1963.

Bandura, A., and Whalen, C. K. The influence of antecedent reinforcement and divergent modeling cues on patterns of self-reward. *Journal of Personality and Social Psychology,* 1966, *3,* 373–383.

Barker, R. G., *et al. Adjustment to physical handicap and illness: a survey of the social psychology of physique and disability.* Bulletin 55 (rev.). New York: Social Science Research Council, 1953.

Benedict, R. *Patterns of culture.* New York: New American Library, 1950.

_____. Continuities and discontinuities in cultural conditioning. In W. E. Martin & C. B. Stendler, eds., *Readings in child development.* New York: Harcourt, Brace, 1954.

Blair, G. M. Personality and social development. *Review of Educational Research,* 1950, *20,* 375–389.

Blatt, M. Experimental studies in moral education using a developmental approach. Unpublished Ph.D. dissertation, University of Chicago, 1959.

Block, J. Ego identity, role variability, and adjustment. *Journal of Consulting Psychology,* 1961, *25,* 392–397.

Boyd, W. *The history of Western education.* New York: Barnes & Noble, 1965.

Brittain, C. V. Adolescent choices and parent-peer cross-pressures. *American Sociological Review,* 1963, *28,* 385–391.

Bronson, G. W. Identity diffusion in late adolescents. *Journal of Abnormal and Social Psychology,* 1959, *59,* 414–417.

Bruner, J. S. *The process of education.* New York: Vintage Books, 1960.

Bühler, C. *From birth to maturity.* London: Kegan, Paul, Trench, Trubner & Co., 1935.

Bunt, M. E. Ego identity: its relationship to the discrepancy between how an adolescent views himself and how he perceives that others view him. *Psychology,* 1968, *5,* 14–25.

Buxton, C. E. *Adolescents in school.* New Haven, Conn.: Yale University Press, 1973.

Cattell, R. B., and Scheir, I. H. *The meaning and measurement of neuroticism and anxiety.* New York: The Ronald Press, 1961.

Coleman, J. S. *The adolescent society.* New York: Free Press of Glencoe, 1961.

Comenius, J. A. *The great didactic.* (M. W. Keating, ed. and trans.), London: A. & C. Black, 1923.

Committee on Adolescence, Group for the Advancement of Psychiatry. *Normal adolescence.* New York: Charles Scribner's Sons, 1968.

Conrad, K. *Der Konstitutionstypus als genetisches Problem.* Berlin: J. Springer, 1941.

Constantinople, A. An Eriksonian measure of personality development in college students. *Developmental Psychology,* 1969, *1,* 357–372.

Cross, H. J., and Allen, J. G. Paternal antecedents of identity status in college males. Paper presented at the Eastern Psychological Association Annual Meeting in Philadelphia, 1969.

Darwin, C. R. *The origin of species by means of natural selection.* London: J. Murray, 1859.

Davis, A. Socialization and adolescent personality. In *Adolescence, Yearbook of the National Society for the Study of Education,* 1944, *43,* Part I.

Dennis, W. The adolescent. In L. Carmichael, ed., *Manual of child psychology.* New York: John Wiley & Sons, 1946.

Dollard, J., Miller, N. E., Doob, L. W., Mowrer, O. H., and Sears, R. R. *Frustration and aggression.* New Haven, Conn.: Yale University Press, 1939.

Douvan, E., and Adelson, J. *The adolescent experience.* New York: John Wiley & Sons, 1966.

Erikson, E. H. *Childhood and society.* New York: W. W. Norton, 1950.

————. *Young man Luther.* New York: W. W. Norton, 1958.

————. Identity and the life cycle: selected papers. Psychological Issues Monograph Series I., No. 1. New York: International Universities Press, 1959.

————, ed. *The challenge of youth.* Garden City, N.Y.: Anchor Books, 1965.

————. *Identity: youth and crisis.* New York: W. W. Norton, 1968.

————. *Gandhi's truth.* New York: W. W. Norton, 1969.

————. Autobiographic notes on the identity crisis. *Daedalus,* 1970, *99,* 730–759.

Eron, L. D., Walder, L. O., Toigo, R., & Lefkowitz, M. M. Social class, parental punishment for aggression, and child aggression. *Child Development,* 1963, *34,* 849–867.

Flavell, J. H. *The developmental psychology of Jean Piaget.* New York: Van Nostrand, 1963 (a).

————. Piaget's contributions to the study of cognitive development. *Merrill-Palmer Quarterly,* 1963, *9,* 245–252 (b).

Freud, A. *The ego and the mechanism of defense.* (C. Baines, trans.). New York: International Universities Press, 1948.

Freud, S. Three contributions to the sexual theory. Nervous and Mental Disease Monograph Series, No. 7. New York: Nervous and Mental Disease Publishing Co., 1925.

_____. *New introductory lectures on psycho-analysis*. (W. J. H. Sprott, trans.). New York: W. W. Norton, 1933.

_____. *An outline of psychoanalysis*. (J. Strachey, trans.). New York: W. W. Norton, 1949.

_____. *A general introduction to psychoanalysis*. (J. Riviere, trans.). New York: Permabooks, 1953.

Friedenberg, E. Z. *The vanishing adolescent*. Boston: Beacon Press, 1959.

Fromm, E. Über Methoden und Aufgaben einer analytischen Sozialpsychologie. *Zeitschrift für Sozialforschung*, 1932, *1*, 28–54.

_____. Theoretische Entwürfe über Autorität und Familie: Sozialpsychologischer Teil. In M. Horkheimer, ed., *Studien über Autorität und Familie*. Paris: Alcan, 1936.

Gesell, A. Maturation and the patterning of behavior. In C. Murchison, ed., *A handbook of child psychology*. Second ed. rev. Worcester, Mass.: Clark University Press, 1933.

_____. Reciprocal interweaving in neuromotor development: a principle of development evidenced in the patterning of infant behavior. *Journal of Comparative Neurology*, 1939, *70*, 161–180.

_____. Twins T and C from infancy to adolescence: A biogenetic study of individual differences by the method of co-twin control. *Genetic Psychology Monographs*, 1941, *24*, 3–121.

_____. The ontogenesis of infant behavior. In L. Carmichael, ed., *Manual of child psychology*. New York: John Wiley & Sons, 1946 (b).

_____. *Studies in child development*. New York: Harper, 1948.

Gesell, A., *et al. The first five years of life*. New York: Harper, 1940.

Gesell, A., and Ilg, F. L. *Infant and child in the culture of today*. New York: Harper, 1943.

_____ *The child from five to ten*. New York: Harper, 1946 (a).

Gesell, A., Ilg, F. L., and Ames, L. B. *Youth: the years from ten to sixteen*. New York: Harper, 1956.

Gesell, A., and Thompson, H. Learning and growth in identical infant twins: An experimental study by the method of co-twin control. *Genetic Psychology Monographs*, 1929, *6*, 1–124.

Gilbert, A. R. Recent German theories of stratification of personality. *Journal of Psychology*, 1951, *31*, 3–19.

Greulich, W. W. Physical changes in adolescence. In *Adolescence, Yearbook of the National Society for the Study of Education*. 1944, *43*, Part I.

Gruen, W. Rejection of false information about oneself as an indication of ego identity. *Journal of Consulting Psychology*, 1960, *24*, 231–233.

Haan, N., Smith, M. B., and Block, J. Moral reasoning of young adults: Political-social behavior, family background, and personality correlates. *Journal of Personality and Social Psychology*, 1968, *10*, 183–201.

Hall, G. S. *Adolescence.* 2 vols. New York: Appleton, 1916.

Hampden-Turner, C., and Whitten, P. Morals left and right. *Psychology Today,* 1971, *4,* 39–43, 74, 76.

Harris, D. B. The climate of achievement. *Child Study,* 1958, *34,* 8–14.

Harsch, C. M., and Schrickel, H. G. *Personality development and assessment.* New York: Ronald Press, 1950.

Hartshorne, H., and May, M. A. *Studies in the nature of character.* (Three volumes). New York: Macmillan, 1928–1930.

Hartsoeker, N. *Essai de Dioptrique.* Sect. 88. Paris, 1694.

Havighurst, R. J. *Developmental tasks and education.* New York: Longmans, Green, 1951.

Hetzer, H. *Kind und Jugendlicher in der Entwicklung.* Hanover: Wolfenbütteler Verlagsanstalt, 1948.

Hickey, J. E. The effects of guided moral discussion upon youthful offenders' level of moral judgment. *Dissertation Abstracts International,* 1972, *33,* (4-A), 1551.

Hobbes, T. *Leviathan.* London: 1651.

Hollingworth, L. S. *The psychology of the adolescent.* New York: Appleton-Century, 1928.

Horney, K. *New ways in psychoanalysis.* New York: W. W. Norton, 1939.

Hunt, J. M. V. *Intelligence and experience.* New York: Ronald Press, 1961.

Inhelder, B. Cognitive development and its contribution to the diagnosis of some phenomena of mental deficiency. *Merrill-Palmer Quarterly,* 1966, *12,* 299–319.

Inhelder, B., and Piaget, J. *The growth of logical thinking.* (A. Parsons and S. Milgram, trans.). New York: Basic Books, 1958.

Jones, R. M. *An application of psychoanalysis to education.* Springfield, Ill.: Charles C Thomas, 1960.

Keasey, C. B. Social participation as a factor in the moral development of preadolescents. *Developmental Psychology,* 1971, *5,* 216–220.

Keniston, K. Social change and youth in America. In E. H. Erikson, ed., *The challenge of youth.* Garden City, N.Y.: A Doubleday Anchor Book, 1965.

Keniston, K. Youth: A "new" stage of life. *The American Scholar,* Autumn 1970, *39,* 631–654.

————. The tasks of adolescence. In *Developmental psychology today.* Del Mar, California: CRM Books, 1971, Chap. 20.

Kiell, N. *The adolescent through fiction.* New York: International Universities Press, 1959.

King, M. L. *Why we can't wait.* New York: Harper & Row, 1964.

Kinsey, A., et al. *Sexual behavior in the human male.* Phila.: Saunders, 1948.

Kohlberg, L. The development of children's orientations toward a moral order. *Vita Humana,* 1963, *6,* 11–33.

_____. Development of moral character and moral ideology. In M. L. Hoffman & L. W. Hoffman, eds., *Review of child development research.* New York: Russell Sage Foundation, 1964.

_____. Moral and religious education and the public schools: a developmental view. In T. R. Sizer, ed., *Religion and public education.* Boston: Houghton Mifflin, 1967.

_____. Stage and sequence: the cognitive-developmental approach to socialization. In D. A. Goslin, ed., *Handbook of socialization theory and research.* Chicago: Rand McNally, 1969.

_____. Moral development and the education of adolescents. In R. F. Purnell, ed., *Adolescents and the American high school.* New York: Holt, Rinehart & Winston, 1970.

Kohlberg, L., and Blatt, M. The effects of classroom discussion on level of moral development. In L. Kohlberg & E. Turiel, eds., *Recent research in moral development.* New York: Holt, Rinehart & Winston, 1972.

Kohlberg, L., and Gilligan, C. The adolescent as a philosopher. In J. Kagan & R. Coles, eds., *Twelve to sixteen: early adolescence.* New York: W. W. Norton, 1972.

Kohlberg, L., and Kramer, R. Continuities and discontinuities in childhood and adult moral development. *Human Development,* 1969, *12,* 93–120.

Kretschmer, E. *Körperbau und Character.* Berlin: Springer Verlag, 1951.

Kroh, O. *Entwicklungspsychologie des Grundschulkindes.* Langensalza: Hermann Beyer, 1944.

_____. Psychologie der Entwicklung. In *Lexikon der Pädagogik,* vol. 2. Bern: A. Francke, 1951.

Kubie, L. S. Introduction. In R. M. Jones, *An application of psychoanalysis to education.* Springfield, Ill.: Charles C Thomas, 1960.

Kuhn, M. H., and McPartland, T. S. An empirical investigation of self-attitudes. *American Sociological Review,* 1954, *19,* 68–76.

LaFleur, N. K., and Johnson, R. G. Separate effects of social modeling and reinforcement in counseling adolescents. *Journal of Counseling Psychology,* 1972, *19,* 292–295.

Lersch, P. *Aufbau der Person.* München: Johann Ambrosius Barth, 1951.

Lewin, K. Environmental forces in child behavior and development. In C. Murchison, ed., *Handbook of child psychology.* Worcester, Mass.: Clark University Press, 1931.

_____. *A dynamic theory of personality.* New York: McGraw-Hill, 1935.

_____. *Principles of topological psychology.* New York: McGraw-Hill, 1936.

————. The conceptual representation and the measurement of psychological forces. Duke University Series, *Contributions to Psychological Theory,* 1938, *1* (4).

————. Field theory and experiment in social psychology: concepts and methods. *American Journal of Sociology,* 1939, *44,* 868–897.

————. Studies in topological and vector psychology: I. formalization and progress in psychology. *University of Iowa Studies in Child Welfare,* 1940, *16,* 9–42.

————. Field theory and learning. In *The Psychology of Learning, the Yearbook of the National Society for the Study of Education,* 1942, *41,* Part II.

————. Behavior and development as a function of the total situation. In L. Carmichael, ed., *Manual of child psychology.* New York: John Wiley & Sons, 1946.

————. *Resolving social conflict.* New York: Harper, 1948.

————. *Field theory and social science.* New York: Harper, 1951.

Locke, J. *An essay concerning human understanding.* London: 1753.

————. Treatise on civil government. In *The work of John Locke.* London: 1768.

Maier, H. W. *Three theories of child development.* New York: Harper & Row, 1965.

Malinowski, B. *Sex and repression in savage society.* New York: Harcourt, Brace, 1927.

Marcia, J. E. Development and validation of ego identity status. *Journal of Personality and Social Psychology,* 1966, *3,* 551–558.

Marcia, J. E. Ego identity status: relationship to change in self-esteem, "general maladjustment," and authoritarianism. *Journal of Personality,* 1967, *35,* 118–133.

Marcia, J. E. The case history of a construct: ego identity status. In E. Vinacke, ed., *Readings in general psychology.* New York: Van Nostrand Reinhold, 1968.

Marcia, J. E., & Friedman, M. L. Ego identity status in college women. *Journal of Personality,* 1970, *38,* 249–263.

Mead, M. The primitive child. In C. Murchison, ed., *A handbook of child psychology.* Second rev. ed. Worcester, Mass.: Clark University Press, 1933.

————. Educative effects of social environment as disclosed by studies of primitive societies. *Environment and Education: A Symposium. Human Development Series,* 1942, *1* (54).

————. What is happening to the American family? *Journal of Social Casework,* 1947, *28,* 323–330.

————. *Male and female.* New York: William Morrow, 1949.

————. *Coming of age in Samoa.* New York: New American Library, 1950.

————. Adolescence in primitive and modern society. In G. E. Swanson, T. M. Newcomb, E. L. Hartley, *et al.,* eds., *Readings in social psychology.* Rev. ed. New York: Henry Holt, 1952.

————. *Growing up in New Guinea.* New York: New American Library, 1953.

————. Age patterning in personality development. In W. E. Martin and C. B. Stendler, eds., *Readings in child development.* New York: Harcourt, Brace, 1954.

————. The young adult. In E. Ginzberg, ed., *Values and ideals of American youth.* New York: Columbia University Press, 1961.

Mead, M., and Macgregor, F. C. *Growth and culture.* New York: Putnam, 1951.

Miller, N. E., and Dollard, J. *Social learning and imitation.* New Haven, Conn.: Yale University Press, 1941.

Mills, C. A., and Ogle, C. Physiological sterility of adolescence. *Human Biology,* 1936, *8,* 607–615.

Mischel, W. *Introduction to personality.* New York: Holt, Rinehart & Winston, 1971.

Mowrer, O. H. A stimulus-response analysis of anxiety and its role as a reinforcing agent. *Psychological Review,* 1939, *46,* 553–565.

Muuss, R. E. *First-aid for classroom discipline problems.* New York: Holt, Rinehart & Winston, 1962.

————. Adolescent development and the secular trend. *Adolescence,* 1970, *5,* 267–284 (a).

————. Puberty rites in primitive and modern societies. *Adolescence,* 1970, *5,* 109–128 (b).

Nixon, R. E. An approach to the dynamics of growth in adolescence. *Psychiatry,* 1961, *24,* 18–31.

Offer, D. *The psychological world of the teen-ager.* New York: Basic Books, 1969.

Ojemann, R. H., and Pritchett, K. Piaget and the role of guided experiences in development. *Perceptual and Motor Skills,* 1963, *17,* 927–940.

Parnell, R. W. Simplified somatotypes. *Journal of Psychosomatic Research,* 1964, *8,* 311–315.

Piaget, J. *The moral judgment of the child.* (M. Gabain, trans.). New York: Harcourt, Brace, 1932.

————. The moral development of the adolescent in two types of society primitive and modern. Lecture given to the United Nations Educational, Scientific and Cultural Organization. Paris, 1947 (a).

————. *The psychology of intelligence.* (M. Piercy & D. E. Berlyne, trans.). New York: Harcourt, Brace, 1947 (b).

————. *The origins of intelligence in children.* (M. Cook, trans.). New York: W. W. Norton, 1952.

————. *The construction of reality in the child.* New York: Basic Books, 1954.

————. *The language and thought of the child.* (M. Gabain, trans.). New York: Meridian Books, 1957.

————. Three lectures. *Bulletin of the Menninger Clinic,* 1962, *26,* 120–145.

————. The attainment of invariants and reversible operations in developmental thinking. *Social Research,* 1963, *30,* 283–299.

Piaget, J., and Inhelder, B. *The psychology of the child.* (H. Weaver, trans.). New York: Basic Books, 1969.

————. *The child's conception of space.* London: Routledge & Kegan Paul, 1967.

Plato. *The republic.* (B. Jowett, trans.). Oxford: Clarendon Press, 1921.

————. Phaedo. In *The dialogues of Plato.* (B. Jowett, trans.), vol. 1. Third ed. New York: Random House, 1937.

————. Laws. In *The dialogues of Plato.* (B. Jowett, trans.), vol. 4. Fourth ed. Oxford: Clarendon Press, 1953.

Podd, M. H. Ego identity status and morality: the relationship between two developmental constructs. *Developmental Psychology,* 1972, *6,* 497–507.

Podd, M. H., Marcia, J. E., and Rubin, B. M. The effects of ego identity and partner perception on a prisoner's dilemma game. *Journal of Social Psychology,* 1970, *82,* 117–126.

Rank, O. *Will therapy and truth and reality.* New York: Knopf, 1945.

Rasmussen, J. E. Relationship of ego identity to psychosocial effectiveness. *Psychological Reports,* 1964, *15,* 815–825.

Remplein, H. *Die seelische Entwicklung in der Kindheit und Reifezeit.* München: Ernst Reinhard, 1956.

Rosen, G. M., and Ross, A. O. Relationship of body image to self-concept. *Journal of Consulting and Clinical Psychology,* 1968, *32,* 100.

Rosenberg, M. *Society and the adolescent self-image.* Princeton, N.J.: Princeton University Press, 1965.

Rousseau, J. J. *Émile.* (W. H. Payne, trans.). New York: Appleton, 1911.

Rubin, K. H., and Schneider, F. W. The relationship between moral judgment, egocentrism, and altruistic behavior. *Child Development,* 1973, *44,* 661–665.

Saltzstein, H. D., Diamond, R. M., and Belenky, M. Moral judgment level and conformity behavior. *Developmental Psychology,* 1972, *7,* 327–336.

Schoeppe, A., and Havighurst, R. J. A validation of development and adjustment hypotheses of adolescence. *Journal of Educational Psychology,* 1952, *43,* 339–353.

Sears, R. R. *Survey of objective studies of psychoanalytic concepts.* New York: Social Science Research Council, 1943.

————. A theoretical framework for personality and social behavior. *The American Psychologist,* 1951, *6,* 476–483.

Sears, R. R., Maccoby, E. E., and Levin, H. *Patterns of child rearing.* Evanston, Ill.: Row, Peterson and Co., 1957.

Selman, R. L. The relation of role taking to the development of moral judgment in children. *Child Development,* 1971, *42,* 79–91.

Sheldon, W. H. *The varieties of human physique.* New York: Harper & Brothers, 1940.

Sherif, M. & Cantril, H. *The psychology of ego-involvements.* New York: John Wiley & Sons, 1947.

Shock, N. W. Physiological changes in adolescence. In *Adolescence, Yearbook of the National Society for the Study of Education,* 1944, *43,* Part I.

Spiegel, L. A. A review of contributions to a psychoanalytic theory of adolescence: individual aspects. In R. S. Eissler *et al.,* eds., *The psychoanalytic study of the child.* New York: International Universities Press, 1951. Vol. 6.

Spranger, E. *Types of men.* (P. J. W. Pigoros, trans.). Halle-Saale: Max Niemeyer, 1928.

————. *Psychologie des Jugendalters.* Twenty-fourth ed. Heidelberg: Quelle & Meyer, 1955.

Staffieri, J. R. Body build and behavioral expectancies in young females. *Developmental Psychology,* 1972, *6,* 125–127.

Stoltz, H. R., and Stoltz, L. M. Adolescent problems related to somatic variations. In *Adolescence, the Yearbook of the National Society for the Study of Education,* 1944, *43,* Part I.

Stone, L. J., and Church, J. *Childhood and adolescence.* Third ed. New York: Random House, 1973.

Stratz, C. H. *Der Körper des Kindes und seine Pflege.* Stuttgart: F. Enke, 1923.

Sullivan, H. S. *The interpersonal theory of psychiatry.* New York: W. W. Norton, 1953.

Turiel, E. An experimental test of the sequentiality of developmental stages in the child's moral judgments. *Journal of Personality and Social Psychology,* 1966, *3,* 611–618.

————. Developmental processes in the child's moral thinking. In P. Mussen, J. Langer, & M. Covington, eds., *Trends and issues in developmental psychology.* New York: Holt, Rinehart & Winston, 1969.

Waterman, A. S., and Waterman, C. K. The relationship between ego identity status and satisfaction with college. *Journal of Educational Research,* 1970, *64,* 165–168.

White, G. M. The elicitation and durability of altruistic behavior in children. *Research Bulletin* No. 67-27. Princeton, N.J.: Educational Testing Service, 1967.

Williams, F. *Adolescence-studies in mental hygiene.* New York: Farrar and Rinehart, 1930.

Witham, W. T. *The adolescent in the American novel 1920–1960.* New York: Frederick Ungar, 1964.

Wolf, T. M. Effects of a live modeled sex-inappropriate play behavior in a naturalistic setting. *Developmental Psychology,* 1973, *9,* 120–123.

Wylie, R., and Hutchins, E. B. Schoolwork-ability estimates and aspirations as a function of socioeconomic level, race, and sex. *Psychological Reports,* 1967, *21,* 781–808. Monograph Supplement 3-V21.

Zeller, W. Über den Entwicklungstypus. *Psychologische Rundschau,* 1951, *2,* 76–80.

————. *Konstitution und Entwicklung.* Göttingen: Psychologische Rundschau, 1952.

Index

Theories of
Adolescence
Third Edition

Consulting Editor:

L. JOSEPH STONE

Vassar College

Theories of Adolescence

Third Edition

Rolf E. Muuss

Goucher College

 RANDOM HOUSE   NEW YORK

Third Edition
987654321
Copyright © 1962, 1968, 1975 by Random House, Inc.

Library of Congress Cataloging in Publication Data

Muuss, Rolf Eduard Helmut, 1924–
    Theories of adolescence.

    Bibliography: p.
    1. Adolescent psychology. I. Title.
[DNLM: 1. Adolescent psychology. WS462 M993t]
BF724.M8 1974   155.5   74–10575
ISBN 0–394–31867–6

Manufactured in the United States of America

Grateful acknowledgment is made to Basic Books, Inc. for permission to quote
from *The Growth of Logical Thinking from Childhood to Adolescence*, by Bärbel
Inhelder and Jean Piaget, © 1958 by Basic Books, Inc., Publishers, New York.

Cover by Carol Dethloff